Praise for *Three Weeks in October*

"A compelling account of what it means to be a police chief in a major American metropolitan area, and a very pointed account of what it means to be an African American police chief.... A very candid story of [Moose's] conversion from a youth who believed all cops were bad to a career law enforcement officer [who acted] with grace while under the enormous pressure of one horrible event after another."   —*The Washington Post*

"An inside look at the operation that led to the capture of prime suspects John Allen Muhammad and John Lee Malvo [and] an in-depth portrait of a proud and powerful black policeman who battled racism and adversity."   —*The Daily Oklahoman*

"Tells his own remarkable story in a gutsy, endearing, no-nonsense way, from growing up in an all-black neighborhood in North Carolina ... to his unlikely entry into law enforcement and his even more unlikely rise to the top of the profession."   —*Publishers Weekly*

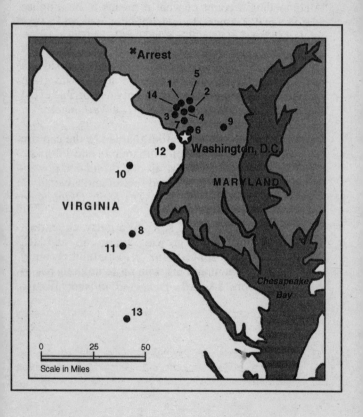

SNIPER VICTIMS AND LOCATIONS

1. 5:20 PM Wednesday, October 2: Windows shot at Michael's, a Maryland craft store. No one hurt.
2. 6:02 PM Wednesday, October 2: James D. Martin, fifty-five, of Silver Spring, MD, killed in a Maryland grocery store parking lot.
3. 7:41 AM Thursday, October 3: James L. "Sonny" Buchanan, thirty-nine, of Arlington, VA, killed while cutting grass at a Maryland auto dealership.
4. 8:12 AM Thursday, October 3: Taxi driver Prem Kumar Walekar, fifty-four, of Olney, MD, killed at a Maryland gas station.
5. 8:37 AM Thursday, October 3: Sarah Ramos, thirty-four, of Silver Spring, MD, killed outside a Maryland post office.
6. 9:58 AM Thursday, October 3: Lori Ann Lewis-Rivera, twenty-five, of Silver Spring, MD, killed while vacuuming her van at a Maryland gas station.
7. 9:15 PM Thursday, October 3: Pascal Charlot, seventy-two, of Washington, DC, killed while standing on a street in Washington, DC.
8. 2:30 PM Friday, October 4: Forty-three-year-old woman wounded in a Michael's parking lot in Fredericksburg, VA.
9. 8:09 AM Monday, October 7: Iran Brown, thirteen years old, wounded as he is dropped off at his Bowie, MD, school.
10. 8:15 PM Wednesday, October 9: Dean Harold Meyers, fifty-three, of Gaithersburg, MD, killed at a gas station near Manassas, VA, about thirty miles west of Washington, DC.
11. 9:30 AM Friday, October 11: Kenneth H. Bridges, fifty-three, wounded while pumping gas at an Exxon gas station in Massaponax, VA, just south of Fredericksburg, VA.
12. 9:15 PM Monday, October 14: Linda Franklin, forty-seven, of Arlington, VA, killed outside a Home Depot store in Falls Church, VA.

13. 8:00 PM Saturday, October 19: A man, thirty-seven, wounded while leaving a Ponderosa steakhouse with his wife in Ashland, VA.
14. 6:00 AM Tuesday, October 22: Conrad Johnson, a thirty-five-year-old bus driver, killed on a commuter bus in the Aspen Hill area of Montgomery County.

ARREST: 3:19 AM Thursday, October 24: Police arrest John Allen Muhammed, forty-one, and Lee Boyd Malvo, seventeen, while they're sleeping in their car at a rest stop in Frederick County, MD.

THREE WEEKS IN OCTOBER

THE MANHUNT FOR THE SERIAL SNIPER

CHARLES A. MOOSE

AND CHARLES FLEMING

A SIGNET BOOK

SIGNET
Published by New American Library, a division of
Penguin Group (USA) Inc., 375 Hudson Street,
New York, New York 10014, U.S.A.
Penguin Books Ltd, 80 Strand,
London WC2R 0RL, England
Penguin Books Australia Ltd, 250 Camberwell Road,
Camberwell, Victoria 3124, Australia
Penguin Books Canada Ltd, 10 Alcorn Avenue,
Toronto, Ontario, Canada M4V 3B2
Penguin Books (NZ), cnr Airborne and Rosedale Roads,
Albany, Auckland 1310, New Zealand

Penguin Books Ltd, Registered Offices:
80 Strand, London WC2R 0RL, England

Published by Signet, an imprint of New American Library, a division of
Penguin Group (USA) Inc. Previously published in a Dutton edition.

First Signet Printing, September 2004
10 9 8 7 6 5 4 3 2 1

This book is dedicated to
my best friend and wife, Sandy.

CONTENTS

INTRODUCTION

My name is Charles A. Moose. I have been a police officer, at the writing of this book, for more than twenty-eight years. That's more than half of my life. It's the only real job I've ever had.

I didn't start out wanting to be a police officer. In the town where I grew up, at the time when I grew up—in Lexington, North Carolina, in the 1950s and 1960s—all a young black man wanted from the police was to be left alone. I was afraid of them. I never had any interaction with them. I was never arrested, or even harassed. That's because I knew enough to stay away from all the places where I'd run into them. I wasn't a criminal. My family wasn't victimized by criminals. I didn't go near the Do Drop Inn, which was a nightclub in our part of town, where the criminals hung out, so I didn't see firsthand any of the arrests that I heard about taking place there.

I didn't know the police. I never met a police officer or a sheriff. But I knew they were bad. I believed they were associated with the Ku Klux Klan. I believed they beat up black people, and put them in jail, and worse. I believed they were involved in cross burnings and lynchings. I believed they made up cases, falsified evidence and told lies. If you were black, and you were arrested, God help you.

When I was a senior in college, I started planning to go to law school. I still had no contact with the police, and I didn't know anything about the law, but I knew which side I wanted to be on: I wanted to be on the side of the people defending themselves against the police. So I took a class in criminology. I thought it would help me be a better defense attorney.

Then I got tricked into meeting a recruiter from the Portland Police Bureau in Oregon. One of my professors told me he'd let me skip a test if I went and met with the recruiter. I was always eager to skip a test, so I went. I met the recruiter and took a qualifying examination. I passed. That led to my being offered a job. I took the job, thinking only that it would give me a perspective on the police that would be useful for my work as a defense attorney. It was a look at the inside. I'd see how the police made up cases, falsified evidence and stretched the facts.

I was hired by the Portland Police Bureau on an eighteen-month probation, which was standard for all new recruits. This meant going to the police academy, getting trained, being partnered with another officer, then learning how to be a patrol officer on your own. I told myself I would do the eighteen months. Then it would be on my résumé. I would have the credit for becoming a police officer.

But something unexpected happened to me. As a police officer, I got a close look at crime, and the people doing the crime and the people being victimized by crime. I saw people taking advantage of other people. I saw people hurting other people. I didn't see the police hurting them, even though I didn't see the police doing all that much to help them, either.

And I saw that I had the opportunity to do something about that.

The power goes out in a thunderstorm, and you're driving by the JCPenney in your district. You find the back door kicked in. Inside, you find people stealing everything in sight.

You get a call on a "rape in progress." You go in, and find a guy who's been raping and beating an old woman, and he's running out the back door.

You get a child abuse call, and find someone who's been trying to have sex with babies.

You get a call on a burglary, and the victim is a poor black woman. This isn't some rich suburban family, where the thief has stolen the woman's diamonds and pearls. It's a poor black woman who lives in government housing, and the thief has stolen her cheap costume jewelry and her TV set and her food stamps.

And here was the big surprise to me: The people doing this terrible stuff were black people. It was real black-on-black crime. It's not what I thought. It wasn't black people being victimized by the police. It was black people being victimized by criminals, and the criminals were black people, too.

The crime was very real to me. These were innocent people, and they were being hurt.

Two things became apparent to me, right away.

First, these people looked like me, and they needed help.

Second, the police were not the bad guys. The criminals were the bad guys. But the police were not working very hard in the black community. Someone needed to help these people, and the police were not really doing all they could. There was a sense, at that time, in that city, that black people must want the environment they lived in—because they kept living there.

It was an awakening for me. The way I had been seeing the world was wrong. I made a decision. I told myself that I was not going to make up anything. I was not going to falsify any evidence. I was going to make arrests, and I was going to make them solid, and I was going to make them on really bad people who needed to be put away.

I decided to be the best police officer I could be, and see what happened.

What happened was I stayed in Portland. I stayed a

police officer. I became a sergeant, then a lieutenant, then a captain, then a deputy chief, then the police chief. I was the police chief for six years. I left the job to move to Maryland, to become chief of police for the Montgomery County Police Department. I had been there more than three years when the serial sniper started shooting. I became the head of the task force whose job was to capture the killer.

This book is the story of how I got from the beginning to the end of that journey. It's the story of how a black boy from the segregated Deep South became the police chief of two predominantly white communities. It's the story of how a person raised in a town where a black man could be beaten or killed for even looking at a white woman could grow up to be happily married to a white woman. It's the story of how a rookie police recruit with no plans to become a police officer became the head of the largest single manhunt in American police history. It's the story of how I went from being lionized for helping bring the snipers to justice to being vilified for writing a book about it.

It's the story of the changes—the changes in me, the changes in law enforcement, the changes in my country—that made this journey possible.

1. This Doesn't Happen Here

I was in my office, at the Rockville, Maryland, headquarters of the Montgomery County Police Department, when the first call came in. It appeared to be a homicide. The call came in from Captain Barney Forsythe, who was a thirty-year veteran of the police force and the director of the major crimes unit, at around 6:30 P.M.

"Chief, we have a homicide," he said. "And it's a little out of the ordinary."

It was Wednesday, October 2, 2002. I got a second call a few minutes later from the media office, from Captain Nancy Demme, a veteran undercover plainclothes officer whom I had recently made the public information officer for the force.

The few known facts were the same. A middle-aged white man had been shot once in the back, in the parking lot of the Shoppers Food Warehouse, in the community of Wheaton, at 2201 Randolph Road. There were no witnesses. There were no suspects. The shooting had taken place at 6:02 P.M.

It sounded strange. We don't get a lot of murders in Montgomery County, especially compared to Portland. That was a city of five hundred thousand residents, with a murder count that ran as high as seventy killings a year. Montgomery County was almost twice that population, and rarely had more than fifteen killings a year.

Besides that, the details were unusual for Montgomery County. We don't get many killings on the street. We don't have drive-by shootings. There have been bodies dumped in the street, in the night, and found in the early morning hours. But for someone to be shot, in public, on the street like that—that was strange.

I asked Captain Forsythe the usual questions. Did anybody see anything? Was there some kind of a fight? Did we have anybody in custody? Did we know the guy? In other words, was there a criminal record or profile of the victim?

The answer to all those questions was "No."

He added one unusual detail. He said it appeared that a rifle had been used—a high-powered rifle.

There was one additionally unusual factor. Forty-five minutes earlier that evening there had been an incident near the Shoppers Food Warehouse. Two miles away, and less than an hour before, someone had shot a bullet through the plate glass windows into a Michael's craft store, at the Northgate Shopping Center, at 3800 Aspen Hill Road. No one was injured. The call on the shooting had come in just before the call from the Shoppers Food Warehouse. There didn't appear to be any connection.

The shooting at Shoppers was so near the District 4 police station that two police officers heard the sound of a shot fired and responded on foot. One of the officers got to the victim and began CPR—to no avail. They had the location roped off and secured within minutes. Forsythe got the call not long after, from his deputy, Lieutenant Phil Raum, who told him there was a homicide.

Forsythe asked a series of questions: Was it a smoker?—his slang expression for "smoking gun."

Raum said it was not a smoker.

"Was it a robbery?"

Raum said it wasn't.

"Was it a carjacking?"

Raum said it wasn't.

"Was it a domestic dispute?"

Raum said it wasn't.

Forsythe said, "I'm on my way."

One of my assistant chiefs had already been at the scene. John King had spent the day at the FBI National Academy in Quantico, Virginia. He was there as part of an eleven-week training program the bureau does for a select group of police officers. It's the same program I'd participated in as a lieutenant from Portland. King had come home for the evening to see his family—he and his wife and three children live in the Montgomery County town of Damascus—and was driving back to Quantico. For sentimental reasons, he decided to swing by the Wheaton station, where he had been district commander. He saw the police tape and the police cars with their lights on, and stopped to find out what had happened.

King headed on to Quantico. Forsythe made sure investigators jumped on everything available from the Shoppers shooting—interviewing witnesses, store employees, family members, friends and colleagues—and decided to check out the shooting at Michael's.

In my phone conversation with Captain Demme, she told me she had been visiting with a friend from the force who was laid up with a bad knee when she got the page on the Shoppers shooting. She rushed to the scene, met with the few reporters who were covering the shooting, and then called me. She said, "I don't know what we have here, but it's different from your regular homicide." She told me the victim appeared to be a nice, normal, middle-aged guy. He had his sleeves rolled up and his tie loosened, and his company I.D. badge pinned to his shirt, and his lunch box was sitting on the passenger seat, like he was just going home after work. She told me the victim had not been robbed, and that the shots came from a distance. The officers who heard them said they sounded like a truck tire blowing up. She told me the forensics officers were going to the

Michael's store to see if there was any connection between the two shootings.

I went back to my paperwork. That evening I had more than usual. My wife, Sandy, and I were leaving town the following day for a national police conference in Minneapolis. I was going to be on the Major City Chiefs roundtable, and in a Civil Rights Committee meeting. If there was time, I was also going to get tickets to a Minnesota Twins play-off game. I would be gone from Thursday to Sunday, so there was a lot to do before I went home for the night.

I left the station around eight o'clock. My mind was at ease. My only concern that night was getting home in time to pack, and getting up early enough in the morning to get Sandy to the airport for her flight.

There had already been one change in our original plan. We were supposed to fly out together Thursday morning. But early in the week I had been informed that one of our officers, Corporal William Foust, had died of a heart attack the previous weekend, while attending a wedding. He was to be buried Thursday. I immediately changed my flight. Sandy would leave early Thursday morning. I would stay behind, to attend Corporal Foust's funeral, and then join Sandy in Minneapolis in the late afternoon.

I had a little anxiety about the funeral. I had only been in Montgomery County for three and a half years. I didn't know all the officers personally. I didn't really know this officer very well. I didn't know who his close friends were. I had never met his family. Foust was a motor officer—he rode a police motorcycle. Forsythe had been his commander, at the District 3 station in Silver Spring. I knew that many of the people most affected by his death would be his colleagues on the motor division, and that they would be riding their motorcycles as escorts to the motorcade after the funeral. Over the years, I have been to a lot of funerals for fallen police officers. The police in attendance are often very emotional. I was worried how they'd hold up.

It was only about a ten-minute drive from the station to the condominium we had bought in Gaithersburg, Maryland. When I got home, I told Sandy about my day, including the killing at the Shoppers Food Warehouse. It wasn't because it was so unusual. I always told Sandy about my day, every day—not every fact, or every detail, but a recap of the big events. She's a lawyer. She's been around police almost her entire working life. She wants to know what's going on. I told her the murder was a little strange.

We didn't dwell on it. We spent the evening talking about a house we had wanted to build. Our three-thousand-square-foot "traditional," with a wide, wooden front porch and gabled windows on the second floor, was going up just a few blocks from our condominium. We had to discuss some details about that—what kind of tile should go in the master bathroom, or what kind of light fixture should go in the living room. It was going to be a $500,000 home. That meant $500,000 worth of details to decide. We were talking about the garage apartment we wanted to include for my son, David. He was twenty-two years old that fall, and had just begun his junior year at Howard University in Washington, D.C. He'd been living with us since September 2001— the first time I had lived with my son in many, many years. Our relationship was growing into something strong and new. Sandy and I wanted to make a place that would be comfortable for him.

About eleven o'clock that night, the phone rang. It was Captain Forsythe. He was calling to tell me what they had on the Shoppers shooting. They had no good witnesses. They had no criminal background on the victim. They had done all they could for the night, and had no place else to go. During the hours since the first call had come in, there had been few people on the street. A lot of the businesses were closed. There weren't that many possible witnesses to interview.

He did tell me that he had seen a very clear videotape, taken by a store security camera mounted outside the store, that showed the victim at the moment of the shooting. He had been walking from his car toward the store. Two other people were visible in the frame. The victim just dropped—bang, like that, shot from behind. Forsythe said the investigators were guessing the victim was shot with a high-powered rifle, from some distance away. There was a small entrance wound, and a large exit wound.

He also told me he and Lieutenant Raum had been over to the Michael's location. The store was closed, but they found the place where the bullet had hit the glass, and they could see into the store enough to follow the trajectory of the bullet. It had struck one of the lighted signs over the cashier's aisles. The sign for cashier number five had a hole shot through it.

Forsythe told me he had no evidence to support this, but he assumed the two incidents were probably related.

Lieutenant Raum had also called Assistant Chief Dee Walker, the third of the three assistant chiefs, around the same time. As head of the ISB, or investigative services bureau, Assistant Chief Walker was in charge of major crimes, family crimes, drug crimes, auto theft, special investigations, vice and intelligence. She oversaw about two hundred officers.

She listened to Raum's report and thought, *This doesn't happen here. Maybe it's a drug deal, or a gambling debt. Maybe it's a hit. Maybe the guy was having an affair. But this is weird.* Later, when she learned about the Michael's shooting, that introduced what she called "the first hint of the randomness." That made it weirder.

The investigators were going to start again in the morning, but they wanted to let me know I could stand down. Captain Forsythe knew I was leaving town. He wanted me to know the case was in good hands.

Going to sleep, I thought this shooting might turn out to be one of those that is hard to figure out, and one that might take a while. With most homicides, everything happens in those first few hours. Everything is wrapped up quickly. The detectives run really hard for the first eight to ten hours—when everything is still hot. That doesn't mean they solve the killing right away. But that's when you have the best chance to get witnesses, to get evidence, to build the case.

That first eight to ten hours is also the time when most murderers give themselves away. Killing a human being is generally so personal, and so emotional, that when someone does that they usually have trouble following their routine. They have trouble appearing normal. They may have blood on their clothing. They may be emotionally overwrought. They may not go home. They may show up at their favorite bar, acting strange. People who know them will know something is wrong. If you've had a terrible fight at work, or at home, someone who knows you is going to know about that. Then, if the person you had the fight with turns up dead, they're going to have an idea what happened. And they're going to call the police.

But when there's nothing—no crime scene, no evidence at the crime scene, no witnesses at the crime scene, no way of guessing a motive—that's going to take a little more time to figure out. I thought this might be one of those. That's what I went to bed thinking about. I thought, *Tomorrow morning the detectives will find a witness, and this will start to make more sense.*

I remember thinking that night about a killing we had in Portland. A man had walked into an office one morning and started yelling about robbing the place. Then he had gone over to this one female employee and shot her. He said something else about money and left.

It didn't make any sense. The office was a charitable organization designed to help underprivileged children get access to better health care, schooling and after-school programs. Who would rob a charitable organization? In the daytime?

For a while, we thought maybe it was an attempt on Ron Herndon, the black activist who was running the organization at that time. We thought the killing might be racially motivated. Then we discovered an insurance angle. The dead employee's husband had taken out a large insurance policy on her. He had hired someone to go into her place of business and stage a robbery, and kill her for the insurance money.

It took a while to clear that up. I thought this shooting might be something similar.

Sandy and I were at Baltimore Washington International Airport at six the next morning. I had picked up a copy of the *Washington Post* on the way. I remember telling Sandy it was strange, and sad, that a man could be shot down on the streets of Montgomery County and not even get a mention in the morning paper. I pulled the big black Crown Victoria to the curb—that is the police chief's car in Montgomery County—and got Sandy's bags out. I kissed Sandy good-bye and told her I'd see her in Minneapolis. I drove myself back to the police station.

My schedule for the previous day had been busy. I was out of the house before 7:00 A.M. By 8:00 I was at Rolling Terrace Elementary School, in Takoma Park, for a "Safe Walk to School" presentation. At 9:00 A.M. I was back at the station to conduct interviews at 9:30, 10:00, 10:45 and 11:30, meeting with candidates for promotion. We were about to promote some people into lieutenant and captain positions. I had to conduct a brief interview with each of them. At 1:00 I was at a quarterly police/fire meeting. At 2:00 I had attended the graduation of a K-9 class, held at the police academy out on the Great Seneca Highway.

That evening there had been a "viewing," or a wake, for Corporal Foust, at the Hines-Rinaldi Funeral Home, in Silver Spring. Captain King had come up from Quantico, in part to attend it, so I knew that police management had been represented. I was planning to attend the funeral, rather than the wake, and it was scheduled to take place at the same location, at 10:00 A.M. the following morning. The burial would take place at the Gates of Heaven cemetery, also in Silver Spring. I had

already arranged to drive out there with one of my assistant chiefs, Bill O'Toole. The plan was to meet at the
station, dress for the funeral, and go from there.

I always go to work in my street clothes. I change into
the uniform in my office. The so-called "uniform of the
day" is tan slacks and tan shirt. (The K-9 officers and the
SWAT officers have a black uniform of the day.) I also
wear a black tie with my uniform, most days. There are
two small gold stars on my collar.

Most of the police chiefs in Maryland are called
"Colonel." They wear gold eagles on their lapels. Each
of them has a deputy chief called "Lieutenant Colonel."
Below the deputy chief, in Montgomery County, were
three assistant chiefs, who were called "Major." This was
a merit job, but not exactly: You had to take an exam to
become a major. But I found that some of the majors
had not been selected for promotion by following that
process. They had filed grievances, and won their grievances, and become majors that way.

I wasn't too wild about that, or the title of Colonel. I
used to get memos addressed to "Colonel Moose, Chief
of Police," which was like having two titles where only
one was needed. "Chief" was good. I had become ac-
customed to it in Portland.

More important, though, I didn't like the structure of
one deputy chief and three assistant chiefs. When I got
there, Montgomery County had one lieutenant colonel,
who managed three majors, who managed the three
main bureaus—management services, field services and
investigative services. I thought that having a number
two person created a layer between me and the people
managing the bureaus, and I wanted more direct access
to them. I felt it was important to flatten the top of the
organization, and make it more of a team structure.

So I instituted some changes. I retired the lieutenant
colonel/deputy chief position. I took over appointment
of the assistant chiefs.

To signify these changes, I retired the eagles, and took
two gold stars for myself, and gave each of the assistant

chiefs one gold star. Somehow, because we live in such a military area—Andrews Air Force base is nearby, as are Bolling AFB, Fort Detrick, the Pentagon—the star looks more like a military rank. The chief of police in Washington's Metropolitan Police Department wears four stars. I wonder if anyone calls him "General." No one calls me "General." But at least no one calls me "Colonel" anymore, either.

For me and many of my officers, the uniform also includes a T-shirt and, over that, the body armor vest. In summer the uniform shirt is short-sleeved. In winter, it's long-sleeved.

All ranks have a dress uniform. That's what I started putting on for the funeral. It's the tan slacks and tan shirt, under a green coat. That's what you call the uniform, in fact—"green coat." All officers from lieutenant and above wear the same coat for formal events. Officers below lieutenant wear the same uniform but with a Sam Browne leather belt.

I got dressed and put on a weapon just the same. I always wear a weapon, no matter what clothes I'm wearing. That morning, I put my Smith & Wesson 9mm into a belt holster. For the regular uniform, I'd carry the standard Berreta 9mm, which is a little bigger and bulkier than the Smith & Wesson.

That's what I wear to work most Mondays—the Smith & Wesson, under a dark suit. That's because I teach courses in criminology on Monday evenings at Montgomery College. I wear a dark suit to the station, change into the tan uniform of the day, and then change back into the suit in the evening before I go out to teach. I wear the slimmer Smith & Wesson, so it doesn't stick out of my suit coat.

I had finished dressing. I was standing at my desk going through papers. The only things on my mind were getting through the funeral and getting to the airport. I was confident, having stayed late the night before, that the department would be in fine shape for a few days without me watching over it.

Then the call came in—first from Captain Demme, in the media division, and second from Assistant Chief O'Toole.

A man had been killed. He was mowing the lawn in front of the Colonial Dodge car dealership at the Fitzgerald Auto Mall, on the Rockville Pike, in Bethesda. He was pushing the lawn mower, and then he just dropped, with a deep wound in the upper body. It was 7:41 A.M.

At first it wasn't clear what had happened. The call came in as a shooting, but there was a competing theory that something went wrong with the lawn mower—that it blew up, or that the mower blade kicked up something that hit the victim.

That sort of resonated for me. When I was about eight years old I was in the yard watching my brother David mow the lawn. I was envious. I wished I was old enough to run the lawn mower. He was running it over the grass when suddenly he screamed and fell down. There was blood pouring out of his leg. He didn't know what had happened, but he was in terrible pain. We got him to the hospital. He had to undergo surgery to remove what turned out to be a length of wire coat hanger—picked up by the lawn mower and spun out with such force that pieces of it pierced his leg.

For years afterward my brother kept a little baby food jar in his room in which was the piece of the coat hanger they'd removed from his leg.

The lawn mower theory made sense to me as a possibility, as it did to some of the others. Captain Demme had received a page that morning as she was getting ready to leave home. She was putting on her dress green uniform for the funeral of Corporal Foust when the first one came in. It was a lawn mower accident. She figured it was one of those ride-on lawn mowers, with a gas engine, and it had exploded and caught fire.

The two calls, from Demme and O'Toole, contained the same information. But I was glad to get both calls. This is a system of redundancy I used in Portland and instituted in Montgomery County. It's my way of making sure that I always know what's going on. If one side forgets, or thinks the other side is calling, I still get the information. And this way, I get two sets of facts. Sometimes one side knows something the other doesn't, so I get the complete picture.

This morning, the complete picture wasn't very complete. An ambulance was on the way. We didn't have much information. There were no witnesses. No one saw or heard anything. The victim had no criminal record. It was just a guy cutting grass who fell over dead.

Just like last night it was a guy in a grocery store parking lot who fell over dead.

I remember thinking, *This is strange.* We got murders weeks apart, or even months apart. Two men being shot like that, in less than twenty-four hours, that was strange.

But there was no connection, in my mind, or in anyone else's. I was assured that people from the major crimes unit were on it. Because of the shooting the night before, a lot of people had come in early to get working on that. So we had people assembled, even before 8 A.M., and ready to go.

I went back to my paperwork. I had asked the media office what they were planning to do. I wanted to know more details about the Fitzgerald Auto Mall shooting. In my experience, you have to get the media questions answered fast. You have to know what the crime scene looks like, how public it is, whether it's a volatile situation, whether it's a low-key situation, and is the media on it yet.

That's partly because the answers to those questions will determine how fast you have to move and with how many officers. If there is a shooting in a house on a dead-end street, you have a lot more time than if you have a shooting in front of a liquor store on a busy street. In that case, you'll have people standing around who threaten to contaminate your crime scene. You'll have witnesses who will walk off before you get a chance to interview them. You may have other problems, too. In Portland, we had instances of gang shootings where members of a rival gang might show up. This could turn volatile, and involve more killing. You have to know how public the crime scene is, and who's there, and what the mood is, before you start dispatching teams of officers.

You have to be cognizant of what you're going to tell the public, too. You don't want people to be afraid. You want maximum disclosure, with minimum delay, but you want the message to be the correct one. You want to be able to say to people, in essence, "You are not in danger."

That morning, I had no reason to think anyone was in danger. So far, it was off the routine, but it wasn't unmanageable. I wasn't worried about how the major crimes guys or the media office people were going to handle it.

Especially the media office. We had a good relationship with the press. This was the result of some hard work on our part. When I arrived in Montgomery County—and it's one of the main reasons I was hired to be the chief in Montgomery County—the department was near the end of a three-year Department of Justice (DOJ) investigation. It had begun as a "pattern and practice" investigation, looking into complaints of police profiling and brutality. The investigation turned up no pattern of brutality, but it did demonstrate there was a pattern of African-Americans receiving more than their fair share of traffic stops and traffic tickets.

This was during a time when there was a heightened consciousness about racism and racial profiling in police departments all over the country. The Montgomery police took quite a beating from the press.

In the end, an agreement was reached with the DOJ. The police would make improvements in its internal affairs division, make improvements in its training procedures and hire a monitor to make sure the improvements were being instituted. And the police would also collect and analyze all its traffic ticket data—to demonstrate that there was no racial profiling there. Every patrol officer was given a hand-held computer, and told to record the race, sex and age of every motorist stopped, questioned or ticketed.

It turned out to be a little redundant, because later that year the Maryland legislature passed a law requiring all Maryland police departments to collect traffic stop data for the same reason. But we continued with the program, which was the most inclusive ever conducted.

This had strained the police department's relations with the media. When I arrived, I made changes to address that problem. I took the corporal who was in charge of media relations and replaced him with a lieutenant. Shortly after, I upgraded the position to a captain's position. I told all the officers to forget the department policy on not talking to the press. I told the media office I wanted us to take charge of the story of our department, and that I wanted them to generate at least one press release a day that told the story of a police department doing a good job. I told them that it might happen that none of these press releases would wind up being a story, but that at the end of the year I wanted there to be a big stack of press releases showing what a good job the police officers were doing.

It worked. We got a lot of positive stories. Police officers started being treated like heroes. Whenever one of them was profiled, I'd have copies of the stories made and framed, and I'd hold a little ceremony to present the officer with the framed copy. The officers always acted like this was stupid, like they didn't even want the copy at all. We didn't hang them up in the station and the officers never hung them up in their offices.

But I've been to their homes. I see these framed stories, on the walls. I've been to their mothers' homes. They have *two* copies on the walls. So I know this was a good idea.

By this time the DOJ review was over. The Montgomery County police had nothing to hide, nothing to apologize for, nothing to worry about. We were doing a good job.

There was no reason to think this second shooting wouldn't be wrapped up pretty soon. In my office, I was listening to the activity on the police radio. There was no massive call-out—to bring in officers who are not on duty. The dispatch stuff was going to uniformed officers. They were setting up a perimeter around the auto mall. They had an ambulance going there. It was a routine response to an incident of this nature.

I wasn't worried about leaving town. I wasn't worried about having to be at a funeral. I wasn't thinking about calling my boss, the county executive. That's how relatively routine this seemed—unfortunate and tragic, for the people involved, but relatively routine. If it had not been, I would have been on the phone, scrambling to change my flight plans and making an emergency call to my boss.

At some point I walked over to the media office to see how things were going. There wasn't much new information. The lawn mower was a big, powerful Lawn Boy. The guy doing the mowing was James L. Buchanan. He was thirty-nine, and a landscaper, a Maryland man who had recently moved to Virginia but returned to Maryland to help his dad build a house. He came into Bethesda once a week, as a favor to Dottie Fitzgerald, the owner of the auto mall. We later learned he was the son of a former Montgomery County police officer. He was known as "Sonny."

Sonny had stopped for a sip of water right before he fell. He clutched his chest and began to stumble toward the auto mall. He'd walked almost two hundred feet before dropping. The first person to get to him was Al Briggs, a service director at the auto mall.

The 911 operator who took the call heard a voice saying, "This guy with a lawn mower did something, man. It chopped him up. He's bleeding real bad."

It turned out he had a wound to his stomach "as wide as a coffee cup," one witness would later say.

By then we had gotten a little more information on the previous night's death, too. The victim was James D. Martin, fifty-five, father of an eleven-year-old son and a program analyst at a lab in D.C. He had just gotten out of his car and was on his way into the Shoppers Food Warehouse. The shot that killed him came less than an hour, it had been established, after the shot that was fired into the nearby Michael's craft store.

Then the next call came in.

There had been another shooting, at a Mobil gas station in the Aspen Hill section of Rockville, at 4100 Aspen Hill Road—just three blocks down the road from the Michael's shooting the night before, and less than three miles from the spot where Sonny Buchanan died. A man was pumping gas, and he just fell over. And died.

Assistant Chief Bill O'Toole came in just then. He had come through the back door of the police station, and had run into Barney Forsythe outside the major crimes room. Forsythe, seeing O'Toole in his green suit, said to him, "You might want to forget about the funeral." O'Toole said he'd already heard about the guy with the lawn mower. Forsythe told him, "It's not that. There's been a shooting at a gas station."

O'Toole is a real Irishman, and looks the part. He has bright red hair and wears a mustache on a handsome face that often looks a little flushed, like he's a bit embarrassed. At that moment, he looked more flushed than usual.

O'Toole and Forsythe had already spoken with Assistant Chief Walker. She had come into work early, and was getting ready to go to the funeral, when she heard about the Mobil shooting. She told them she was probably going to miss the funeral, and headed over to the Aspen Hill area right away.

That's very much in keeping with Assistant Chief Walker's background and personality. She's a career police officer. She went to work for the Montgomery County Police Department six months out of college, in

1985, and never worked anywhere else. She carries herself like a career cop, too—trim build, little or no makeup, hair cut short and combed straight back, a no-nonsense, no-excess look about everything she does.

Walker got into a car and went through the rush hour traffic "lights and siren," she remembered later. It was the only way to get through the traffic, she thought, and not spend a half an hour fighting her way to the scene.

O'Toole suggested that I go on to the funeral alone. He and Forsythe told me what they knew about the Mobil shooting. Then I turned to Captain Barney Forsythe. He's more senior in age and experience than O'Toole. He's also a no-nonsense guy, a real straight cop, who wears his gray-white hair combed straight back in a kind of fifties style. I asked him to remind his people to put on their vests—the bulletproof body armor I'm always telling all my officers to wear—and then said that I was going to ride down to the crime scene, too.

This was not typical for me. I don't go out to crime scenes. I have police officers, detectives, investigators, captains and assistant chiefs to go out to crime scenes. They are all professionals. They know how to do their jobs, probably better than I know how to do their jobs. If I show up at the crime scene, I just get in the way most of the time and waste the officers' time by getting them to answer questions that don't need asking, while they're trying to do their work.

But this felt different. I'm not sure why. I didn't think it was the beginning of some big crime spree. I did not know we were seeing the work of a serial killer. I certainly did not think this was the start of the largest manhunt in American police history. But this was three deaths, three *unusual* deaths, in one night and one morning.

I went back into my office and began to change clothes, mostly because I needed to put on the body armor. I don't wear the vest when I'm in the formal uniform. But I've made a big deal to my officers about wearing the vest whenever they're in the field, and I wanted to make sure I was setting the right example.

I told my aide, "We may have to miss the funeral."

The Mobil station was only a short drive from the Rockville headquarters of the Montgomery County Police Department. I got into the black Crown Victoria and drove myself down. When I got there, though, instead of pulling into the gas station, I parked across the street. I snuck my car into a mini-mall parking lot with a bunch of other cars. I wanted some perspective. I wanted to see what the scene looked like from a distance. I just wanted to be there, and see it, and feel it, and kind of not be there.

I didn't want to get in the officers' way. And I didn't want to start any kind of panic. You see the police chief showing up at a crime scene, that sends a message. I didn't have any message to send.

It was only eight-thirty in the morning, but it was already starting to warm up. I could feel it was going to be a very hot day. There was a little breeze blowing. The trees had started to change color. This is what they call Indian Summer in that part of the country—warm and dry, with the fall already coming on.

I remember thinking how normal everything looked. The traffic was heavy with people going to work. There were people on the street. There were people waiting for a bus. No one was panicking. The responding officers had closed the gas station. An ambulance had taken the body away. There was yellow police tape around the perimeter. There were probably three or four police cars already on the scene. But it was not getting much attention.

I found myself standing next to Detective Terry Ryan. He's a burly plainclothes detective. He was wearing slacks and a shirt—and the vest. This was odd. The plainclothes guys, almost as a point of pride, never wear the body armor. I remember wondering what that meant, if he knew something I didn't know that was making him take extra precaution. I found out later that

Captain Walker had issued an order, from the car, as she went "lights and siren" down to the crime scene: "No investigator is allowed to respond to the Mobil station without a vest on." She was already thinking about the implications of a sniper with a high-powered rifle, and she wanted her people protected.

Detective Ryan didn't know anything special. We stood for a while talking. Or rather he was talking, and I was listening. You can't learn anything from talking. Besides, I didn't want to contaminate the officers' ideas by sharing my thoughts, any more than I would want to contaminate a crime scene with my fingerprints.

I asked questions. What do you have? What do you think? What is the common theme here? What are the possible connections? What is the possible motive? Do we have any witnesses? Did anyone hear or see anything?

And, of course, I was wondering, *Can we solve this? Is this over?*

Obviously there are things you can rule out, right from the start. One of my concerns, as a police chief, is always whether any officers are involved. We knew that wasn't the case.

We also knew it was not a question of killings taking place during the commission of some other kind of crime. The victims all had their wallets. They weren't being robbed. And they weren't famous people. It's not like they were all senators or congressmen or something, even though we had a lot of those living in Montgomery County. So it was probably not a question of kidnapping, or extortion, or anything like that.

The other thing we knew, straight off, was that these weren't family killings. They weren't domestic disputes, or some kind of simple disagreement with a friend or even a stranger. We had enough witnesses to know that no one had come up and started yelling and then pulled out a gun and shot someone.

That's often the case. Killings are emotional, and volatile, and personal, most of the time. It's two guys at a bar trying to date the same girl. It's a guy who gets fired from his job and comes back to shoot his boss. It's a wife who thinks her husband is cheating. It's a crook trying to rob a drug dealer, or a john trying to kill a prostitute. And almost always someone has heard something. Someone has seen something. It was very unusual for us to experience a murder in Montgomery County that occurred with no clues or witnesses, and that went unsolved. So the absence of information here was all the more alarming.

It's important, on several levels, for us to know what someone has seen or heard. First of all, that's often the beginning of the investigation. You establish a relationship between the victim and the suspect, and you start to know where to look for the suspect.

You also could make a guess about whether there would be any other victims. If a man kills his wife and his children at home and then leaves, and you know there are other children in school or something, you might want to do something about locating those other children.

You also can prepare to make some kind of statement to the public. Through the media, you are going to want to minimize panic, and let people know they are not in danger. If it's two guys fighting over a girl at some bar, the average person can say, "I wasn't in that bar trying to date that girl. I'm okay." If it's a family matter, the average person can say, "It's a personal thing. My children are safe."

I didn't have any theories. Detective Ryan didn't have any theories. I remember having a very unsettling thought, as I stood there: *What if the guy is watching me, right now?* I didn't feel afraid. I didn't think of myself as a target. I remember thinking the guy could be observing this all, right now, and really enjoying himself.

O'Toole told me later that he'd had the same idea. He was thinking about arsonists, and how they often light a fire, disappear, and then come back to watch the firefighters try to extinguish their blaze. He was wondering whether the sniper was standing around someplace watching us clean up his mess.

Captain Walker was thinking the same thing. She had been the commander of the Wheaton station, right across the street from the Shoppers Food Warehouse. She had a cousin who lives right around the corner from there, and who walks with her children to do her marketing at the Shoppers Food Warehouse. She had a sister with children who go to Rockville schools. And Captain Walker, unlike most of my people, was born and raised in Montgomery County. She was very conscious of being a target herself, she said, but she was even more conscious of her family members being exposed and in danger.

The crime scene in the gas station, from our perspective, didn't yield much. At some point, I went across the street to take a closer look.

The gas station was locked down. The officers had all the gas station employees and some of the customers locked down, too. They were in the gas station office and the repair bay, being questioned. The dark gray taxicab that belonged to the victim was just sitting there. There wasn't much in the way of blood or anything. There wasn't much to see.

There wasn't much information, either. The victim was a male in his fifties. He bought a lottery ticket, a pack of Juicy Fruit gum and $5 worth of gas for his taxi. He went outside and started pumping. There was a bang, which one of the mechanics said sounded like a car backfire. The cabdriver clutched his side and leaned over against the passenger door of another customer's silver minivan, smearing blood on it. The victim called out for help, and then fell to the ground.

There was a doctor in the gas station at the time, pumping gas. The doctor tried to help the victim. There was nothing to be done. The victim was unresponsive.

The first responding officer was one of our people, Corporal Paul Kukucka. He was in his patrol car, stopped at the intersection in front of the Mobil station, when the shooting occurred. He had not seen a suspect, and did not see the victim as he was shot. Now he was inside, talking to the gas station customers. Unfortunately, he had not learned much.

But the media was starting to arrive. One news crew had parked its van and was already setting up on the sidewalk. I knew something was going to have to be said pretty quickly. I didn't know what there was to say.

In my head, I was sure this was going to end soon. I was still thinking that we were going to find a witness, very shortly, who saw something. We would establish a connection between the victims. We would find out they all worked at the same place, or drank at the same place, or belonged to the same health club, or dated the same girl, or something.

Or we would learn that this was all a bizarre coincidence.

Either that or, I was beginning to think, the person responsible for the shootings was insane. The killer was freaking out, having some kind of complete breakdown. If that were the case, then we would find this person very shortly. He couldn't freak out like that for very long and not draw attention to himself. Whoever it was would turn up. His family would notice something. His boss would notice something. Some citizen would notice something. Because this person had flipped, and when you flip you can't control that.

I was thinking, the next thing we're going to hear is there is a person sitting on a corner somewhere with a gun in his mouth. We'll get there in time to see the person commit suicide. Or we'll get there in time to stop him from committing suicide. It would be bizarre, but it would be over.

I was confident that I would be able to tell the media, "We can take care of this."

The next call we got was not about a guy on a corner with a gun in his mouth.

The next call was about another shooting.

A Hispanic woman had died, sitting on a bus-stop

bench, in front of a post office and a Crisp and Juicy chicken restaurant, across the street from Leisure World, in Silver Spring, at 3701 Rossmoor Boulevard. This was, again, only a few miles away.

The first report, probably based on the first 911 call, indicated this was a possible suicide. The victim had what appeared to be a gunshot wound to the head. It appeared to be self-inflicted. She was waiting for a bus and reading a book. No one ran up to her. No one was sitting on the bench with her. There were no witnesses with anything to offer.

It was not quite 8:40 A.M. There had been four killings in sixteen hours.

I made the decision, right away, not to go to the Leisure World crime scene. I had to do something else. I had to be the police chief.

By late morning we made the decision to set up a command center there, using the command bus in the Aspen Hill area. Captain Forsythe, in response to the first shooting, had already issued an order to have the command bus sent down to the Mobil station location. He and Assistant Chief Walker had arranged to have it parked behind a Home Depot. Assistant Chief Walker's plan was to place it in a location that would offer the media and the police officers maximum cover and security.

I didn't like that idea so much. I wanted the police to have maximum visibility, not maximum security. The security was for the citizens. Plus I knew the media would never participate. They have to set up their stuff where they can take pictures of an interview and also take pictures of the crime scene. They wouldn't be able to see the crime scene from behind the Home Depot.

I told Assistant Chief Walker, "We're not worrying about protecting the police. We're worrying about protecting the public. Get the command bus out into an open location."

Next to the Mobil station, where the cabdriver was shot, was a Korean Baptist Church. I sent an officer to see whether we would be allowed to move in and use their parking lot, and to find out whether they had bathrooms, telephones, electrical connections and other things we would need to create a field headquarters. When it was clear that we could use the facility, I requested the command vehicle be brought into the parking lot.

The command vehicle is a kind of bus, turned into a mobile police station. It has a conference room at one end and office space at the other, and it's equipped with telephones, fax machines, internet hookups, televisions and so on. This would be the home base for the investigation.

There was a lot of work to be done in it already. I was meeting with my assistant chiefs. I was meeting with the forensics people. I was on the phone to Doug Duncan, the county executive, which in Maryland is the equivalent at the county level to the mayor—he's the guy that hires and fires the police chief, for example—telling him what we knew. He had been out of town, and he wanted to know whether he should come home.

I told him, "We have a mess here. It's not an impossible situation, but it's a difficult situation, and it's going to take some serious police work." I gave him all the facts I had. I told him it would be helpful if he came home, at once.

When I finished with that, I went again to speak with my media people and my other staff. I needed to know how many units we could get into the Aspen Hill area. I didn't think we could protect anyone if there were more shootings—because there were just too many people on the street, and too much going on, for it to be possible to prevent them from being targeted—but I did think that more visibility on the street might serve as a deterrent. I needed to know how many of those units we could get into the area without causing a scheduling crunch for the next day. I wanted as many units as possible, but I didn't want to exhaust our resources all at once. I needed to know what the forensics guys were thinking, how many teams they had available, and whether they'd need more. I needed someone to notify the forensics lab at the Bureau of Alcohol, Tobacco and Firearms in Rockville that we would need their services.

In other words, there was a lot to be done.

And nothing was going right. The command vehicle kept breaking down. The electricity went out. The air-conditioning went out. The day was very hot, by now, and we had to go out and find a shade tree or some other cool place to work every time the bus broke down.

By then, we had received more information on the Leisure World shooting. It was not a suicide. There was no handgun or other weapon found anywhere near the body. We knew it was a homicide. We didn't have witnesses yet, but we knew it was probably going to be connected.

Then there was another shooting.

It came in over the radio as a "possible 0-100." That's police talk for a homicide. The shooting occurred at 9:58 A.M., at a Shell station at 10515 Connecticut Avenue in Kensington, Maryland—less than one mile from where we were standing, in the parking lot of the Mobil station.

The victim was a twenty-five-year-old white woman. She was shot once, in the upper back, while vacuuming the floor of her minivan. Witnesses said she fell to the ground, blood pouring out of her nose and mouth.

Captain Demme remembered later that we all stood there staring at each other for quite a while, as we listened to this report come over the radio. Captain Demme is not easily ruffled. She's a law school graduate who worked in private practice before she returned to police work. She's very tough and very firm—despite the blond hair she keeps tied up under her police officer's hat—and doesn't take any nonsense from anyone. But at that moment she looked stunned.

Assistant Chief O'Toole would later use the word "surreal." That's a good word. We were hearing these voices come over the police radio. What we were hearing just didn't seem possible. I was standing there. Demme and O'Toole were standing with me. Sergeant Roger Thomson, another career police officer, was there with us. These announcements would come in. We'd look at each other. There was nothing to say. None of us had any experience with anything like this. It felt like we were sort of suspended in time. And every few minutes, the radio would crackle again and there would be another victim.

What we were hearing almost didn't make sense. O'Toole got out a notebook and began making a map, trying to figure out what kind of route the killer would have had to take to get from one shooting scene to the next. So far, the killings were very localized, and all centered on the Aspen Hill area. So we had every reason to think the next shooting, should there be another, would take place fairly close by.

Thomson was a real veteran cop. He had spent most of his career working homicide. He had been to the most gruesome crime scenes. He had had to be professional under the most trying circumstances. I had never seen him show the slightest emotion on the job. And yet this morning he looked unnerved. I am sure he would have said the same thing about O'Toole and me. We all probably looked uncertain, and off-balance, because we were.

I told O'Toole we should start concentrating on establishing a connection between the victims. That would be the place the investigation could begin to make sense of who was being killed, which might explain who was doing the killing, which might explain why, and which might point ahead to more possible targets.

At this point it didn't even occur to me to go to the new crime scene. I knew there was nothing for me to contribute there. I understood by now that this was the work of a serial sniper. I suspected that the victims were not connected by anything but their availability as targets. I didn't say this out loud. I couldn't announce it. But I knew.

I continued to set up the command center and oversee the scheduling of my officers. The Shell station was locked down. The witnesses were interviewed. The family of the victim would be interviewed. The body would be removed and taken to a hospital. The medical examiner would get the evidence. There was nothing I could do for the victim.

There was plenty I could do at the command vehicle. Throughout the day Thursday, I continued to bring more visible units into the Aspen Hill area. As the hours passed, more manpower was becoming available. Police officers started hearing things, on their radios or from the media. A lot of them left the funeral for our fallen officer and came directly into the station, without being asked. They just started showing up, even though some of them were not scheduled to work for another couple of days, and asking where they could be assigned.

We were also getting calls from the Maryland State Police, wanting to know how many troopers we needed, and where we needed them deployed.

I also ramped up our tactical capacity. I was still convinced at that time that this was someone who was going to show his hand very shortly, that day or the next day. This person had gone berserk. We had to have the capacity ready to confront him, and take him out, as soon as he showed himself.

I was moving up the SWAT officers and equipment. I had helicopters in the air for flyover surveillance. I was bringing up officers who had long guns, with more firepower. The regular officers have 9mm handguns, and some have shotguns, but now we needed long guns—and the people who knew how to use them. If this person was flipping out, and was going to be holed up somewhere, we needed sniper teams to take him out from a distance. We also needed negotiators. We needed an armored personnel carrier. All that equipment had to be moved into the area.

We were also spending a lot of energy scheduling officers for the next day. We wanted visible patrols out, especially around schools, so we had to make certain we had the manpower for that, and that we didn't exhaust our staffing options on the first day.

We also started doing low-altitude helicopter flyovers at the schools, partly in case there was a sniper lurking in the woods, but largely because we wanted the community to see that we were there.

In the command vehicle that Thursday afternoon there was a lot of back-and-forth between me and the assistant chiefs about why this was all occurring. We were asking each other whether there could be a racial connection, whether this could be some kind of hate crime.

That all fell apart pretty quickly, because no one could find the common thread. Here were two white guys getting shot. Then there was a man who was originally from India. The fourth victim was originally from El Salvador. The fifth victim was white. It was difficult to argue that there was a racial or religious or ethnic thread suitable for a race or hate crime.

Another theory that fell apart pretty quickly was the terrorist theory.

In the very beginning, perhaps because the 9/11 attacks on the World Trade Center and the Pentagon were still so fresh in everyone's mind, and because of the anthrax scare that followed—with anthrax and other strange powders appearing in mail sent to Washington, D.C., offices like those of Senator Tom Daschle and newsman Tom Brokaw—some of our people started thinking the killings might be the work of terrorists. It seemed to me that the FBI people, particularly, were interested in developing this theory.

We had an additional reason to consider this. That morning, while we were all at the command vehicle, Captain Forsythe had received an intelligence briefing from the FBI or the ATF (Bureau of Alcohol, Tobacco and Firearms). The briefing was a warning that the agency had received intelligence that Al Qaeda operatives were being trained to assassinate members of the

U.S. Senate and Congress in the metropolitan Washington, D.C., area—on golf courses.

Forsythe brought the briefing to me and said, "I just want to alert you to this."

I didn't see the connection. The victims weren't senators or congressmen. They weren't celebrities or rich people. They didn't seem likely targets for anyone with a financial or political motive. I didn't rule the terrorism angle out, but I didn't make it a priority, either.

Most of our investigative energy that first day was focused on the idea that someone must have had some beef with someone, and that the connection must be through some association—work, neighborhood, PTA, something—that would become visible if we could connect the victims to each other.

We were eager to know what that something was. If we learned that, then we could learn why the shootings were occurring. If we knew why, that would lead us to the perpetrator, and perhaps even tell us where to look for the next victim. We could bring some peace of mind to the community, as well. If there was a pattern, and it didn't fit them, they might not feel so frightened.

More information continued to come in from the earlier crime scenes. The woman gunned down on the bus bench near Leisure World was named Sarah Ramos. She was a part-time baby-sitter and housekeeper. She had a seven-year-old son. She was shot once, in the head. The bullet passed through her head and shattered the window of the storefront behind her. She didn't even fall over. A witness described her, in death, as "just sitting there." One witness, who was inside an adjacent place of business, reported hearing a "popping" sound.

The second woman shot was Lori Ann Lewis-Rivera. She was married, and had a daughter, and worked as a nanny. She had moved to Silver Spring six years ago, from Idaho. She had removed her child's car seat from her purple minivan and was vacuuming the floor when she was killed.

We learned more about Premkumar Walekar, the taxi

driver shot at the Mobil station, too. He lived in Olney, Maryland. He had a wife and two children. He usually went to work around noon, driving a shift for Presidential Cab. But today he had started work early, so he could get off early and spend the afternoon with his family. In what I thought was a kind of eerie detail, the sign on the top of his taxi read "Call 911." That's because you dialed "911-TAXI" to order a cab from his company.

At some point, I overheard Bill O'Toole say, "Hey. It's been an hour. We haven't had a shooting in over an hour." I remember thinking how weird that was, that we should be happy not to have had any new shootings in an hour. That's how under siege we felt, that first morning. Later in the day, O'Toole noted again that it had been five hours since the last shooting. It felt like such a break.

By Thursday afternoon, too, we had our first clue. A witness was absolutely certain he had seen a white van or box truck leaving the scene of the Ramos shooting across from Leisure World. At first the information was a little uncertain. The witness was Spanish-speaking, and it wasn't clear that the person interviewing him spoke Spanish fluently. So we had to find a fluent Spanish speaker to go back and talk to the witness. We found one, a Wheaton station crime analyst named John Desoulas who Forsythe remembered spoke Spanish. Desoulas got the witness to confirm that he had seen this white box truck, or van, in the vicinity. He didn't say, as was later reported, that he saw someone shooting out of the box truck. Just that he had seen it. We didn't want to make too much of it, but it was a possible lead, in a situation where we didn't have that many leads.

The white box truck lead didn't add much. We didn't have a license plate number on the vehicle. We didn't have age, facial characteristics, hair or even race on the driver. It might be one guy. It might be two guys. All we had was a white box truck.

We tried to get that out there, that afternoon, through the media. And maybe we all began to obsess on it. Assistant Chief O'Toole told me later that as we stood out there by the Mobil station taking in this information about the truck, he was watching the intersection in front of us. It was still rush hour. The streets were filled. And he said, "All I could see was white box trucks. Everywhere I looked, there were white box trucks. How were we ever going to find the needle in that haystack?"

We later learned, from the Ford company, that the company had sold more than fifty thousand Econoline vans in the Washington, D.C., area over the last decade.

The first press briefing was held Thursday morning. It went very badly. Captain Nancy Demme led the briefing, standing on the sidewalk near the Mobil station crime scene. The reporters pressed in on her so aggressively that she was backed up to the edge of the sidewalk, and then onto the curb, and then into the street. Captain Demme later said the reporters looked scared, or nervous, as if they were afraid they might become targets of the next shooting. As a group, they were like a mob. They pressed forward, pushing Captain Demme off the sidewalk and into the street. And there was a lot of traffic moving down the street. It wasn't safe. One of the reporters actually said, "Back off! You're going to get her killed!"

I had assigned Captain Demme to the media position almost a month earlier. But she had several projects she felt obliged to finish with the undercover work she was doing. So she actually hadn't taken over the position until October 2. That afternoon—just two hours before James Martin would be shot down at Shoppers Food Warehouse—I sat down with her and told her what my expectations were. I shared with her my theories on how to keep the press happy and still do your job at the same time. I told her I had two rules: feed them material for stories, or they'll go find or invent material on their own, and use maximum disclosure with minimum delay, so they feel you are keeping them abreast of everything as it happens.

I specifically told Captain Demme that she was going

to be the one doing all the press interface, and that she'd be the person the public associated with our police department. I said, "I want you out there ninety percent of the time. They're only going to see my face ten percent of the time. And when they see my face, they're going to know it's very serious, or very bad."

Well, this was serious and bad. I took Captain Demme aside afterward and told her that while I always wanted her to be the face of the police department during regular, ordinary police business, this was no longer regular or ordinary. I wanted the people of Montgomery County to see the police chief out there, to know that the police chief was responding.

She said, "Chief, I think your ten percent is about to kick in."

I didn't think I'd be bullied by the media the way she'd been. So, at my first press briefing, I tried to establish some ground rules.

When I came out, practically before I even introduced myself, I laid down the first ground rule. I told the media that I was going to read a statement, that I was going to give them all the information we had at that time, and then I was going to leave. I was not going to take questions, because I was already going to give them all the information that we had. And my ground rule was this: I said, "After that, I'm going to walk away. And I don't want any of you guys to try and make me look like an asshole, by calling out questions and film me leaving and make it look like I'm running away. Don't make me look like an asshole."

What I didn't know was that the cameras were already running while I made this speech. I found out later that some of the stations ran this more or less in its entirety. When the press conference tape was played on the news that night, a lot of my officers at the station saw it. Someone told me later that they applauded. Someone shouted out, "Way to go, Chief! Somebody finally told them!"

The *Washington Post* reported the following day that

I had used "profanity." I probably should have said, "Please don't make me look uncooperative." But that wasn't what I meant. I meant, "Don't make me look like an *asshole*." So that's what I said.

Sometime that afternoon, through one of the press briefings, I made the decision to ask people to start phoning in anything they'd seen that seemed suspicious. Even though it was not the way you usually go about it, I asked people to phone 911, if they'd seen a white box truck, if they'd seen any suspicious behavior. I asked them to try to think, if they were in the vicinity of any of the shootings, of what they might have seen or heard. Usually you would wait to do this until you had time to set up a hot-line number and get it staffed. We were working on that—trying to find volunteers, trying to round up retired police officers—but we hadn't got it set up yet. And this was all breaking so fast, and we had so little information, that I just didn't think we could afford to wait. By the end of the day, the 911 people were starting to get inundated with calls.

Most of it was nothing. But the system was working. We were getting leads. We were getting tips. We were assigning these to investigating officers. They were running down the most promising ones. The investigation was under way.

By nighttime, I was starting to wonder whether this thing was over. The last shooting, at the Shell station, had been at 9:58 A.M. We'd had an entire day, and nothing else had happened.

That created two contradictory feelings. I was afraid there would be more shootings. And I was afraid there *wouldn't* be any more shootings. It sounds weird to say that, but I knew that if there weren't any more shootings there wouldn't be any more evidence—and without more evidence we were going to have a hell of a hard time finding out who was doing the killings. Of course I didn't want anyone else to be hurt, but I knew that if the shootings just ended, like that, we might never catch the person responsible.

I was hoping for time. I knew I didn't have much information. It was going to take time to do the investigating. I was still hopeful. I knew I had great people doing the investigation. One of them was going to catch a break. I hoped that the shootings would stop for long enough that we could crack this thing and make an arrest before anyone else was hurt.

But I also knew that if there was another shooting, that would increase the chance that someone would see something, and that would increase the body of evidence, which would give the investigators a better chance to catch a break.

My great fear was that the person responsible for this would be arrested for doing something else. He'd get picked up on some warrant or something, in some other jurisdiction, and he'd go to jail for two months. The shootings would stop. We wouldn't be able to solve the crime. Then he'd be out on the street in two months and the killings would start again. I had a lot of this kind of anxiety in my head.

Sometime late in the day I also had a couple of conversations with my wife. Sandy had landed in Minneapolis and been picked up by a car. She had started chatting with the driver. He asked where she was from. She said she was from Montgomery County, Maryland.

"Oh yeah," the driver said. "That's where they just had all those killings."

Sandy corrected him. She said it had just been one killing, the night before.

The driver said, "No. I mean all the killings today." He told her what he knew.

Sandy said, "Take me back to the airport."

It took her all day and well into the night to get home. There was no direct flight back. She had to book something that took her through St. Louis. There were delays. We talked a couple of times on the phone. She told me she had already spoken to my son David, and that he'd agreed to pick her up at the airport when her flight got in around midnight.

I was trying to wrap it up for the day. I had held several press briefings. I had met with the county executive. He and I had briefed Constance Morella, the congresswoman from our district. I had made the scheduling assignments for the next day.

And then we got the call. There had been another shooting.

A man in his sixties or seventies was crossing a street in Washington, D.C., just over the Montgomery County line. He stopped or slowed down to light a cigarette. He fell to the ground—shot once, fatally, in the upper chest.

And immediately following the shooting, we had a suspect. Or a suspect vehicle. A car had run a red light, very near the shooting location. When police gave chase, the driver sped off. Police pursued him into Montgomery County, where our officers became involved. By the time the driver was apprehended, some of the officers had concluded he must be connected to the D.C. shooting—which might make him the serial sniper.

He wasn't. He had run the red light and then tried to run from the police because he had an expired driver's license, or something stupid like that. He was not connected to the shootings in any way. So much for our first suspect. We were back where we started.

Only now we had another police agency involved. We now were running the risk that the chain of evidence would be broken, if the Washington, D.C., police force decided to pursue this shooting as an individual case. They might take their evidence to a different forensics lab. They might not want to cooperate. This could complicate things.

The details that came in on the shooting in the District did not clarify the situation much. The victim was a seventy-two-year-old retired carpenter, originally from Haiti, named Pascal Charlot. He was a walker. Neighbors said he went out walking daily on Georgia and Connecticut Avenues, in the area around his home. Reports from the hospital showed the bullet that killed him went through his chest—after first passing through his hand. Maybe he was reaching up for the cigarette, or waving to an acquaintance.

We didn't have a suspect. But we had caught a break. The ATF had brought canine units to the scene. These are specially trained dogs capable of detecting various kinds of explosives. When a rifle is fired, for example, gunpowder is expelled on the shell casing and through the ejection port where the shell leaves the rifle. This is a minute amount of gunpowder, not visible to the eye, but the dogs can pick it up.

The ATF keeps teams of these dogs all around the country. They have thirty agents specially trained to handle the dogs, and they have forty local police agencies around the country who've been given trained dogs in exchange for their availability during a crisis. Michael Bouchard, special agent in charge of the Baltimore field office of the ATF, had sent down a team of dogs earlier in the day.

In this case, the dogs "alerted" on a wall that surrounded a parking lot near the shooting scene. There wasn't any evidence on or near the wall, but we had for the first time a clear picture of where the shooter had been standing, or lying down, when he took his shot. From that, we could start to get a clearer picture of what kind of weapon he was using and what degree of expertise he had.

There was not much other information available, but one witness described seeing a dark-colored car leaving the scene. The witness later said the car was a burgundy Chevrolet Caprice. Washington, D.C., police would eventually locate this car. It had been abandoned, and burned out, and had no connection to the sniper.

There was more confusion the next day. After initially deciding to handle the forensics investigation themselves, the MPD people finally agreed to work with us, and let the forensics evidence be handled by the ATF people in Rockville. This was a great relief. We now wouldn't run the risk of breaking the chain of evidence—if the shootings were all connected—by having different pieces of evidence handled by different labs.

But then the forensics evidence got lost. Somehow the team of people driving the evidence from Washington into Montgomery County took a wrong turn, or a shortcut, and they got lost. And for two hours no one could find them. We were feeling a great deal of pressure. We didn't know when the next shooting was coming, or where, or how many there would be after that. We had a serial killer on our hands, and we knew he was going to strike again. We felt like every minute mattered. And now the evidence had disappeared in the Friday afternoon rush hour.

It was just a little mistake. And, in the larger scope of things, two hours was nothing. But at the time it was incredibly frustrating.

The location of this latest shooting told me that all our concentration on the Aspen Hill area might be a waste of time and manpower. This shooting wasn't that far into the District. In fact, it was so close to the line between D.C. and Montgomery County that the shooter might have been *in* Montgomery County, even while the victim was in D.C. But it was still not in the Aspen Hill area. And it was at night. And it was an elderly person. And, we learned later, he was a black man. So, again, there was nothing at all to connect this to anything else. There was no pattern.

The randomness was so confusing. Part of what I was having such trouble with was the question of why the person doing this was choosing only one victim at a time. There had been multiple targets available, at each of the shooting locations. There were lots of people in the Shoppers parking lot. There were several customers in the two gas stations. There were plenty of pedestrians on the street in front of Leisure World. There were many other people walking down that street in D.C.

The person doing the shooting was choosing one target, and firing one fatal round, and then moving away. I couldn't figure out why.

These were the things on my mind that night. When I finally got home and got into bed, it wasn't for long. There had been some kind of mix-up. My son and my wife had not connected at the airport. The phone rang, and it was Sandy. I told her to sit tight. I got up, got dressed and made the thirty-minute drive out to BWI.

Driving back in, I told Sandy everything I knew, and I shared with her some of the anxiety I was having. I didn't share this with anyone else. My police officers needed to know I was feeling optimistic and totally confident in their abilities. The people of Montgomery County needed to know I was feeling optimistic and totally certain that my officers were going to solve this crime. But privately I had real doubts about how all this was going to play out.

2. A Southern Childhood

I was born into a middle-class family in August 1953. My father was a schoolteacher. My mother was a nurse. I had an older brother named David, named for my father. He and I were both born in New York City. Shortly after my birth, we moved back to near where my father was from, to Lexington, North Carolina. My little sister, Dorothy, was born there. Until I left home for college, it was the only home I ever knew.

The life my father made for us was orderly, structured and safe. The house was a solid, one-story, three-bedroom brick house, with white trim, set under pine trees in the southern part of Lexington. We were in the black part of town—it was black then, and it's still black now—on Smith Avenue. Of course it wasn't the nice part of town. It's still not the nice part of town. You can still see the broken-down clapboard houses with the boarded-over windows and the sagging old porches, and the shotgun shacks where you could shoot a bullet through the front door and have it go out the back door and not hit anything. There are still tar-paper shacks all over that neighborhood. There are still the Federal Street "projects," called South Side Village, that were built around the time I was in grade school.

But we had one of the nicest houses in the black section. We were middle-class black, not poor black. Smith Avenue was a quiet, leafy street with a gentle slope to it, and there were even a few white families living at the high end of the slope. Down the block lived the richest guy in the neighborhood—the dentist. He was very wealthy, by our standards. When his son graduated from high school, the dentist bought him a brand-new Corvette. When his daughter graduated, he bought her a Porsche 914.

We weren't doing *that* well, but we were doing fine. My father drove a Buick LeSabre—he was a dedicated Buick man, although later in his life he surprised us all and began driving a Pontiac Grand Prix—and my mother drove a Plymouth Valiant. I don't remember ever going hungry, or wanting for clothes, or not having schoolbooks or shoes. I didn't have my own bedroom, in our three-bedroom house, but my sister did—and in the room I shared with my brother, I did have my own bed. We didn't have air-conditioning, but we had a covered back porch and a fenced backyard and a nice collie dog named "Beauty" running around it. We were well taken care of.

I didn't have much consciousness of our status. I didn't have a very clear picture of poverty and wealth and the difference between the two. I remember driving with my brother into the projects one time. He was going to drop off a classmate of his. We passed this house that had a really fancy car parked in front of it. I said, "Now, how in the world can anybody afford a car like *that* if they're living here in the projects?"

My brother got so mad at me. After we dropped the guy off, he said, "How could you say something like that in front of him? Don't you have any sense at all?"

I guess I didn't—not any sense of that, anyway. Maybe the owner of the fancy car was just visiting. Maybe he lived there. Who knows? But it shows how in-sensitive I was to the whole question of class and money and status.

We went to church in Greensboro every Sunday, as

regular members of the Lutheran Church. My mother would make me dress up in a shirt and tie—it was the only time I *ever* wore a shirt and tie, and I had to wear it every single Sunday—and we'd drive the thirty miles or so into Greensboro. It was part of the rhythm of the week, part of the routine. The life in our house at 124 Smith Avenue was a little uptight and extremely focused. Life was about staying out of trouble, staying ahead of the bills and getting ahead.

For as long as I remember, both my parents worked. My mother was a night nurse at a veteran's hospital in Salisbury, North Carolina. For my entire childhood, she worked either the late shift or the graveyard shift. When I got up in the morning, she'd just be coming home from work. She'd make us breakfast and get us off to school. We lived just a few blocks from South Lexington Elementary School. We walked there every day. When we had gone, my mother would take care of the household chores and then go to bed.

She'd be awake again when we got home after school. She'd make us a snack and see that we were doing our homework. Then she'd get dinner together, and have that on the table when my father came home. We'd eat dinner together. She'd clean up. Then she usually went back to bed for a little bit.

When I'd wake up the next morning, my clothes would be all laid out for me. There would be a clean shirt and nice slacks. And leather shoes. We had to dress nice to go to school. Coming home after school, you'd always have to change into your play clothes before you could do anything. If you did something in your school clothes, and got them dirty, that was trouble.

Other things were trouble, too. We all got punished pretty regularly. You could get into trouble for not doing your homework, or not cleaning up your mess, or not doing the dishes, or breaking something. I got into trouble for fighting with my sister. Once I got into trouble for stealing some change off the dresser.

The punishment could be severe. When I was very

young, my mother handled the discipline. She'd go outside and get a switch—a small branch, off a bush, with the leaves stripped off—and you'd get a whipping. It was usually a series of whips on the back of your legs. It stung, and left a nasty series of little welts, but it didn't hurt all that long. What hurt more was my mother's attitude. She'd let you know she was upset, or hurt, and she'd keep letting you know that for a couple of days. You'd get the cold shoulder. She wouldn't let you forget your transgression.

My father was more businesslike about it, but the punishment was more damaging. He used a belt. He'd tell me to go to my room. I knew that meant I was going to get beat. He'd tell me why I was getting punished. He was never angry, but he was very diligent. I wasn't really scared of him, but I was scared of the beating. I knew he wasn't going to be lenient. He'd say, "You better not cry," but then he wouldn't stop sometimes until I did cry.

I remember one day I went riding on my bike, far away from the house, in a part of town I wasn't supposed to be in. I had a fall—a really bad fall—and I tore my thumb up. This old guy offered me a ride home. I managed to keep myself together pretty good until I got back to the house, but as soon as I saw my dad I started crying.

He took one look at my thumb and we were off to the emergency room. I got stitches, and they wrapped my thumb up in this big bandage.

When we got home, my father said, "Go to your room. We got some other business to attend to now." He took out the belt and I got a whipping, for riding my bike in a part of town I wasn't supposed to be in.

It was like "I love you, and I'm going to take you to the hospital and take care of you. But you've disobeyed me, so I have to beat you now."

Most of the really bad things didn't end with me getting punished. There weren't many of them, but I generally didn't get caught. Some friends of mine and I spent one whole afternoon busting the windows out of this guy's tractor with our slingshots. I have no idea why we didn't get caught. It probably would have been my first personal experience with the police.

As it was, I only heard about kids having trouble with the police. One time a wild kid I knew got arrested and carried off for doing what at the time was called a "crime against nature." We didn't have any idea what that was. It sounded bad. It sounded serious. He went away for a long time. I don't know if he even came back at all. Years later I understood that he had gotten involved in a homosexual relationship, or some kind of homosexual act. Nobody would explain it to me. I was given to understand that it was very unusual and very serious. It was the act of an insane person.

My brother and sister and I usually got to watch a little TV after dinner. There was only one TV, and it was always tuned to whatever my father wanted to watch. So we'd watch what he was watching. And even when he fell asleep in front of the TV, we couldn't change the channel. If we did, he'd wake up and make us change it back. We watched a lot of boring TV that way.

Sometimes my father would get excited. He'd tell us that Nat King Cole was going to be on *The Ed Sullivan Show*, for instance. He was a big fan of Nat King Cole, and of Duke Ellington, and he got very excited when a black person was on television. He'd say, "They got some colored folks on TV tonight!" He'd make us come and watch.

Not that we needed asking. We loved watching TV. When the rich family down the block became the first people we knew with a color TV, it was the most exciting thing going on. We couldn't wait for the parents to go out for an evening. Then we'd tear down there and rush in and watch color TV. That was pretty big stuff on Smith Avenue.

At ten or eleven o'clock, after we'd already gone to bed, my mother would get in the car and drive the fifteen or twenty miles to the hospital. I don't know this for sure, but I always suspected that if she'd been white she could have gotten a good job at the hospital in Lexington. She was a very qualified nurse. Driving twenty miles, each way, five or six days a week, on the midnight shift, was a strain. I am sure she could have had a job at a closer hospital, but it would have paid her less money. In our house, making less money was not acceptable.

My father was an ambitious man. He became a high school biology teacher, but I don't think that was his ambition in the beginning. He'd imagined bigger things for himself.

He was raised in New York and went to school there. After doing his undergraduate work in Greensboro, he went back to New York and studied at Columbia University. He met my mother there. She had gone to nursing school in Greensboro and Winston-Salem, and was working as a nurse at the Frances Delafield Hospital in New York when she met my dad.

I know from stories they told me, and from photographs I saw later, that they were a pretty swinging couple. My dad was a very sharp dresser, and a dancer and singer who performed in nightclubs. My mother was a piano player. We always had a piano growing up, and sometimes my father and mother would play together. She'd sit at the piano and he'd sing. When they had parties, they'd play all the old songs.

I look at the photographs of them now and they seem like a happy, good-looking couple. My mother was quite light-skinned and had soft, wavy hair and soft, brown eyes. My father had a high, wise forehead, an intense stare and twinkly eyes. He looks like a man who'd be fun to be around, but who also might be scary if he lost his temper.

When I look at those pictures now, I see that I got my mother's smile. So did my sister and my brother. We all have that, from my mother. I think Dorothy and I have her eyes, too, though I guess I got more of my father's build. If I look at my high school football team picture, and his high school football team picture, it's almost like the same guy. My brother and sister got more of my mother's physique, longer and leaner.

My brother David was the firstborn in my family. He was born in New York. I was born in New York, too, four years later. Shortly after that, my father decided to move back to the South. He loved New York, loved the nightlife and the nightclubs and the music, and he had better job opportunities there, too, but he and my mother reckoned that North Carolina was a better place to raise kids. They moved. My father did some postgraduate work at North Carolina Agriculture and Technology College in Greensboro, and got some kind of job there, too. We settled in the town of Lexington, North Carolina, a low, flat factory town in the low, flat Piedmont area of the state, where he got a job teaching in the high school.

This was a good beginning for him. He had studied at Columbia University. He had done postgraduate work at North Carolina Agriculture and Technology. He might have been a college professor, but he was a high school biology teacher. He was on the track to become an administrator, and his ambition was to be a principal or a vice principal.

But this was the second ambition he'd had in life. He had started out wanting to become a doctor.

He worked hard at everything he did, and he did a lot. I have been a college professor for almost twenty years. I know what goes into that, so I can guess what goes into being a high school biology teacher. It's a huge amount of work. But it's only a fraction of the amount of work my father did. He always had so many side jobs that he was never idle.

Every summer, for example, David "Doc" Moose ran the public swimming pool at Washington Park, which was a few blocks over from where we lived. This was a city pool. I guess my father got a salary of some sort from the city. But he also ran all kinds of other stuff there to make extra money. He ran a concession stand. He'd buy boxes of candy bars and drinks and sell them at a profit. At night, when the swimming pool technically wasn't supposed to be open, he'd run it like a nightclub. I don't think he had permission from the city to do it, but since he was "Doc" Moose and ran the pool, nobody asked any questions. He'd bring kids in for night swimming and sell them tickets—it cost a dime—to get in. There were some kids who didn't have a dime, but if he knew them he'd let them in for free. He'd hire lifeguards to watch the swimmers. He'd haul in a juke-box, and let the kids stick nickels in that and play music and dance. He'd roll out the concession stand, and hire a kid to run it. He was quite an entrepreneur, and the swimming pool was a hot place for the neighborhood black kids to hang out.

Right around the corner from the pool was the corner where I used to work as a volunteer crossing guard. I had the sash and everything, and I'd stand out there in the afternoons helping the little kids get safely across the street. That was my first job in law enforcement.

At tax time, my father took in people's taxes. For a month or so before April 15, he'd be up half the night, every night, poring over people's taxes.

During football season, he worked the security gate at the football field. I think his job was to keep an eye on the back gate and make sure no one snuck into the game, and also to make sure the gate was unlocked in case a kid got injured and they needed an ambulance on the field. I was on the team. I don't think my father ever actually saw a single game I played in, because he was working that gate. He was at the game, and afterward he always seemed to know whether I'd been involved in a big play—if I'd run back a kickoff or something. But he wasn't there to watch me. He was working. If we had an away game, on the road somewhere, he didn't come for that. Later, when I was on the wrestling team, even when I wrestled in the all-state competition, he didn't come to see those events either. He was always working.

He'd even bring singers to the house to coach them for performances or recitals they were going to give, be-cause of his background in New York as a singer in nightclubs. He still sang in church, and at funerals, and he found a way to make a little extra money by coaching people at the house.

When he was at home, and not working, he was never still. He helped my mother run the house. He was always looking for something else to do. He'd do the laundry. He'd iron his shirts.

On Sunday, he cooked all day, preparing all the meals for the week. He'd buy a huge amount of groceries and spend the whole day making a full week's worth of food. He'd make a meat loaf and a pot roast and a vegetable soup and some sweet potatoes and a pot of green beans, or something like that, and fill the refrigerator, and we'd make meals out of it for the week. We might have a pot roast, greens and sweet potatoes on Sunday night, and then have sweet potato pie on Monday and Tuesday, and leftover pot roast on Thursday. On Friday, it was always fish for dinner. Saturday nights, depending on how the bank account was doing, we might have something fancier or something pretty plain. My dad might grill something on the barbecue, like hamburgers, or we might go out for fast food. If things were going really well, my mother liked to cook the fancy meals.

She was fancier than my father in general. She was big on etiquette, and table manners, and was always trying to teach us the finer points of things like that. She wanted us to be sophisticated and worldly. One year the movie theater in town had a special series of "cultural" movies. My mother bought tickets for the series, and once a month for several months she'd get me to dress up and accompany her to these movies like *Gigi* or *Cat on a Hot Tin Roof.* I don't remember whether any of those films made an impression on me, but I know it was a big deal for my mother to take me to them. That impressed me, that she would want to include me in something like that.

With everything they did, it was all about making sure we had a better chance than they had.

My mother worked hard, too. My whole childhood, she ran the house during the day and then worked all night. She had worked for four years as a nurse in North Carolina before she met my dad, then had worked in New York for two years before he married her and moved her back to North Carolina. She got a job at the Veterans Administration hospital in Salisbury in 1955, and she never worked anywhere else.

They weren't very social, my parents. They didn't go out much. My father had one good friend, a man named Benny Goodman, like the band leader, who lived in Greensboro. He and my dad had met at college in Greensboro, and like my dad Benny was a high school teacher. He taught "industrial arts," which is to say he taught wood shop and subjects like that. He and his wife were certainly my parents' best and closest friends. His wife was my sister Dorothy's godmother, in fact.

Every once in a while, my mother and father would go out with Benny and his wife, or have them to the house. And even less often my father would have people in to our house for a party. We had finished out the basement, and there would be a party down there, with music and drinking.

That didn't turn out too good. My mother didn't like the way it turned out, anyway. Things always got broken. Things always disappeared. The house was always a wreck afterward, and my mother would complain.

There was a piano upstairs in our house. My mother read music, and she would play church songs and other music for my father to sing. During those parties, the ones in the basement, it wasn't church music that was playing. It was drinking and getting-into-trouble music, playing on the record player. My mother tolerated that, but just barely.

All that musical talent jumped past me. My mother tried to teach me piano when I was young, but I couldn't get with it. In college, I almost flunked the music class I had to take to graduate. I can't even dance right, in fact. None of that black stereotype works for me. I can't dance, I can't sing, and I can't play basketball. When I was in high school, I was a running back on the football team. I had a pretty good season. The basketball coach approached me and told me I should go out for basketball. I said, "I don't think I should. I can't play basketball." He insisted, though. So I went out for basketball. The coach watched me play for a while. Then he said I shouldn't go out for basketball after all. I said, "I told you that already." The coach was white. He fell for the stereotype. He saw a black kid who was fast on the football field, and he thought, "I got me a basketball player here." Wrong.

I don't know how old I was when I first began to understand the difference between black people and white people, but it was pretty early. I understood that all the black kids went to one school, and all the white kids went to another school. And I understood that other things were separated, too. I don't remember anyone explaining this to me. It was just a fact. Explaining it would have been like explaining gravity.

There was one movie theater in Lexington, and it had two entrances. There was the main entrance, under the marquee, where the box office was. That was for white people. They'd go in, stand in line for the popcorn and candy, and sit in the main room.

There was another entrance for black people. It was a little door off to the side of the marquee. It led up a flight of stairs. You'd buy your ticket up there, and you'd sit in a balcony overlooking the main room. There wasn't any popcorn or candy up there. You'd watch the same movie the white people watched, but you knew you were not allowed to sit down where they sat.

All the restaurants in town were the same way. We used to get barbecue from a place in town called City Barbecue. There were two rooms. One was where white people sat down and ate or ordered their food to take out. The other was for the black people.

My parents made sure I understood things like that. They didn't tell me *why* this was the way it was. But they made sure I understood it was important. You used this door, not that door. You drank from this drinking fountain, not that drinking fountain. There were certain neighborhoods that you stayed out of, certain places you stayed away from. These were survival tips.

There was the threat of violence, certainly, if you didn't follow these rules. A few blocks over from Smith Avenue was a juke joint called the Do Drop Inn. That was a sort of boundary. You didn't go past that corner, especially after dark, unless you were interested in real trouble. There was a market on another corner, around where Oak Street or Hickory Street came in, and sometimes we'd be sent down there after school or in the evening to pick something up. You understood that was another boundary. You didn't go past there, especially at night, or else you were running the risk of getting hurt.

Or worse than hurt. The Ku Klux Klan was very active in our town. They marched down Main Street. They held rallies on the outskirts of town. They burned crosses in the fields. Once, in the town where my father's mother lived, they burned a cross on a man's front lawn.

My father, for that reason, always carried a gun. He wore it when he went out. He kept it in his car. It was a little "Saturday night special" pistol. He didn't have a license for it, and he didn't advertise it. But he didn't go out without it, either.

He wore it for protection. A lot of the men did. You'd hear them talking about something that had happened. You'd hear them talking about using their guns.

Everybody was afraid of the Klan. Everybody was afraid that one day they'd come. Nobody knew what was going to happen. The newspaper was always full of stories about crimes that black people had supposedly committed against white people. There was always a story about a black man raping a black woman. Remember, this was not that far away from the time of "eyeball rape," when a black man could be beaten or even lynched for "eyeballing" a white woman—just for looking at her.

When I was in high school, I knew a couple of boys

who were always sneaking around with these white girls who were interested in black boys. There was a lot of talk about what would happen to them if anyone found out. The assumption was they would be killed.

That's a pretty rotten way to grow up, scared like that. Martin Luther King Jr., in his famous "Letter from a Birmingham Jail," wrote so eloquently about how hard it was during that time to be an African-American living in this country. Expressing his people's unwillingness to sit quietly and wait for America to give African-Americans the civil rights guaranteed by the constitution, Reverend King wrote,

> Perhaps it is easy for those who have never felt the stinging dark of segregation to say, "Wait." But when you have seen vicious mobs lynch your mothers and fathers at will and drown your sisters and brothers at whim; when you have seen hate-filled policemen curse, kick and even kill your black brothers and sisters; when you see the vast majority of your twenty million Negro brothers smothering in an airtight cage of poverty in the midst of an affluent society; when you suddenly find your tongue twisted and your speech stammering as you seek to explain to your six-year-old daughter why she can't go to the public amusement park that has just been advertised on television, and see tears welling up in her eyes when she is told that Funtown is closed to colored children ... when you are harried by day and haunted by night by the fact that you are a Negro, living constantly at tiptoe stance, never quite knowing what to expect next, and are plagued with inner fears and outer resentments; when you are forever fighting a degenerating sense of "nobodiness" then you will understand why we find it difficult to wait.

That was the climate around me, around my family, when I was a child. The marches and demonstrations were televised, and pictures of the violence were in the newspapers. I saw black men set upon by police dogs, beaten with billy clubs, blasted by water cannons. It was made clear to me that this was what happened to black people who stepped out of line.

My father wasn't into the civil rights movement or, later, the black power stuff. He didn't march. He sympathized, but he was no activist. When we'd drive through downtown Lexington, or stop at the post office, he'd point at the old Davison County Courthouse and say, "They used to sell slaves on the steps of that courthouse. Never forget that."

He kept his opinions on the race question to himself. Around us, there was a lot of disagreement about what should be done. One camp said we should stand and fight, go get our guns and defend ourselves. Another camp said we should all just try to get along. My father probably would have been in the first camp. Privately, I think he was very angry.

Publicly, though, he was a high school biology teacher. He needed his job. He needed to provide for his family. He wasn't going to rock the boat too much. He knew his place.

He was probably influenced in his opinions by what he had seen outside Lexington. He never talked about it much, but he had been a soldier. He had served in France. He was a medical sergeant in the Army. That's where he got the nickname "Doc." He got interested in medicine serving in the Army, and he planned on attending medical school when he got home from doing his military service. He couldn't afford it, though. He never got into medical school. I think that hurt him. It had been a big dream, and it didn't come true. The only thing that stuck was the nickname. Forever after that, for his whole life, people referred to him as "Doc Moose." It was a term of respect. He was a very respected guy. But on some level it must have hurt, to always be reminded that he was not, in fact, a doctor.

He was in an all-black unit in the Army. While he was overseas, he had a white, French girlfriend. Now, that would never have happened back home. When he told me about it, what he was saying was "This is a big world. Lexington is a small world." It was also his way of saying there was more to him than what you could see every day. He was different. He had been places and seen things.

Later on, he was very frustrated about not becoming a school administrator. He had been a teacher in the Lexington school system a long time. He believed, or was led to believe, that he would climb the ladder from teacher to school administrator—a vice principal, first, and then a principal, and then maybe something higher up in the school system itself.

That didn't happen. Instead, integration came to the Lexington schools. New schools were built to educate the newly mixed classes of white and black students. For reasons that were not clear to me, the integration of the Lexington schools worked against him. He had been a successful teacher in the all-black high school. But he was not welcomed, or not needed, as a teacher in the integrated high school. He got bounced down, against his wishes, to the integrated junior high school. And that ended, permanently, any dreams he might have had about becoming a principal at the high school.

He talked about this for years after. It was very damaging to him. He felt he had been treated badly. He felt he had been discriminated against. He knew that, as a black teacher, he had been edged out by white teachers who had less experience, less talent and less ability than he had.

But he had a wife whose health was failing. He had one son in high school, one son in junior high school and a daughter in grade school. He couldn't afford to kick up too much of a fuss—not without risking the loss of his job. He was a responsible family man. I know he was spoiling for a fight, and would have loved nothing better than getting in there and raising a ruckus over not getting a job at the high school. He didn't even raise his voice. He took it, because he had to take it.

Maybe he played that wrong. Maybe he should have

filed complaints and threatened lawsuits. Maybe he should have kissed more ass, been more politically astute about protecting his position. Maybe it wouldn't have mattered if he had. But not doing that created a lot of turmoil for him.

His experience became a kind of lesson for me. He used what had happened to him to teach me that I should never let anything like that happen to me. He used to say to me, "Work hard, establish your credentials, be prepared, but watch out." He had gotten hurt, trying to get ahead. So he ended with "But watch out."

The lesson he always stressed was that I had to be better than the other guy, especially if the other guy was white. I had to be smarter. I had to work harder. I had to score higher. I had to come in earlier, and stay later. I had to be more moral, more ethical and have a cleaner record. Otherwise, if there were two candidates for a job or a promotion, and I wasn't far and away the more qualified—the white guy would get the job, and I wouldn't.

I don't think I shared his anxiety at that time. I was doing well. Up until junior high school, anyway, I was going along fine. Then, when I was in the seventh grade, everything changed. When integration came to Lexington, it hit me, too.

They didn't call it integration. They called it "Freedom of Choice." A black student from the black middle school had the freedom to choose—stay at Dunbar High School, the all-black school for grades seven to twelve, or start up at Lexington Middle School, the brand-new integrated school.

I didn't want to change schools. At Dunbar, I was the smartest kid in my class. I was good at sports. My father had been a tennis player, and I became a tennis player, too—good enough to get a spot on the high school team. I was ranked number three or four in the seventh grade, even though I was much younger and smaller than these high school juniors and seniors. I was pretty happy to stay at that school.

My father had other ideas. He was looking forward to this integration thing. He saw it as an opportunity. He sat me down and said, "When you grow up, you can't go to any all-black city. You can't get any all-black job. You are going to have to figure this thing out sooner or later. You might as well figure it out now."

That fall, I started up at Lexington Middle School. I went from being the smartest person in the room to one of the average kids. I was just okay. I went from being number three or four on the tennis team to not being able to get on the tennis team at all. These other kids, these white kids, had read so much more than I had, and had been to better schools than I had. As tennis players they were just that much more experienced. I went from being the top dog to being just another mutt in the pack.

This was painful for my father. He had seen a lot of trouble. I remember, when I was five or six years old, we had gone to Greensboro, about forty miles from Lexington, to see the circus. My mother and father had scraped and saved their money to take us, me and my brother and sister, to the big circus in the big city. And it was wonderful. We had a great day.

On the way home, my father said we were going to stop at a restaurant. This was a special treat because we hardly ever ate out. Sometimes we took home barbecue, or we took home fish, but we almost never ate in a restaurant. Today was a special day.

We stopped in at this hamburger place. My dad said, "Go on, now. You go on up to the counter and tell the man what you want."

We stood at the counter, my dad and me. I was all excited, ready to place our order, and the kid behind the counter said, "What are you doing here? We don't serve niggers here."

We went back to the car, and drove away. We didn't stop to eat anywhere else. My father was quiet all the way home. It was very traumatizing for him, to have us see that happen to him and his family. I had never seen anyone hurt my dad, until that moment.

*   *   *

We never took family vacations when I was a boy. There were only two places we ever went. We drove up to New York, to see my aunt Betsy, and we drove down to Concord, North Carolina, to see my father's mother.

My father was one of four children. I think he was the oldest. He had a brother and two sisters. For some reason, the family split up. I never knew what happened to his father. He was just gone, and I guess his mother couldn't handle raising all the children. So my father was sent up to New York to live with this Aunt Betsy.

I don't think she was really a relative at all. But at that time it was common for folks to refer to an old family friend that way, as "Aunt" this or "Uncle" that. There's a lot of Southern families that have more aunts and uncles than is biologically possible. I think my father's aunt Betsy was that kind of aunt.

Every summer, for a long time, we'd drive up to New York to stay with Aunt Betsy. It seemed like a very long road trip. And Aunt Betsy's world couldn't have been more different from our lives in Lexington. She lived right in the city. Her world didn't make any sense to me. They sent me out one time to get a newspaper. I went to the guy on the corner and tried to buy a newspaper. He wouldn't sell me one. I couldn't figure it out. He had some newspapers. I had the money. But he wouldn't sell me a paper.

I found out later he was a numbers runner. He wasn't really in the business of selling newspapers. He was running a numbers racket, and I was getting in the way.

My father had very ambivalent feelings about Aunt Betsy. She had raised him almost like a mother, but she had been very severe with him. She had treated him almost like a servant. He had to work constantly. Because he'd grown up and gotten a college education in New York, he had benefited a great deal from Aunt Betsy's help, but he had been treated pretty roughly, too.

After his parents separated, my father's mother set up house in Concord, which is not that far south from Lexington. We'd drive down there, sometimes as often as once a week. Like New York and Aunt Betsy's house, it could hardly have been more different from our house.

Our house in Lexington was very well ordered. It was clean. It was middle-class. We knew there was a rough part of town where colored people lived rough, disorderly lives, but we didn't ever go to that part of town. We kept to Smith Avenue, where the fathers went off to work in the morning and the children went off to school and the mothers, for the most part, stayed home cooking and cleaning.

My grandmother's house in Concord was the opposite. Nothing about it was orderly. First of all, she was a bootlegger. She sold whiskey—illegal whiskey. I guess the county she lived in was a dry county—a lot of North Carolina counties were, well into the 1960s. Davison County, where I grew up, was dry. People had to drive to the next county, to the town of Salisbury, to get booze. That was true all over the state. If you wanted liquor, you had to drive to the next county or know a bootlegger in town. My grandmother was the local bootlegger.

She lived in a little two-bedroom house with one of her daughters. Neither one of them was married. But they both had boyfriends. Sometimes I think the boyfriends lived with them. Sometimes, I think they were *sharing* boyfriends. My grandmother had a guy named George who was around, but my father didn't approve. He was supposed to be some kind of handyman, but he didn't seem all that handy at anything but drinking and loafing. He wasn't supporting my grandmother. In fact, she seemed to be supporting him. Which meant my father was kind of supporting him—because my father had bought this house for his mother and took care of some of the bills. He didn't approve of the bootlegging and the other things she did at her house, either, even though they were things she was doing to make money and survive. But I guess he was a dutiful son, because we went down to Concord as often as once a week, to check on her and see that she was doing okay.

There were always all kinds of men around, dangerous-looking men. There was lots of noise and music and dancing and drinking—tons of drinking. People would come to the house to buy liquor and just not leave. My grandmother sold shots of bootleg liquor for 75 cents. The men stood in the kitchen, drinking shots, getting loud. The house was in a pretty rough section of town. The street didn't look like our street in Lexington, with the lawns all mowed and the cars all washed in the driveways. This street looked like a place where there was going to be trouble.

Some of that trouble got my uncle Bobby. My father's brother was a rough character. He never had a job. He was a drinker and a gambler and a sort of gangster. He was killed, right in that neighborhood—someone shot him over a gambling debt.

There was another sister, though, who like my dad stayed out of that kind of trouble. Her name was Mary. She lived in a nice house in Concord and had a nice, straight husband. Sometimes we'd go visit them after we visited my grandmother, and it was a nice change. The house was clean and tidy. The only problem was Mary kept the living room furniture covered in plastic and collected little knickknacks. There were zillions of them, all over the house, and we were always sure we were about to break one of them and get in trouble. Mary had an adopted daughter, named Alice, who we thought was spoiled rotten. As kids, we were convinced that she got *everything*.

I guess she was my cousin. I had other cousins, who were Uncle Bobby's kids. And there was one more, sort of. My grandmother and my aunt had a girl who lived with them. Her name was Gail. She wasn't a blood relative. She wasn't really even adopted, I don't think. They took her in, though—and worked her like a slave. Just like my dad had grown up with Aunt Betsy in New York, Gail was like a servant girl. They made her do everything. She didn't play with the other kids, when there were kids around. She hung back and did menial chores. I guess it was better than where she was living before they took her in, but it seems awfully hard now when I look back on it.

We went down to Concord almost every week, all through my elementary school days, into junior high school and high school. Things got worse down there. My grandmother got sick. She had her legs amputated. Bobby got killed.

I don't know why, but it wasn't scary to me. It was exciting. It was so different. There were always all these people around. They were drinking and talking rougher than I heard people talk at home. And if they were drinking and in a good mood, they'd send me off to the store to buy something, and then they'd always give me some money to buy something for myself.

That was a big thing. We were doing all right in Lexington, but I never had much spending money. I did some chores around the house, and sometimes I'd get a dollar or even a dollar and a half to mow the lawns and clip the hedges and rake the leaves out of the yard. But I didn't have much pocket money. Getting paid 50 cents for going to the store was a pretty big deal.

The partying at my grandmother's house was exotic, although both my parents drank. Not to excess, but they drank. My father was a Jim Beam man. Sometimes he'd go a little too far with it. But he was always a happy drinker. He and my mother would go out to Greensboro for some party or some dance. When they came back, he'd be lying in the backseat with his shoes off and my mother would be driving.

Other than that, there wasn't much goofing off around my house. There wasn't much leisure time. My father had a kind of "office" in the house, and there was a bookcase in there that was just full of books. All kinds of books: history, fiction, biography. My father and mother used to say they were going to sit down and read every book in that bookcase when they retired.

I began to get used to the transition to the integrated school. I struggled pretty badly the first couple of years.

Then I began to adjust. I began to feel more like I belonged there.

The difference between the old all-black high school and the new integrated high school and junior high school was pretty amazing. The new buildings were these grand brick buildings, solid and beautiful, two-story constructions with a grass lawn and a split-rail fence running all around them. They had everything you'd dream about having in a high school. Next to the school, they had a "tennis center." It was like nothing I'd ever seen—great courts, with new nets and new surfaces. At the old school, there was hardly a court at all.

After school, we had football practice. And right next to the football field there was a special training room for the football players. We had our own little gym. It had some weight training equipment in it and lockers for our gear. I felt so special, being part of that team.

By the time I got to high school, I was completely involved in sports. I weighed in at about 150 pounds. I was a running back on the football team. I thought I was going to be the next Jim Brown. He was my big hero at that time. When he was carrying the ball, it was the most beautiful thing in the world. I had ambitions to be a pro football player just like him.

My ambition didn't last too long. I had high hopes of being picked for the varsity football team when I was in the tenth grade. I thought I'd jump right past the junior varsity team and start with the serious football players. I knew I wouldn't be able to start every game, but I'd be able to practice with the varsity team and travel with them to out-of-town games. I was real excited about that.

Then I broke my ankle. I was running, in practice, and I fell and broke my ankle. That wiped me out for the tenth grade. Even though the ankle healed, I lost an entire season. This took some of the energy out of my plans to be the next Jim Brown. There were guys around me who were making all conference or all state. There were guys getting recruited to go to the bigger schools. Later, when I got to college and saw the size of the guys who were playing on the college team, I understood why I wasn't being recruited. I was average size for a high school running back, but at 150 pounds or so I wasn't nearly big enough to play college ball.

The worst of it was I had to wear shorts to school for several months, because of the cast on my leg. I was more of a long pants guy then, and wearing shorts was real embarrassing to me. In fact, I'm pretty much a long pants guy now. I own a couple of pairs of shorts. I've only ever worn them in Hawaii, and even there I feel kind of uncomfortable in them. I guess that's left over from being self-conscious about it in high school. It isn't that I have ugly legs. But shorts, even today, feel weird to me. Maybe they're too informal. I've been a police officer for a long time, and when you're a police officer you're always sort of in uniform, because you're never really off duty. If I retire and manage to get to Hawaii, I plan to wear shorts a lot someday.

I had already lost my ambition to be a big tennis player. Before that, tennis was a big deal. I used to wear out two or three pairs of Converse sneakers every summer, playing on those old asphalt courts—at a time when my family couldn't really afford two or three pairs of sneakers every summer. But then in junior high school, at the integrated school, I was in a regional competition. I ended up matched against John Lucas—the same John Lucas who later became a big star playing for the NBA. I thought I was a pretty good tennis player. But Lucas beat me so bad, it was like he was just wasting his time on the other side of the net. I don't know if I got a single point. It was like 6–0, 6–0. He wiped me out. I had never suffered anything like that my whole life. After that, I didn't play too much tennis.

Instead, I did other stuff. I played football. I ran track. I was on the wrestling team. I did really well. I was given the "best blocker" award my senior year. And I lettered in wrestling. In my senior year I won the all-AAA wrestling championship. The winners were given this large card with their names in brackets. There was a trophy, too, but the name in brackets seemed more personal. I was proud of that.

At home, things weren't going so well. When I was fifteen, my mother got sick. To my mind, it was real sudden. She started being tired and then got real sick, real fast. She started having trouble getting to work. Then she had trouble even getting out of bed. She started losing weight.

My sister, Dorothy, who later became a nurse, thinks my mother had been sick a long time before she started showing it. She thinks my mother had Raynaud's disease, which is an inflammation and deadening of the nerves and muscles in the hands, that causes terrible pain and loss of strength and control. Dorothy remembers my mother not being able to braid her hair, and having to help her get dressed. Dorothy remembers my mother having terrible trouble with her teeth, too, and lots of pain associated with that.

The doctors couldn't figure out what was wrong with her. Then they admitted her to the hospital. For some reason, they administered a spinal tap. I don't know what they were looking for, but they didn't find it. They failed to come up with any diagnosis whatsoever.

And then it didn't matter. She died. She was just gone. We buried her in the cemetery in Greensboro around the corner from the Lutheran church where we worshipped every Sunday.

She was only forty-three years old. I was two months shy of my sixteenth birthday.

My father was really broken by it. He was convinced the spinal tap killed her. He'd get these bills from the hospital and he'd go into a rage. He'd shout, "I'm not paying. It was that damned spinal tap! I'm not paying for it!"

He would have been in his late forties then, about the age I am now. He was a single father. He had a son in college. He had a boy in high school. He had a daughter in junior high school. He was on his own. I inherited my mother's Plymouth Valiant and didn't have to walk to school anymore. Every day I'd drive my sister to school, and every afternoon I'd drive her home. Somehow my father managed to get dinner on the table every night. The house continued to run along almost like it had.

But my brother was having trouble at school. He had gone away to Fisk University, in Nashville, Tennessee. He got into the fraternity scene and pledged Omega. He had the insignia burned into his arm. He changed the way he dressed, the way he acted, the way he talked. He was changing in a radical way.

Then something happened. It had to do with drugs. Someone got killed. Someone was after my brother. Someone—maybe the law—was looking for him. Was he a suspect? I never knew. I just knew he was in trouble. And then he ran off. He left the country. We heard nothing, for several years. He was just missing. Just gone.

It was painful for me to lose him this way. As my big brother, he had shown me a lot, and he had answered a lot of questions for me. He helped me avoid doing some of the dumb things, or saying some of the dumb things, I would have done or said otherwise. He helped me stay out of trouble. He exposed me to ideas I wouldn't have had on my own. Sharing a room with him helped me grow up.

As much as I love my sister, Dorothy, and as much respect as I have for her, she and I weren't close the way my brother and I were. We have never talked the way my brother and I talked. I don't know how she feels about having me as an older brother, but I often wonder how life would have turned out for David if he had grown up with an older brother the way I did, and had someone close to him to help him grow up the way he helped me.

I managed to finish high school. I knew I was going to college. This was a given. My brother and sister and I had known, since we were little, that we were going to college. Beyond that, though, I didn't have any fixed plan. I thought, for a while, that I'd take an athletic scholarship and go to one of the state universities. I had a scholarship offer from Livingstone College, which was an all-black college located in Salisbury, North Carolina, the small town where my mother had worked as a nurse, and from North Carolina Agricultural and Technical, where my dad had gone to school before Columbia. I could have gone either place and played football.

But a lucky thing happened. There were some guys at my school who were going to Carolina—to the University of Carolina at Chapel Hill. I didn't know a thing about this university, even though it was only a couple of hours' drive from where I'd lived my whole life. I'd heard of it. If you were into sports, and you lived in North Carolina, you'd have heard of it. But I hadn't *thought* of it, as an option, for me.

These guys were talking about it. I got interested in it. I went through the application process and I was accepted as an undergraduate.

I knew that going to Chapel Hill meant I wasn't going to play football. I knew I couldn't make the team there, and they hadn't offered me any scholarship. And I kind of knew I wasn't going to be any kind of academic star there, either, like I might have been at one of the smaller schools. But I made the decision to try and get the better education rather than rely on the football and the scholarship.

I also made the decision never to pledge a fraternity. Since I didn't know what had really happened to my brother, I was scared. Somehow the fraternity, with its rituals and its secret handshakes, seemed responsible for what had happened to him. I realize now that fraternities have done great things for some people, but in those days I was reluctant to get involved with that kind of group.

It's hard for me to even imagine how different my life would have turned out if I had gone the other way. Where would I have gone from, say, a football scholarship at NCA&T? Or with a lifelong series of friendships and connections from a fraternity?

I probably wouldn't have been thinking of law school, so I probably wouldn't have been exposed to courses in criminology, so I probably wouldn't have been introduced to the idea of being a police officer. I might have become a teacher, like my dad. Or a high school or junior college football coach.

I don't think I would have completed four years of undergraduate work and then gone on to get a master's degree, and then gone on to do my doctoral degree. I wouldn't have wound up as a Ph.D. police chief.

I had a girlfriend by then. My first serious girlfriend. Her name was Joy Franklin. I had started going out with her in high school. She lived in a somewhat rougher part of town, just off Fifth Street, near the center of Lexington. Her mother, whom I knew as Mrs. Hargove, was the principal of the elementary school I attended. I never did find out why she was called Hargrove and Joy was called Franklin. I knew that she wasn't really Joy's mother, but you didn't ask questions about things like that. They lived in a little frame house, and I spent a lot of time hanging around that house.

For some people, that would have been it. I would have married Joy Franklin, and we would have settled in to some kind of life in Lexington. I think we had our eyes on other things, though, and by the time we were going to college, we were going to different colleges. Joy went off to Shaw University, in Raleigh, and I wound up becoming a cop. Life put us in different places and we never met again.

My father never entirely recovered from my mother's death. He went about his business. He taught at the junior high school. He eventually retired. He took to driving into town every day to run errands and check for mail at the post office, his Saturday night special tucked into his pocket, ready for trouble that never came. He never got to the bookshelf bulging with books in his little office.

By the time he was in his middle fifties, he was already suffering the early onset of Alzheimer's disease.

Around this time, we were contacted by someone from overseas, someone from the U.S. Embassy in India. David was being held there. He had gotten into some kind of mess with the local authorities. He was broke and had no way of getting home. We were told to send some money to pay for his airfare, if we wanted to see him again. My father had some money wired to the embassy, and David came home.

He wasn't the same. He was half-crazy. He talked a lot of nonsense. It was difficult to understand what was going on with him. He argued a lot. I don't know if it was mental problems, or problems with drugs, or mental problems exacerbated by problems with drugs. In the end, David disappeared again. He took to the streets. It would be years before we would ever know where he was or what had happened to him. And when the news came, it wouldn't be good news.

3. A Ghost with a Gun

The Rockville headquarters was starting to get out of control, less than twenty-four hours after the first shooting had occurred. Six of Montgomery County's citizens had been murdered—six citizens that I was called upon to serve and protect. It took a lot of faith, at that point, to believe there wasn't going to be another killing.

We had made the decision Thursday afternoon to move the command vehicle back to the station, to concentrate all our people in that location and to bring the media up to the parking lot in front of the station. That's where we traditionally do all our media briefings. Even when we don't speak to the media, that's where they set up and do their shots, with the police station in the background. "Live, from the Montgomery County Police Department . . ."

The people at the Korean church hadn't started complaining about having us in their parking lot, but they were becoming uncomfortable. They were afraid their church was going to end up associated with this terrible thing. We didn't want to inconvenience them any more than necessary. Plus the command vehicle was so undependable. We moved everything up to what became known as "Camp Rockville."

Police officers from every division had started showing up. There were also people from other police agencies. There were state police, and police from neighboring departments, and officers from the ATF and the FBI. It wasn't a multijurisdictional task force yet. All these people were coming in, on their own, and setting up shop in the major crimes unit. There were people sitting on chairs in the hallways, running down leads on their cellular phones. There were makeshift desks set up in the laundry room. The stuff was spilling out into the parking lot.

We were hoping to get something from forensics. The previous day, the victims had been taken to the hospital. Then they were taken from the hospital to the medical examiner. There was a rush on the M.E.'s work. He was looking for bullet fragments. When the M.E. found fragments, they went to the case detective. The case detective got them to the forensics lab.

By midday Thursday the forensics labs had bullet fragments from five bodies. They didn't have anything from the Michael's shooting on Wednesday. But they would, soon: Two weeks later, a customer would buy a bolt of fabric, and when she got home she'd unroll it and find a chunk of metal in there, and some holes in the fabric. She would contact the police and we'd have that fragment to work with, too.

On Friday afternoon, the detectives working the killings as individual cases got together, for the first time, to share their information. Nothing they had, unfortunately, created a pattern. They had been out to speak with the victims' families, and to see their workplaces. They had talked to wives and husbands and friends and coworkers. They had tried to learn everything they could about these people, to try and figure out what the connection between them could be. It was clear, by Friday afternoon, that there was no connection at all. We were becoming convinced that this killer might have the worst method any law enforcement person can encounter: He was choosing his victims at random.

We were starting to get some help with the weapon question. That's when I heard again from Mike Bouchard. Bouchard was the special agent in charge of the Department of Treasury's Bureau of Alcohol, Tobacco and Firearms, working out of Baltimore, who'd sent down the dog team Thursday. I'd met him before. In fact, he had come down to our office in Rockville about three weeks before, just to look in. One of my assistant chiefs, Dee Walker, had just been put in charge of the investigative branch. Bouchard, who was a determined-looking career agent who wore metal-rimmed glasses and a neatly trimmed mustache, had come down to say hello and ask us how we were doing.

We were doing fine, then. Now we weren't doing so fine. Bouchard showed up and in his quiet, efficient way put himself at our disposal. He said he was there to assist in any way he could. I don't imagine he had any way of knowing how long he was going to be involved in this thing, or what a commitment he was making that day. But there was plenty for him and his people do to. We had all kinds of questions about weapons, ammunition and ballistics, which was their area of expertise.

The forensics people, especially those with the ATF, were able to begin making some conclusions about what kind of killer was at work and what kind of weapon he was working with. Investigators conducted a "trajectory analysis" at each of the crime scenes. Using statements from witnesses, and the condition of the body of the victim after the shooting, investigators could sketch out the likely route the fatal shot had taken. If the victim was standing sideways, with an arm on his car, putting gas into his car, and there was an entrance wound on the left side of his upper chest and an exit wound on the right side of his lower back, that told investigators that the bullet came from a particular direction at a particular angle. Working backward, they could begin making calculations about the place from which the shot was fired.

They could also make assumptions, based on the bullet fragments pulled from the bodies of the victims, about what kind of weapon was being used. By the end of the first day, investigators were certain the killer was working with a high-powered rifle, firing from a distance of 100 to 150 yards, using ammunition in the .22 family—a .221 or .223. They could narrow the type of weapon down to one of perhaps twenty-five specific models.

Sometime that afternoon, Bouchard participated in his first press briefing—the first of dozens and dozens of them—and we put out some information about the kind of gun the killer might be using.

While this was going on, there was a seventh shooting, and a seventh victim. A forty-three-year-old woman was shot once in the upper back, standing in a parking lot, at 2:30 in the afternoon, while loading packages into a minivan. The woman was rushed to Inova Fairfax Hospital. She had a chance of surviving, but for now she was listed in critical condition.

The shooting took place at 3000 Plank Road in Fredericksburg, Virginia, and was handled by the Spotsylvania County sheriffs. This was out of our jurisdiction, but we were pretty sure it was connected—sure enough, anyway, that I had detectives rushed to Fredericksburg by helicopter.

As before, however, there were no witnesses. No one heard or saw anything. Later that day we would determine that the bullet wound was consistent with a .223-caliber rifle, fired from a considerable distance. Later still, we would find that the bullet may have hit the woman's vehicle first, before it hit her, passing through the raised rear door of her SUV before striking her in the back. Ballistics tests would connect the bullet fragments to the other shootings.

It would have been easy for us to feel frustrated by the continued killings and our continued lack of definite forward motion. We had officers, detectives, special agents, analysts and others working very hard, and new talent and new technology to help with data assessment was coming in almost by the hour. Knowing how many good people we had working, and with what great resources, I felt confident that we were going to get a break.

Privately, I was anxious that it come soon. The tension in the community was terrible. People's lives were being affected in a very real way. No one felt safe. No one knew when the sniper would strike again, or who the victim would be. We really needed a break in the case.

By that evening, we had started to get some real leads, and one was very promising.

Sometime earlier a woman had called our 911 line and told the operator that she thought her husband might have something to do with the killings. He had a gun like the one the ATF guys showed on TV and had been missing for the same amount of time as the killings had been going on. Investigators contacted her after the 911 call and collected more information. They got an I.D. on the guy and on some of his credit card numbers and his vehicle. The investigators made sure everyone on the task force received this information. The word went out that we were looking for this individual in connection with the shootings. He wasn't a suspect. We were very clear on that. He was just wanted for questioning.

What we knew was that he was thirty-three, lived in Rockville, was a former resident of Raleigh, North Carolina, and had a warrant out for him on an auto theft issue in Florida. What we'd been told is that he owned a .40-caliber handgun and a .223-caliber rifle.

The ball had landed in Mike Bouchard's court. He called some of his people in the ATF division office in Charlotte, North Carolina. He told them to contact people down there and tell them about the latest shooting. He explained that it was possible the killer was moving south, because this latest shooting had occurred in Spotsylvania County, below the Montgomery County area where the other killings had taken place, and maybe he was headed for North Carolina. Mike told them the person might be a military person, and was using an assault rifle. He encouraged them, if there was a shooting in their area, to immediately "expand the crime scene," to look beyond the location of the body, to consider that the shooter might have been at some distance from the victim when he fired.

At around the same time, my people in the Montgomery County Police Department issued what we call a "bolo," a warning to "be on the lookout for" a suspect or missing person, in this case Benson, who was identified as a missing person. The "bolo" said anyone with information should call the Montgomery County Sniper Task Force.

So far, so good. Mike Bouchard's people in Charlotte called their people in Fayetteville. The Fayetteville people called the North Carolina Highway Patrol. The Highway Patrol called some people in local law enforcement in the Fayetteville area. Those agencies put out notices to their police officers and Highway Patrol officers.

Still so far, so good—but not for long. Some local newspaper people in North Carolina had been listening to their police scanners. They heard the two announcements—one about a missing person and one an advisory about shootings in Montgomery County and Spotsylvania County. They put two and two together, and they figured this missing person guy must be the sniper suspect.

Pretty soon Mike Bouchard was getting calls from every news organization imaginable. He told me later that he worked from midnight to 6 A.M., and spoke to thirty newspeople or more, trying to convince them they were making a mistake and trying to get them not to go out with a story that this man was the sniper suspect. Apparently all of them agreed to hold the story.

But the next morning it was front page news in the *Raleigh News & Observer*. They had all this background on the guy, because he used to live there. The Associated Press picked up the *Raleigh News & Observer* story and put it on their national wire. So a lot of the other news organizations felt they had no choice now but to go out with what the *Raleigh News & Observer* and the AP were reporting.

I was pretty upset about this. I felt like it had been a mistake—and that the mistake was not my fault, or the fault of my police department.

But I was supposed to be running this investigation, so I did the only thing I knew to do. I went out and held a press briefing and took responsibility for it. I said we had released a "bolo" that was not as clear as it should have been.

Some people on the team expressed surprise at this. In my experience, from a leadership standpoint, there would have been no point in assigning blame—except to alienate the people who had made the mistake, and whose help I needed. I felt like I was in this big mess. I didn't know if I was going to be able to dig myself out of it. So I didn't want to alienate anyone who could help me.

By Saturday morning, we had put together a nearly complete case on this man. We learned that he had a business that had gotten into trouble, and his wife had more or less taken it over. We learned that he had tattoos, maybe of a neo-Nazi nature. We learned that he had a drug problem. His wife told us that he sometimes just disappeared for days at a time, on these drug binges. He would hole up in a cheap motel to do his drugs and then sleep it off, then he'd buy more drugs on the street and go back to the motel.

Apparently he used a credit card or an ATM card at a motel south of Alexandria, Virginia. That popped up. We had a location. And we had his vehicle at the location. We kept him under surveillance for several hours. It became clear that he was not moving. So we went in.

Fairfax County police apprehended him. And it wasn't our guy. He wasn't the sniper. He was just a drug addict, holed up in a cheap motel with a hooker. He didn't even own the weapon his wife thought he was using. He had owned one, but when he brought it home his wife objected to him keeping it in the house, so he sold it back to the guy he'd bought it from.

It was a great disappointment to us, especially because the man's name had gone out as a suspect. Since it had been in one newspaper, it had been picked up by all the TV people, too, and all the other newspapers. It had been everywhere. So we had to explain that we'd found him and that he wasn't the guy.

I wasn't surprised. It had looked a little too easy, somehow. I hadn't gotten all that excited about the possibility that this was our suspect, because experience has taught me that you can't get too excited about every lead. You get burned out emotionally if you do that. But I was pleased that they'd located him. Either he was our suspect, and we had him, or he wasn't, and we could be done with it. I was very unhappy with how public it had become. I'd been afraid he'd rabbit on us, and we'd never find him. I was upset because his wife had not intended for this to be published in all the papers. I was concerned that other people, who might have information for us, wouldn't call it in because they'd be afraid we wouldn't keep it confidential.

Word had gotten out in the press by that afternoon that we were developing a "psychological profile" of the sniper, but I cautioned against getting too excited about that, either. "I'm not convinced that there is anything we can say about the person responsible for this," I said. "Until we bring the suspect or suspects into custody, get an indictment and get a conviction."

There were a lot of reasons for this. I hated to think what would happen if someone identified some guy as a suspect when he was not, and one of the officers involved with the task force wound up being influenced by that. What if he treated the wrong person as a suspect? What if he went off on some person who was wanted for questioning, thinking he was really a suspect? What if he killed that person?

There were several more suspects. I know that later on the media depicted the investigating team as a bunch of bumbling flatfoots who just sort of wandered around until the two suspects we finally arrested threw themselves at us.

But there were real, active, ongoing investigations of dozens and dozens of suspects. We'd get a tip, begin checking it, put a name up on the suspects board in the major crimes room and begin investigating. We'd conduct surveillance, do interviews with neighbors, family members, coworkers and friends. We'd get search warrants, and confiscate weapons, and conduct ballistics tests. Time after time, suspects would go up on the board and suspects would come down.

That first Friday, we had two extremely promising leads.

One of the ATF agents working on the Pascal Charlot murder scene in the District found himself in conversation with a guy who casually mentioned that he knew the very first sniper victim—James Martin, who was shot at the Shoppers Food Warehouse. Now he just happened to be at the crime scene in Washington, D.C. In conversation, the man said he happened to own a .223 rifle, as well. The man was a white male, middle-aged, which fit the general profile many people thought we were looking for.

It would have been easy to get excited about this guy being our suspect, despite my reservations about getting excited by any leads. But almost as soon as we had him, we eliminated him. We got a search warrant. We confiscated the weapon. We fired it in the lab. It didn't check out. He was eliminated as a suspect.

At almost the same time, we got a tip from a commander over in Prince George's County. There was another suspect, with two or three key things to identify him as a promising suspect. The closer we looked, the better he looked. We got a search warrant and—same thing. We spent hours developing the suspect, then spent hours preparing and getting a search warrant, and then the available evidence eliminated the suspect. In that case, I think we got the search warrant at around midnight, and by morning we had eliminated him as a suspect.

This sort of thing happened again and again and again. We didn't announce these suspects to the media. In the first forty-eight hours, though, we had more than a dozen "good" suspects, all of whom we eliminated within hours. We didn't tell anyone we were getting all these search warrants. We didn't release names of the people we were investigating or had under surveillance. We just kept going, day after day, from one to the next. Once we eliminated one suspect, we forgot about it and moved on. There were always new leads, always new tips, always new people to investigate. I don't think we spent a lot of time being sorry about someone coming down off the board. At least we'd ruled that person out, and could concentrate on the next one.

But sometimes, if you came into the major crimes room at just the right time—or just the wrong time— you could sense a change in the energy. You'd see disappointment or frustration in people's eyes. You'd see their chests and shoulders slumping. You could feel the loss of momentum.

But the good investigators wouldn't spend much time in that kind of mood. Most of the good investigators are extremely dogged. Persistence is probably the most important trait of a quality investigator, in fact. There's a lot of up and down, a lot of promise and a lot of disappointment. The good investigator is just as glad when someone comes off the board as when someone goes up onto it. He or she wants the wrong person eliminated, wants to move on to the next person. A good investigator has to have that bulldog mentality, or he or she will just want to give up. And the quality investigator never gives up.

We reminded people in the media about the man we'd rousted from the hotel several times after that. We asked them to remember Richard Jewell, the man who was wrongly suspected of having planted a bomb during the 1998 Olympics in Atlanta, Georgia, but who was named as the prime suspect and featured in news reports, all over the country, for weeks running. His life and his reputation, and the reputation of the police agencies investigating him, were severely damaged.

By Saturday, we weren't thinking too much about that. We had another good lead.

A car had been spotted leaving one of the shooting locations. The driver had actually made some evasive moves to get around a police roadblock. He ran from officers who tried to chase him down. Someone got a license plate. He wasn't named as a suspect, but he was someone we needed to see.

We learned some more about him: we got an address, found out he lived with another guy who had a criminal record, learned that he had a gun. An ATF guy went to interview him.

It turned out he didn't have a driver's license. That was it. He didn't own a gun, or he didn't own the right kind of gun. He wasn't the killer. He had run from the police, and driven around the roadblocks, because he was afraid of getting arrested for driving without a license. He was interviewed and dismissed as a suspect.

But the weird thing is, he did it again. We had to send people back to interview him again, because he drove around some police barricades again, after a different shooting, apparently for the same reason. He was still afraid he'd get arrested for driving without a license.

Later on, the police department and the task force would be criticized—and I would be criticized—for not giving more information to the public about possible suspects. We were perceived as withholding information from the media, and even from possible targets.

But this is police work. You get a tip. You develop a lead. You compare what you know about this person with what you know about the killer. If enough things compare favorably, you try to find the person. If you find the person, you begin surveillance. If the surveillance confirms your suspicions, you interview the person, or arrest the person.

But where in that process is it wise, and safe, to inform the public? If you do it too early, you run the risk of naming an innocent person as a suspect, or of causing a guilty person to try to run. If you do it too late, you run the risk of aggravating the media. We decided that was a better risk. Every day names would go up on the board. And every day names would come down off the board.

For example, a week into the investigation we got interested in a dentist. He fit the description we needed; he made a good suspect: He had a gun. He had flexible office hours. He was not in the office during the times that we knew a couple of the shootings had occurred. We set up surveillance at his office and we waited.

He returned to the office—right after another shooting had occurred. There would have been just enough time for him to have left the crime scene and made it back to his office. Our officers stopped him. They asked him whether he had a gun. He said he did. They asked where it was. He said it was in the trunk of his car.

The officers had to decide whether they needed a warrant. They decided they did, just to be safe. So they detained the dentist while the warrant was arranged. Then they got the trunk open and looked at the gun. It fired a .223 bullet.

Then the officers wanted to see the dentist's office. Inside, they found maps on the walls. And on the maps they found arrows pinpointing the locations of all the shootings. This was the guy! It *had* to be the guy! So the officers took him in—him and his gun.

The gun was turned over to ballistics. The tests were performed. There was a lengthy interrogation of the suspect. He insisted he didn't shoot anyone, that he was just interested in the case. Well, what would you expect him to say? The officers didn't necessarily believe this story. Besides, while the tests were being performed, there were no new shootings. We had him.

Then we lost him, as a suspect. The gun didn't match. His story checked out. He was just a freaky guy. He wasn't the killer. He was just very, very interested in the case.

We were lucky not to have identified this man, at any time, as the suspect, or to have announced that we had arrested him. Because we would have been wrong. His name would have been made public. His picture would have gone out there. And why? Because we turned some coincidences into possible evidence and got sloppy with it. As it was, we managed to keep him out of the media and were able to let him go about his business and not harm him.

At the next press briefing on Saturday, I told the media that the shooting in Fredericksburg looked like another incident in the same series of shootings.

What I didn't stress for them was this complicating detail: The shooting occurred in front of a Michael's craft store.

This caused us to speculate that the connection between the first shooting and the last was the Michael's store chain, and that the connection between the victims must hinge on some connection to Michael's. Someone created a map of the Michael's stores in the D.C. area, so that we could predict where the next shooting would occur.

Well, forget it. There were six or seven Michael's stores in Montgomery County alone. There might have been as many as thirty in the greater D.C. area. There were a lot of suburbs, and a lot of homeowners in the suburbs who wanted to make their houses look nice. So there were a lot of Michael's. Covering them all, against the possibility of another shooting, would not be possible.

I suspected, still, that there might be no connection between one Michael's store and another. I was thinking it might be nothing more than coincidence. If you've got that many locations—including a shop near a big, wide parking lot, where there are plenty of potential victims standing out in the open, in the suburbs, where there is probably lots of wooded cover within shooting distance of the parking lot ... It's like saying the connection was through gas stations, when in fact a gas station was simply a convenient location for the kind of killings we were experiencing. But we still had to assign officers to run down possible leads. By late Friday, we had people going back through Michael's employee files, back through customer complaints, looking for some connection between the victims.

We had also posted a reward. We announced that we would offer $50,000 for any information leading to the arrest and indictment of a suspect in the shootings. We urged people to call the Montgomery County hot line with any information they might have.

It did not occur to me that there was anything unusual about the fact that the Fredericksburg shooting victim had not died. I did not think the sniper was now shooting to scare and not to kill. I thought we were just lucky this time.

But it did start to occur to me that this shooting might not be related, that it might be a copycat event—someone taking advantage of the headlines to kill someone they had wanted to kill already. I didn't like to think about that. It would make our investigation far more complicated if we were to discover there was more than one person doing these shootings.

We were hoping the ballistics tests would tell us we were looking for just one weapon. That would mean that if we caught the person shooting that weapon we would bring an end to the killings.

If ballistics said it was not just one weapon, then the odds of stopping the killings went down very fast. You could arrest someone, and it could be the right person for one particular killing, but the shootings would continue.

I have thought several times since then about the copycat angle. When I consider the impact of the sniper shootings on the people of Montgomery County and the greater D.C. area, I wonder what would happen if some terrorist group decided to use the same approach.

Twenty teams of two guys each could paralyze entire cities.

The law enforcement response to multiple shooters would be similar to what we were already doing with the sniper. Once you realize you have a pattern, you try to mobilize into a team. You get your schools, neighborhoods, shopping malls and other locations to reduce likely targets while also continuing to function. You run a traffic shutdown, as we did. You begin to collect and collate and cross-check all the available data, as we did.

The big difference with a mass series of shootings would be the increased likelihood that citizens would be eyewitnesses to the crimes as they were being committed. The eyes and ears of the police would be greatly expanded. Law enforcement representatives would collect these pieces of information through tip lines, as we did, but there would be more information.

Lastly, if multiple teams were attacking multiple cities, there would be an agenda. Someone would likely come forward to take credit and issue a list of demands. That communication, as it ultimately did in the sniper case, would enhance law enforcement's ability to narrow and then conclude its investigation.

By late Friday night the forensics and the ballistics people had determined that the bullet fragments found in the bodies of the first six victims were all fired from the same weapon. The reports said the bullet cores and jacket fragments linked the killings of James D. Martin, 55, James L. "Sonny" Buchanan, 39, Premkumar A. Walekar, 54, Sarah Ramos, 34, Lori Ann Lewis-Rivera, 25, and Pascal Charlot, 72. The same ballistics report connected those murders to the attempted murder of the woman outside the Michael's store in Fredericksburg.

Mike Bouchard said at a press briefing early that night, "This evening the forensic laboratory linked the projectile from the D.C. shooting to three of the shootings that occurred in Montgomery County. They're able to tell now that four shootings were done with the same firearm." He said it was not clear yet whether the shooting in Fredericksburg was connected, but it looked like a strong possibility.

We concluded that press briefing by putting out again the number of our telephone tip line, and reminding people of the $50,000 reward for information leading to the arrest and conviction of the killers.

On Saturday, we announced that without a doubt the killings were the work of a serial sniper, and that the shooting of the woman at the Fredericksburg Michael's store was without a doubt linked to the others.

This was the first time that I said out loud that there was probably more than one person involved.

"My experience would say you got a driver, you got a shooter," I said at a press briefing, but added that we had no further clues as to the killers' identities or the relationship between one victim and another. "They still all appear to be random victims," I said. "They don't appear to be anyone's enemy, don't appear to be involved in anything coordinated. Just simply random targets, innocent people who happen to be in the area and have been unduly harmed."

I confirmed that we were looking for a white box truck, possibly a Mitsubishi or Isuzu, with black lettering on the side. I admitted that I was just as unnerved as everyone else by the killings. "I'm on edge," I said. "People in our community are on edge." I felt it was important for people in the community to know we were going through this with them.

The press briefings, by now, were beginning to be enormous, with news organizations from all over the globe. The story had gone from local to national to international in a matter of twenty-four hours. The reason for this, I think, was our proximity to Washington, D.C. There were already news organizations there, assigned to the White House. Every newspaper in Europe had one person in Washington. Every TV news station in the world had a camera crew they used in Washington. If the story had broken in Des Moines, or Detroit, I don't think it would have gotten the same level of attention. But because we were only a half hour from the Capitol, no one had to be flown in to cover it. No one had to be put up in hotels. It wasn't a financial hardship to get people onto the story.

The reporters all had questions. One of the hardest to answer was "What are you doing to protect people?" or "What can people do to protect themselves?"

There was no answer. At one of the press briefings, I said, "We have someone who so far has been accurate in what they are attempting to do. We feel like we have a skilled shooter, and that heightens our concern."

There was very little we could do to keep people safe. Some gas stations had started putting up tarps, so that the people pumping gas were hidden and didn't make easy targets. At other gas stations we found people avoiding the self-serve lines—which was kind of weird, since it really said, "I'll pay extra for someone else to pump the gas, so that *you* can be the one that gets shot, while I sit in my car."

Reporters wanted to know why the schools hadn't been closed. The "lockdown" procedures we had put in place at the schools, in which children were kept in the buildings, didn't play on the yards and were kept away from the windows, didn't seem like enough. The media wanted to know why we hadn't instituted some kind of daylight curfew.

I didn't know what to tell them, except that we wanted people to go about their business and do the things they would ordinarily do. I didn't have any other answers.

I pointed out to them that we had posted officers in front of schools. What I didn't tell them was that this was probably accomplishing nothing other than making targets out of the officers. I didn't know whether having them there was any kind of deterrent at all. I thought it probably wasn't—since one shooting had occurred right across the street from one of our police substations, and another had taken place almost right in front of an officer writing a traffic ticket. I knew the officers placed in these locations weren't in a position to protect anyone.

What I did know was that not one officer that I assigned to this duty hesitated to go out there. They didn't flinch. They didn't complain, or ask what the hell I was doing putting them out there. They went out and they stood guard and they stood tall, and I didn't hear a word about it.

I felt terrible doing it. It was a crazy assignment, to just go out there and stand around with no chance of protecting yourself. But it was very reassuring for the citizens—particularly the schoolchildren—and it did wonders for their self-confidence. It made it possible for them to continue living their lives.

I knew the officers were thinking the same thing I was thinking: Sooner or later, just to prove a point, the sniper is going to shoot a police officer. Despite this, none of my officers ever said no to this assignment. They all just kept showing up.

Through the weekend, their bravery paid off. There had been a shooting Friday afternoon. Then nothing happened Saturday. Then nothing happened Sunday.

No one was relaxing. No one thought it was over—because "over," for us, would mean we had arrested the right person. But all kinds of crazy things started coming up. A lot of it came from the media. They started forming theories:

The sniper is married, and his Little Miss Muffet wife won't let him out of the house on the weekend.

The sniper is a soccer dad, and he's at the game with his kids.

The sniper has to take the weekend off. He has a job that lets him be unaccountable during the week, but not during the weekend.

The sniper works in the Washington area, but goes somewhere farther away on the weekend. His job will bring him back to D.C. on Monday.

The sniper was just passing through. He was in Montgomery County. He went south, into Virginia. The next time we heard from him, it would be a shooting in Georgia.

The sniper was working on some geographical pattern. There was a sort of north, west, east, south pattern to it—from the first four or five shootings. Maybe he was drawing some kind of picture on the map.

None of these theories brought us any closer to figuring out who or where the sniper was. We took advantage of the slower pace. We stood down some of our resources and let some of our people catch their breath. We gathered our strength, and rested some of our officers, in preparation for Monday. There were lots of visible units still in the Aspen Hill area. We wanted lots of visible units around the schools. We didn't want anyone to think we were slacking off, just because two days had passed with no shootings.

I didn't feel like relaxing, even after two days with no new victims. I might have gotten home a little earlier one of those nights—like, I got home at eight-thirty, or nine o'clock, instead of ten-thirty or midnight. I was up at five every day and at the station at six, and hard-charging all day long, right through the weekend.

So were the people around me. Over that weekend, officers and support staff were busy creating the infrastructure for the investigation. In less than forty-eight hours, they installed T-1 communication lines, two hundred telephone lines, and electrical lines sufficient to run an office staffed with over one thousand people. A satellite truck connected our communications with the FBI. A high-speed cable connected us to the Rockville ATF office.

Then the hardware came in. We installed 500 telephones, 250 computers and a battery of photocopiers, fax machines, television monitors and all the usual office furniture. It was like building a company over a weekend, from scratch, and having it operational Monday morning. Only these guys did it faster than that.

There was new departmental architecture, too.

We created something we called the Information

Control Center. In time, once it got rolling, it would be staffed by more than two hundred FBI agents. They handled all investigative tips and leads, through a national toll-free line. These agents would receive and review the tips, and then deliver them to what we called the Intelligence Table.

The Intelligence Table's task was to separate the good tips from the bad, and then prioritize the good into categories—routine, priority and immediate. On a two-hour rotation, as the tips were delivered by courier to the Intelligence Table, these tips were broken out by category and assigned. Depending on how much manpower was available, immediate tips got immediate attention, priorities were handled by other available officers, and routine tips sat waiting until all the immediate tips had been handled.

The tips all went through a sort of criminalistics machinery. The available information was all checked against "want" categories—gun registration, motor vehicle registration, criminal history, etc. Once these questions had been answered, cross-checking against national databases, the tip went into the FBI-designed Rapid Start computer program, which helped us make sure the information was not being processed through a related tip.

Once the tip had been processed by the Intelligence Table, it went forward to the Investigations Table. There, depending on its urgency, the lead might go to tactical operations or crime analysis.

Tactical operations consisted of plainclothes units, from all the participating departments, and SWAT units. The tactical operations were spearheaded by Montgomery's Drew Tracy. His division was responsible for surveillance on suspects and suspect locations, as well as deployment of SWAT units when and if another shooting occurred.

Crime analysis, under the direction of Maryland State Police intelligence section's Captain A. J. McAndrew, was responsible for gathering, developing and coordinating details for the most promising of the leads. After a rapid study of all available software systems, the crime analysis team decided to use a computer program known as the HIDTA case explorer as their primary software, with backup from two related programs called I-2 link-analysis and COPLINK.

This became a huge logistical job, and stayed that way for the duration of the investigation. At one point, the Operations Table was given the job of feeding everyone. We had five hundred people working, at any given time, twenty-four hours a day, seven days a week. We didn't have time for folks to be going out for burgers, and the people working in the middle of the night were going to need something to snack on, so we set up a 24/7 meal system. Three full meals a day were served, and refreshments of all types were made available at all times.

I mention all this pedestrian detail here only because it's an indication of all the little stuff we had to figure out, right away, before the investigation got up to full speed. Since we'd never had a case like this before, there was no blueprint available for us to study. We didn't have anyone to call and ask questions like, "How'd you handle the volume of tips?" or "What did you guys do for food?" It is remarkable to me that this group of men and women, who'd had no experience designing a system like this before, built such a fine operational model, on the fly, with less than a weekend to do it. But a large part of the smooth operation of this multidepartmental machine, made up of over four thousand people who'd never worked together before, was due to the smart design that was invented over that October 5–6 weekend.

I didn't see it, but I heard later that there were some small incidents of friction. There were little moments of frustration, in which someone from one side would start complaining about someone from another side. Some of the Montgomery County Police Department people didn't like the way the ATF people did things. I heard that one officer was griping that the ATF people acted like they'd never even worked a homicide case before.

John King took that officer aside and said, "And how many sniper killings have you solved?"

The officer said, "Okay, Chief. I get your point."

By that Sunday night it was beginning to look to some people like it might be over. We had no shootings on Saturday or Sunday. Some people thought the psychotic episode that had driven this killer to start gunning people down had passed.

Or, some people thought, maybe he was just waiting, and letting us wait, before the shooting began again.

While we waited, we couldn't see him, or hear him. Bill O'Toole summed it up, saying, "It's like a ghost with a gun."

4. Education of a Rookie Cop

I never knew any black cops growing up in Lexington. There weren't any. I never saw black policemen walking the beat. I never saw black policemen driving police cars. I never saw a black man in a police uniform. Now that I think of it, I never saw any of that even in the movies or on TV. I had no consciousness of black people in law enforcement.

What I knew of law enforcement I didn't like. I believed the cops were the bad guys. I thought they lied, and planted evidence, and made up cases. I thought they beat people to get confessions. I thought they beat people just because they could. I thought they killed people and got away with it.

I thought all that because, to one degree or another, all that was true at the time and in the place I grew up.

The furthest thing from my mind when I went off to college was a career in law enforcement. I thought I was going to be a lawyer.

Looking back, I'm not even sure how I got that idea in my head. There certainly weren't any lawyers in my family. Or on my block. Or in my community. I'm sure there were lots of black lawyers in America. I didn't know about any of them, but doing what they did seemed like a good choice, given the available options.

I knew I didn't want to be a teacher, because I saw what a disappointment my father's career had been to him. I knew I didn't want to be a doctor, like he had wanted to be, because I saw how it broke his heart not to go to medical school, and how his hopes for my older brother going to medical school had turned out. I knew I didn't want to be a blue collar worker, because by the time I got to college I had already been that—and I knew I wanted to do more with my life.

By the time I got to college, in fact, I had already had a number of different kinds of blue collar jobs. I had done construction work and been a lifeguard at the city pool my father ran. I had been a factory worker, making furniture at the Lexington Furniture plant in my hometown.

I was a good worker. I worked hard and I had ambition. My father had taught me—or I had learned from watching the way he worked—how to work hard. My mother, too. They both got up and did their jobs, every day, cheerfully and without complaining. They didn't slack off. They didn't call in sick. They went in and did their work.

I worked in the furniture factory in high school, during the summer, as an "off loader." The furniture would come down the line, and I'd take it off and stack it. In the evenings, and on the weekends, I'd make overtime money by working in the lacquer booth, where the pieces of furniture were sprayed with finish. It wasn't brain surgery. It was boring, repetitive, physically demanding work. It wasn't something you woke up excited about doing. It was just a good solid paycheck.

It was also a place where you could do overtime work. That was important to me. In high school, I already had my sights on getting out of Lexington. I didn't go to summer school, which would have been good for my academic career, because I knew I was going to need money to leave town. Even before I knew where I was going, I knew I *was* going.

When I left Lexington for Chapel Hill for my freshman year in college, I hardly looked back. I didn't even go back to spend the summers in my hometown. Instead, I sold books. I was recruited by the Southwestern Book Company to sell dictionaries. For the next couple of summers, that's how I earned my money.

This was a real education, in all kinds of things. The book company would recruit working class kids from college campuses all over the South. They'd bring them in and train them how to work, and how to live. It was an incredibly. rigorous training, too—kind of like boot camp for the kids who go into the military.

Once we were recruited, and had gone though the first part of the training, they formed us into teams and sent us into the Deep South. Some guys went to Pensacola, Florida. Some guys went to Mobile, Alabama. The book company was based in Alcoa, Tennessee. They sent my team to Pensacola.

One of the first things you did was find a room. They told us how to look in the newspaper, at the want ads, and how to ask around the community and in the churches, looking for the right kind of room. What you wanted, they told us, was a room in a house owned by an older couple with no children. A religious couple, if possible. I found a room similar to that in Pensacola.

Then they taught us how to dress and how to carry ourselves. You were supposed to wear jeans and a T-shirt. No nice shirt. No necktie. You wanted to make it look like you were poor. Honest, but poor. They didn't want you to look like a religious person, a missionary or something, because some people wouldn't open the door to someone like that. And they didn't want you to look like you were a bill collector, or someone serving a summons.

They even told us that we should always approach the house at a run, so that we'd arrive out of breath. They said this would give people the impression that we were in a hurry, didn't have a lot of time to spend on them if they weren't interested, and that what we were doing was exciting and very important.

They taught us not to fraternize with each other during the week. They taught us to forget our girlfriends back home, and not try to make any new girlfriends on the road. They taught us that nothing mattered but selling those dictionaries.

They trained us to be familiar with every aspect of the books. You learned how to demonstrate the product and show off its best features. You learned how to flip the pages open to your favorite parts, and how to read those parts out loud—upside down, while you showed them to the customer. You carried the dictionaries in these big blue boxes, and you learned how to slip the book out of the box and hold it like it was the Holy Bible.

I stayed with the McCant family. They were nice, hardworking people. They welcomed me into their home, and into their family. They even took me fishing with them. I didn't tell my supervisors about this, but a few times I'd knock off work early and we'd all go down to the Gulf and go fishing. We would fish off the pier and then cook the fish we caught in a deep fryer they brought with them from home. We'd catch them and clean them and fry them up and eat them, right on the pier. This was great eating, and a different way of life from any I'd been exposed to.

One of their sons, Sam McCant, was an outstanding basketball player with a great future. He was going away to play ball in Salt Lake City. He was a big star in Pensacola—a local player and a local hero. Every Saturday night he'd put on this white suit and do the town. I was a college kid, and just out of Lexington. There was no way I could hang with Sam. He was just too cool, and he had too much charm and style. I couldn't compete. I couldn't even keep up.

At the end of that summer I took some of my book money and hired one of Sam's sisters to make me a white suit. It was one nice suit, but I never felt that I looked as good in mine as Sam looked in his. So I wouldn't wear it. I never wore it. It was ten years before

I finally got around to donating it to Goodwill. I never did develop the style or the guts to wear the suit out on the town the way Sam did.

As salesmen, we'd get up every morning and take a cold shower at six o'clock. We'd have breakfast and go out into the streets. They told us they expected us to be making our first call before eight o'clock in the morning, and to be making our last call after eight o'clock in the evening.

This was designed to help us sell more dictionaries, but it was also designed to help us not spend any money we were making. They wanted their guys to have savings accounts at the end of the summer. That way, we'd feel good about the company. We'd come back again the next summer, and they wouldn't have to waste time training us, and we'd be able to recruit more salesmen by telling them how great the job was working out for us.

Once you'd worked a summer, you would become part of the recruiting team. You'd try to find new guys to join you next summer. I think you got a percentage of their earnings, for every guy you brought in, or a finder's fee or something.

A lot of the time we were calling on customers who were even more down and out than we were. We'd visit a lot of people who didn't have any money at all, and didn't have any need for a dictionary anyhow. Sometimes a woman would say, "Child, I don't have any money for a dictionary. But you sure look hungry. Why don't you come in and let me fix you some supper?"

Making the money was hard. We'd work six days a week, and then on Sundays, which would have been our day off, we had to do our laundry and attend these training sessions from the company.

The black salesmen had it a little tougher than the white salesmen. We spent a lot of time selling dictionaries to families that couldn't afford them. The dictionaries cost $30 each, and the company wanted us to try and get at least a 30 percent deposit to place the order. In the white neighborhoods, the families would often pay for the dictionary outright. For many of the black families, this was impossible. They didn't have $30, or $10, or even $5. So I'd have to visit a family twice or three times, coming back on Friday night, or Saturday morning, or after payday, to demonstrate the product again and try and get that deposit. Then, if I got the deposit, I'd have to make several other visits to get the rest of the $30.

This wasn't racism. It was reality. In the early 1970s, in places like Pensacola and Mobile, very few black families had checking accounts. They couldn't write you a check, so you didn't have checks to deposit for your sales. Instead, you'd get a few dollars as a deposit. Then you had to return on Saturday—after the family breadwinner got his paycheck on Friday—to collect the rest.

I almost always dealt with the woman of the house. It was amazing to watch the determination of these strong black women who were trying so hard to do something to improve the lives of their families. Often these dictionaries we sold them were the only books in the house, the first books the family ever owned. The woman would have to try and rat-hole a few dollars from her husband's paychecks to cover the deposit, or make the rest of the payment. Sometimes you'd have to return several Saturdays until they had enough to cover the whole thing. Sometimes the husbands would be at home, and they'd demand another demonstration of the product before they'd agree to make the rest of the payment.

This worked out all right. It taught me to be persistent. It taught me how hard it is for poor families to bring themselves up, to get up to the equal footing that it is assumed they already have—assumed by people who will later make decisions about who should get into a school, or who should get a job. I had never been exposed to the insides of the lives of very poor people. I learned a lot of compassion watching these black women struggling so hard to put together enough money to buy a dictionary.

The last summer I worked for that company, they sent us to Los Angeles. That was a real big eye-opener for me. I'd never been anywhere like that. It wasn't like Lexington, or Pensacola, or Mobile. In those places, people didn't even lock their front doors. People were pretty poor, but they were real friendly. I'd have people say to me, almost every day, "Why don't you come in and sit down and let me get you a cold drink?"

There wasn't any of that in Los Angeles. We were sent down to Watts. There were bars on all the windows and doors. There were gangs. People wouldn't even come to the door to talk to you. People were scared. You could feel it walking down the street.

I got robbed in Watts. I was walking back from making a sale. I was a sitting duck. The gang members could see I wasn't from around there. I was an unfamiliar face, in their neighborhood, hauling around this big-ass, goofy-looking blue box. They knew I was selling something. They knew I had some money on me. They just put a gun on me and took my money.

It was scary. I hadn't been exposed to much crime before that. I was never a victim of crime before that. I had never had a gun pointed at me before. I didn't like it. I left Los Angeles before the summer ended.

I didn't know this at the time, but all this experience was driving me toward becoming a police officer, and preparing me to become one. But first I had to be introduced to the idea by the right guy. That happened at the University of North Carolina.

As I said in Chapter 2, I almost didn't go there. Carolina wasn't on my list of schools. I was thinking about something smaller, and more local, where I could get a football or wrestling or track scholarship. I got lucky, though, because some people from my high school were interested in Carolina, and life in Chapel Hill, and that got me interested.

Even though I didn't get offered any scholarship, I

did get on the wrestling team. The season started in October and ran until February. I fell into a pattern. There was a lot of practice, and a lot of running, and a lot of emphasis on losing weight. But there was also a lot of emphasis, in the dorms, of hanging out and goofing off and drinking. Then I'd have to go back to practice, and all that running and all that losing weight. But I stuck to it, and I was good at it.

It was a social school, and I got to know a lot of people there. A bunch of us guys would cruise over to James Dorm, which was a coed dormitory, on a regular basis. I guess some of the guys had pretty active sex lives. I wasn't one of them. I wanted to be a ladies' man, but I wasn't. Some guys seemed to get hooked up pretty quick, and they had steady girlfriends. Other guys played the field. We spent a lot of time just hanging out at James Dorm, staying up late into the night, talking, exchanging ideas, flirting or whatever.

I was still involved with Joy Franklin, my girlfriend from high school. For the first three years of college, we had a long-distance romance. She had been accepted at Shaw University, a predominantly black college in Raleigh. I'd get over there as often as I could. I guess it wasn't often enough, though. When I was a senior at Carolina, she broke it off. She had been seeing someone else and had moved in with him. He was a professor at Shaw, and she was very serious about him. I went to see her, and she told me we were through.

I was devastated. I was in love with Joy. I thought I was going to marry her. I thought we would get married and then have children.

I hadn't seen it coming. I hadn't known about this other guy. He was older, and he had a staff job teaching at the university, and he owned his own house, where they were living. He seemed like he had all the things I didn't have. It was a big blow to my pride that she chose him over me.

I'd like to say that my broken heart made me concentrate more on my studies and turned me into a stronger man. That's not really true. Looking back, I would say now that I kind of messed it up in college. I was not as serious as I should have been. I didn't study as hard as I should have and it affected my GPA. No matter how many degrees you get later in life, or how much success you have in your career, you can't do anything to improve your GPA if you've messed it up. I wish now that I'd paid more attention to that and worked harder.

There was one good thing that came out of my breaking up with Joy Franklin. Or with her dumping me. In my senior year, I started going out with a girl named Beryl Wade. She was a prelaw student, and we were pretty serious all through my last year of school. Through her, I started getting interested in law school. She was headed that way, and she sort of pointed me in that direction. She was from Washington, D.C., and she'd seen quite a lot more of the world than I had. She had high aspirations for herself—much higher than I had any reason to have for myself, at that time. Those aspirations turned out to be well founded. She became a lawyer and did very well for herself.

Out of my relationship with her, I started thinking of myself as a lawyer. I started taking the classes to prepare myself for law school. I imagined I would be a defense attorney. It seemed to me like a noble profession, and I didn't have any other big ideas about what I should be. I knew I didn't want to work with my hands, doing something like I'd done at the furniture factory. No one ever talked to me about a career in the military. (I had a draft deferment, so I didn't get called up for Vietnam.) I just knew I wanted to be a professional of some kind. I thought being a lawyer would impress my dad. It would be a good way to make a living, and to help people at the same time.

Then I met Reuben Greenberg. I was in my fourth year at Chapel Hill and heading toward graduating. I enrolled in a class in criminology. I wasn't that interested in criminology, but I needed the credits, and I thought learning something about law enforcement would help me be a better lawyer. The course was called "Guarding the Guardians," which I liked, because I had this idea somebody had to keep an eye on the cops.

More interestingly, the class was being taught by a black man. A black police officer. A *Jewish* black police officer. That interested me a lot.

Reuben Greenberg was a remarkable figure. He was born in Houston, to a mixed-race family. His mother was black. His father was the son of a black woman and a white man, a Russian Jew, from the Ukraine, named Greenberg. The family shortened the name to Green. Reuben and his six brothers and sisters·were raised as Methodists. Reuben's father was in the insurance business. His mother was a cleaning woman.

Reuben went to segregated schools, like I did. When he graduated from high school, he went to California to live with an uncle and attend San Francisco State University. He got interested in Judaism, and changed his name back to Greenberg. He did well in school, and after his undergraduate degree earned a master's in public administration. He went on to be an undersheriff in San Francisco. Later on, he was offered the job at UNC, and that's where I met him.

Later, he became a sort of legendary character in law enforcement—to an African-American in law enforcement, anyway. He went to work in Savannah, Georgia, for a police chief named Dave Epstein. From there, he became the chief of police in several small Southern towns—Opa Locka, Florida, then Orlando, then Tallahassee. In 1982, he was hired to run the police department in Charleston, South Carolina.

This was amazing to me. A black man as chief of police in the very cradle of the Confederacy? It was impossible. But it gave me a great deal of encouragement. I'm not sure what other African-American police chiefs there were in the country at that time. Later, there would be black men running the police departments in Houston, New York, Detroit, Baltimore, Chicago, Atlanta, Miami and Los Angeles, just to name the bigger cities. In 1982, it was still a new thing.

Greenberg had a habit of bringing law enforcement people to campus to recruit possible candidates for their police departments. One day he told me that he wanted me to meet this recruiter who was coming in from the police department in Portland, Oregon. I wasn't all that interested, but Greenberg told me that if I met the man, and took the recruiting test, and wrote a little paper about it, he'd let me skip an examination. Well, I knew I could get a better grade writing a paper than I could taking a test, so I agreed. I met with the recruiter, and took the recruiting test. I don't remember all that much about it. But later on, Greenberg offered me another deal. I could skip another test, and write another little paper instead, if I'd agree to go sit for the oral examination. So I did that, too.

I still wasn't interested in becoming a police officer. I still had a pretty low opinion of police officers. But before I could think up a hundred reasons not to be a cop, the Portland Police Bureau offered me a job. I wasn't real sure about it. My dad encouraged me to take it. He said, "If you don't like it, you can always come home." Reuben Greenberg encouraged me to take it, too. I said, "But what are my friends going to think, if I go and become the police?"

He said, "If they don't like it, they aren't really your friends anyway."

My best excuse for taking the job was that it would help me be a better lawyer. I figured I could get some experience of the corruption of the police department, from the inside. That would prepare me for defending people who were facing trumped-up charges. I could be a better defense attorney if I understood the way the police worked.

So I said yes.

I continued to date Beryl Wade until the end of the year. In May, I moved to Portland. I didn't have any real plans for keeping a relationship alive with someone who was three thousand miles away. And I didn't manage to keep it alive for long. I became preoccupied with learning to be a police officer.

I couldn't say now whether my idea of what a police officer was changed much that semester. I was interested in the Portland job, but only as a stepping stone. I was never intending to be a police officer as a career. I still had the same old ideas about cops being racist, and crooked, and hardly better than the bad guys they were supposed to be chasing.

Maybe people growing up today have a clearer sense of what the police really do. There's so much more information available. For one thing, there are all those police TV shows. Most of them are pretty bad. Most of them don't get any of it right. They misrepresent police officers, and police departments, and police work.

The exception to this is the show called *COPS*—the one in which the viewer gets a chance to ride along with the police while they work. I find this show very interesting. The glamour and the excitement of most of what is represented about police work on television is fake. Real police work is boring, dirty, scary and deadly. Most shows don't accurately portray that.

COPS came to Portland when I was a lieutenant there. I'm not sure who made the decision to bring them in, but some of the police management was fearful of what the cameras would see. What we found was that the officers who had the cameras on them behaved admirably. They worked really hard to make cases and make arrests. Officers who couldn't have spelled the words "yes, sir" were saying "yes, sir" left and right. They were polite and professional and they made the department proud. I am not sure, though, if I were asked, whether I'd be willing to have my officers participate with another *COPS* episode. Despite the fact that the officers behaved so well, I'd worry that having the cameras on would make them take extra chances, like the camera was egging them on to be extra tough police officers.

The only fictional TV show I ever saw that got most of the police stuff right was *Hill Street Blues.* And maybe the first season of *NYPD Blue.* Now I don't know. Maybe they run their detectives different in New York from how they do it everywhere else, but the way it looks on TV is pretty bizarre. There's a lot of excessive force.

All these TV shows have an interesting effect on how people think about the police, and what they think they know about the police.

I've been teaching about police work at the college level for many years. Every semester I do this thing in my classroom. I bring a student up to the front of the class. I tell the students, "This student is going to assault me. He's going to attack me. I'm going to stop the attack. Then I'm going to arrest him and put him in handcuffs and take him to the police station. Do I have to read him his rights?"

And every time, every single student says, "Yes!"

Well, they're wrong. I don't. I'm a victim. I'm a witness. I want to arrest this person. I'm not planning on interrogating this person. I'm not asking any questions. I'm just detaining this person. I don't have to read any rights at all.

But that's the effect of Hollywood. The students have all seen the detectives reading the Miranda rights to the suspects. They've all seen dramas where the case falls apart because the arresting officer didn't read the rights. That's not really the way it works.

Even the TV people are aware of this. I've seen TV shows where the suspect screams out, "You can't do this to me! I want a lawyer! I want a phone call! I know my rights!" And the police officer smiles and says, "You watch too much TV." So I guess the TV people know the way they write it isn't the way it really happens.

I didn't grow up watching police shows on TV. I had to learn everything about being a police officer the hard way—by becoming a police officer. The life of the police officer, I was going to find out, isn't glamorous. It doesn't involve a big salary. It doesn't involve short hours and a cushy assignment.

That makes it good training for life. You're always working hard. You're always in debt. You're always in danger. You could be killed in the line of duty, at any moment. That means you stop worrying about the little things. Not worrying about the little things might be the secret to a successful life.

When I first got to Portland, in 1975, I was taken in by this police officer named Tony Newman. He was this big-hearted guy, married, with a son named Anthony and a basement apartment. He was one of Portland's few black police officers. I started rooming with him, along with another new recruit named Ogie Shaw. Tony took me in and became a lot more than just my land-lord. He set up these bunk beds in the basement for me and Ogie. His wife Rita made us dinner, every single night. And Tony would tell us stories about being a po-lice officer, about how to be a good police officer. He was a real mentor, at a time when I needed someone like that in my life.

I was just a rookie patrolman. I didn't know anything about anything. I didn't have any real life experience of being a policeman. I had barely begun to learn what a police officer was supposed to do.

In those days, the Portland Police Bureau sent its new recruits to a commuter academy within the city limits. It was a small group. Later, the bureau would change this policy and send recruits to a live-in state academy in Monmouth, Oregon. I imagine the instruction im-proved. In my time, there wasn't much instruction at all. You arrived in Portland, and you were sent to qualify for your weapon, and once they knew you could shoot a little they let you borrow $110 from a police fund and sold you a Model 10 Smith & Wesson gun. Then they put you on the street with a coach for a three-month training period.

It wasn't what I'd expected. They put me in a patrol

car with a guy named Stanley Pounds. We were assigned to car 742, in the Southeast. Every day we'd go to breakfast. We'd ride around. There was a young female police officer that we would have breakfast with two or three days a week. We'd make some radio calls. We'd break up family fights, or take a burglary report. We spent a lot of time just riding around talking about things.

I thought, *This seems like a pretty easy job.*

Three weeks into it, we're driving down the street and Stan just stops in the middle of a block. He says, "I've just been shot. Where are we? What are you going to do? How do you get help?"

He hadn't been shot. But what if he had? We were riding around, talking about all this stuff, and it seemed like fun, and guess what? It's not fun. If he had been shot that day, I didn't have a clue where we were, or how to tell someone to come help us.

Stanley Pounds was my first coach. He taught me a lot of basics. Then they switched me up. I rode for a while with Stan McDaniels, who was pretty low-key.

After three months, they sent me to the academy. We learned about discipline, and some academics, but mostly it was very basic. They taught us not to question authority, not to question the instructors, and how to do things like wear our hats properly. They taught us to shoot a gun, which to me was a new experience. My dad owned a Saturday Night Special, but he never taught me how to shoot it. I had never fired a weapon before I fired one on the practice range. I remember the instructors said it was better that way. They preferred to teach people who didn't already have bad shooting habits.

Other than that, I didn't leave the academy much more informed about police work than I had been when I arrived.

This might have been a lucky thing. I might not have been willing to undergo anything more rigorous. Later on, when I joined the National Guard, I was required to go to the Academy of Military Science, in Alcoa, Tennessee, for officer training. (By coincidence, Alcoa was also the home base for the book company I'd worked for every summer during college.) I had to undergo seven weeks of intense, almost prisonlike academy life. I had a roommate, and we had forced inspections. We had to undergo lessons in underwear folding. We had to march, everywhere we went, and stand at attention when we were in line for chow. It almost killed me. I have always, despite what I do for a living, hated "rules." I *enforce* rules for a living, but I don't much like having them enforced on *me*. I particularly hate "rules for rules' sake," and I got a belly full of it at Alcoa. When I was brand-new, I don't think I could have stood it.

In other words, I was green when I got to Portland. Tony Newman looked out for me.

One of the things he did was make me start working out in a gym. He used to kid me. I weighed about 150 pounds. I wasn't short, but I was pretty skinny. He always said, "If you don't get bigger, somebody's going to tear that badge right off your chest one day and take it home."

Tony worked out religiously. He had a thirty-inch waist and twenty-two-inch biceps. He was also a pool player, almost a hustler. He liked to take a drink, and he was a real ladies' man He was a good guy to hang out with.

I worked nights for the first few years on the Portland police force. I'd work from four o'clock in the afternoon to midnight, then go drink for a couple of hours, then go home to sleep, and then be in the gym by ten o'clock. I worked out in Loprinzi's gym, a place run by this guy Sam Loprinzi. This was before the day of Gold's Gym. It wasn't this fancy place with disco music playing. It wasn't a place that women went to. It was me and a lot of bodybuilders and weight lifters, working out in a basement in Sam Loprinzi's house. A lot of the guys I hung out with were sanitation workers. They'd come in after just having done their trash-hauling shifts, and we'd work out together.

I stayed with it for years. I was very serious about it.

I'd eat four or five meals a day, trying to get a lot of protein into my system. I did bench presses and squats. It took me forever to get my weight up to over 200 pounds. That was my goal, though, and I stuck to it. Eventually I got up to 240 pounds. I got so I could bench press 300 pounds, and do eight repetitions. That's a lot of weight for a guy that started out weighing 150 pounds.

The ironic thing, of course, is that I've spent the last twenty years trying for that same goal of 200 pounds. Only now I'm trying to weigh *less* than 200 pounds. I spent all that effort trying to get over 200, and now I'm doing everything I can to get back on the other side.

There were guys at Loprinzi's doing steroids. I was kind of jealous of the results they were getting. They made so much progress, right away—the way they grew, the amount of weight they could lift. But I didn't think it was a good idea for me. I did it the slow way. The old-fashioned way.

It worked. I got big. It didn't make me feel invincible. But it certainly made me feel strong. I think it gave me more confidence. Nobody was going to look at me and think they could tear my badge off my chest, like Tony said. I felt good.

And, after I'd been doing this a few years, when I was thirty years old, I entered the "Mr. Portland" bodybuilding contest. Yes, I did. I got up onstage in my underwear. I had all the poses. I had a routine. I had music by Michael Jackson—something from the *Off the Wall* album. I thought I had a real shot at winning.

I didn't win. I wasn't crushed by that, but I never entered another bodybuilding contest. This was a goal I had set for myself, like getting over 200 pounds, and I had met the goal. There wasn't any reason to keep at it. I wasn't that upset about not winning, because I had realized that I couldn't win unless I was willing to go with the steroids. I wasn't willing. I was worried about the side effects, and I was worried about being a police officer and taking drugs that were not entirely legal—just so I could make my T-shirts fit better. They were fitting pretty good already. The rewards didn't seem to justify the risks.

Being a policeman, at that time, in that place, wasn't all that cool. Socially, it was not cool at all. There were people you couldn't be friends with because of it. There were people you couldn't date because of it. Some women would not go out with a police officer. In the black community generally I'd hear a lot of negative things about being a policeman. There was a lot of hostility toward the police. I got called a "Tom," and an "Uncle Tom" more than once. There were just a lot of people who didn't want to have anything to do with the police.

I didn't have much time for socializing anyway. For the first three months, I'd ride with Stan Pounds all day, come home and eat with Tony Newman and his wife and the other new guy, Ogie Shaw, and then listen to Tony tell stories. After three months, I went to the academy. And right out of the academy, I went undercover.

Going undercover seems like a strange first assignment to me now, but I was black, and young, and new to the department, and the city. Nobody knew me, and if you didn't know any better I probably looked like a criminal. The police department felt a strong need to get people undercover in the black community. There was a lot of crime in those neighborhoods. It was easy for them to put me undercover in the criminal world and think that I'd fit right in. And I did.

It was a very strange way to live. I developed sources. I gathered information and collected informants. It was my job to buy stolen property and make cases against the guys doing the stealing.

Little did I know that what I was doing would turn into one of the biggest sting operations in Portland's history.

We had a district attorney at that time who was committed to bringing down the crime rate. His particular interest was in getting repeat offenders off the streets.

He planned to do this in part by eliminating the practice of plea bargaining with certain kinds of bad guys. The stolen property sting operation was part of that.

I set up shop in this mustard yellow clapboard house on North Mississippi, right in the heart of the Albina section of town. This is traditionally one of the worst neighborhoods in Portland. In the old days, and up until the 1920s, the poorest section of town was the flatlands down by the banks of the Columbia River, down around the shipyards. That's where the poor, working class people lived. But when a flood wiped out that part of town, and killed a lot of the residents, the poor people moved to clapboard frame houses and wooden rooming houses on the bluffs above the river. The white people living there moved out, and Albina became the new black ghetto of Portland.

It was the sort of place a guy who was a fence, like I was supposed to be, would live, dealing with stolen property. This became my home for the next six months.

I started calling myself "Charles Alexander." (Alexander is my middle name.) I had $1,000 in ready money at all times, and I put out the word that I was interested in buying stolen property. I used the money for that, but I also used it to move in the criminal world. I bought illegal guns. I bought illegal drugs. I bought drinks for bad guys, as a way of making friends with them. I moved in with these guys, and moved into their world.

My contact at the police station was a guy named Bill Renoud. He was a wonderful guy, and a good policeman, and a good mentor to me. He taught me how to survive undercover, without anyone learning my real identity or suspecting I was a police officer.

This was a matter of life and death. Most of the guys I did business with were very bad people. Almost all of them had criminal records, and many of them were wanted on outstanding warrants, too—parole violations, probation violations, new criminal charges. At least half of them, it turned out, were drug addicts. Most were "smash and grab" men. They'd smash in the window of a house, or a business, or a car, grab something easy to carry and easy to sell, and run. They brought me stereo equipment, cameras, jewelry, appliances and other stuff like that. They would have hurt me if they'd known I was a police officer.

It was a weird time. I was very alone out there. Bill Renoud was the only cop I ever saw. I'd go in at three o'clock in the morning and file my reports, and drop off stolen property I'd purchased, and he'd help me keep focused on what I was doing.

He loved working robbery. He laughed at the guys who worked homicide. Everyone thought homicide was the big deal, but robbery was where Bill liked to be. He believed you could really make a difference there, going after guys who were on the street scaring and hurting people every day—guys who you could get off the street with nothing more than determination and hard work. With murder, you could catch someone who'd already done something terrible. With robbery, you could actually stop people from doing something terrible.

Bill Renoud was an older white guy, with a house out in the suburbs. He was very good at his job and later wrote a book about conducting criminal investigations.

Despite his age, and his race and his suburban lifestyle, Bill Renoud had a lot of young black informants, and he made a lot of cases through them. That's because he always treated them with respect. He listened to them, and he talked *to* them—not *down to* them. He taught me something important. He said, "If you ever lose your sense of compassion for people, you should get out of police work."

It was exciting work. It was certainly better than having a real job, and it was more exciting than driving around in a patrol car wearing the uniform. I was undercover. I had a bushy Afro and a little mustache. I was on the make and I was making cases.

I was brand-new out of the academy. The values I had learned in the police academy, and the values that

I was beginning to learn as a police officer, had not completely taken root. I had a strong sense of values myself, from growing up the way I did, but some of the other officers did not. It was impossible for them to live in the criminal world, and live with criminals, and still keep their perspective. A female officer—also black, and also from North Carolina—was put undercover about the time I was. She fell in love with one of the criminals. She was later caught taking drugs to him in prison. She left the police department. Several other officers ended up lost to the world of crime, because they could not live in that world and maintain the values of the world of the police officer. They ended up going over to the other side.

I was never tempted. There wasn't anything that big to be tempted by, anyway. In order to become a criminal, I think I would have needed access to a lot more money than I was ever exposed to. If you slip over to that dark side, you know you're going to lose your job and your career and your reputation. So you'd better be able to make a big enough score that you are never going to need a job or a career or a reputation again. I was never offered anything quite that big.

In later years, the police administration passed new rules regarding undercover work. They stopped assigning new officers to this kind of work—for that very reason. They were losing too many of them to the people they were supposed to investigate and arrest. What I found was a flaw in the process: In order to pass through the recruiting process, the background checks, the entrance examination and the battery of psychological tests, most police officer candidates by definition have to come from pretty sheltered, stable, middle-class homes. You wind up recruiting very straight and often very inexperienced young people. When they're sent undercover, some of them are confronted for the very first time in their lives with people who are living a completely different kind of life. They come into contact with people who are taking drugs and drinking and having sex freely. By putting young, inexperienced police officers in this kind of environment, you run the risk that they'll start acting more like these people and less like the officers you hired them to be.

When that happens, is it the officer's fault or the fault of the agency that didn't prepare the officer to work in that environment? I think it's the agency's fault.

Some agencies try to create policies to protect against things like this. Some of them have a rule, for example, that no police officer can live with anyone who's had a felony conviction. That rule has not been challenged, on a civil rights basis, but I don't know why. The idea is to try and protect the officers from getting unduly influenced by the criminal element.

In the end, the undercover sting operation I worked on resulted in forty solid cases. We took forty crooks off the street. Most of the cases stuck, too. Thirty of the cases resulted in jail time, and most of the other crooks went to jail on other charges, like probation violations or weapons charges or whatever. Because the D.A. was so insistent on not doing any plea bargaining, some of the crooks went away for a long time.

One of the biggest crooks in that sting operation was a smart, smart-alecky black man named Al Fortham. He was a drug addict and a thief, and he and I got to be friends when I was working undercover. We really bonded during that time. He trusted that I was a crook. He considered me a friend. When we arrested him, he was terribly hurt to discover I was the police. He felt betrayed. He was outraged that the police were spending all this money and manpower rounding up thieves and putting them in jail. He was angry at the police and angry at the system. He was angry at the way he was being treated—"like an animal," he said—when he should be treated like a sick man with a drug problem. He told the police they should be setting up drug rehabilitation facilities with their money, instead of running sting operations that wound up putting drug addicts in jail.

The investigators didn't seem that interested in his theories.

Al had thirteen prior arrests, and four prior convictions, according to the district attorney, and three of those were for felonies. The D.A. called him a "three-time loser." He managed to get Al a five-year sentence.

I'm not sure how much of his time he served, but Al Fortham got cleaned up and became a useful guy. After he got out of jail, Al and I would go around and give antidrug talks. The friendship we had developed as criminals became more of a real friendship. Police officers who saw us together were always shocked that he called me "Charles"—since that's how he knew me, when I was undercover—and that I let him call me that. My officers could only refer to me as Lieutenant, or later Captain, or later Chief. This former crook and heroin addict called me Charles, and I called him Al. If for nothing else then, I know that undercover work was a good thing because it helped turn one guy's life around.

The case got enough attention that *60 Minutes* came out to Portland and did a big story on us. I rode around in a police car with Dan Rather, explaining to him on camera how we set up the sting. The *60 Minutes* cameras shot film of the arrests and followed some of the crooks through the court system right into their trials.

Rather predicted in one segment that, as the undercover officer who'd done all the buying of stolen property, and who was now back on the street as a uniformed police officer, I must be "a sitting duck." Sooner or later, he said, someone was going to come after me.

I didn't feel all that confident at the time, but there I am on film saying, "I just don't think that's the case. We informed all our uniformed officers and nonuniformed officers to contact everyone and spread the word that the dude that pinched everybody was a police officer. He was doing his job. He wasn't snitching nobody off. Because the life of a snitch, on the street, is very rough. You stand a much higher chance of being in danger if you're a snitch than if you're a police officer."

60 Minutes called the segment "Portland and the 40 Thieves." We were all very proud of that. We had been involved in an extremely successful police operation, and we were all getting a pat on the head from the national media for doing our jobs. This kind of overshadowed any feeling I might have had at the time that I was in danger. Because I made arrests during that time that didn't have anything to do with stolen property, and that involved guys who were much more dangerous than the average "smash and grab" thief.

Indeed, I was shot at for the first time right around then.

I'd been working with an informant named Terry. He knew I was a cop, even though I was working undercover and no one else in the community knew my real identity. Terry was supplying me with information. One day we got into a beef about something, on the back porch of the house where I was living. Terry went into the house and came back outside with a gun. In front of several witnesses, he drew the gun and threatened me and then fired a shot at me and ran back inside the house.

I wasn't hit. Terry later told me he was a crack shot, and had missed intentionally, and was only firing at me to impress the witnesses and destroy any thought in their minds that he was an informant. They would understand there was no way an informant would shoot at me—because an informant would know I was the police.

Terry wasn't all that bright.

He later got into all kinds of trouble. He had a cousin who was dating a guy who wasn't treating her right. Terry climbed up onto the roof of a tavern where this guy was drinking. When he came out, Terry shot him dead.

The crime went unsolved for quite a while. Then one of Terry's neighbors started hearing stories, and a search warrant turned up the murder weapon. Terry did six years in state prison.

I was shocked to learn about Terry and the murder. I realized for the first time that there were people who solved their problems in this way. It wasn't a crime of passion. It wasn't someone who was committing a crime and got into trouble and reached for a gun. It was someone who decided that murder was the best available solution to his problems.

I was just twenty-two years old at this time. I felt good about what I was doing. I felt like I was contributing something useful, and that what I was doing for a living might make my city a better, safer place to live. The work was exciting, and seemed honorable, too.

But around that time I heard there were a couple of guys coming for me. I heard they had targeted me, and they were going to rob me. Since I was buying stolen merchandise, I always had a lot of cash on me. I made a good target for robbery, if you were interested in that kind of thing. They didn't know I was a cop; I was just another criminal to them.

I could have run for cover, but that might have blown the cases I was developing. So I went out and bought a bunch of guns off the street. I got a bunch of guys together—street guys, people I knew from my undercover work, criminals from the stolen property world. I brought them together and told them I was going to be robbed by these two guys. I gave them the guns and said, "I'll give each of you a couple hundred bucks. If these guys come for me, and they've got guns, we're going to kill them."

The guys all agreed. And the other guys did come. Before they could pull out any weapons, however, and make an attempt at the robbery, my guys whipped their guns out and told them to leave. The robbers backed down.

So now I'm a hell of a crook! Later, I realized that was the stupidest possible thing I could have done. If someone had started shooting, and a bunch of guys had gotten killed, I would have had some serious explaining to do. I had done all of this planning to protect myself—buying the guns, recruiting the guys—without any oversight from my superiors. It turned out to be a successful plan, but it could just as well have gone the other way.

I did one more stint undercover after that. I was set up as a clerk, working behind a counter in a store in Portland's Old Town. This was then a very Hispanic section. I was supposed to work the counter and buy drugs and food stamps from the Hispanic criminals. This was not as successful as the Albina setup, for a variety of reasons. One of them: I don't speak Spanish. So I never knew what anyone was saying to anyone while I was dealing with these people. They'd say something to me, and then say things to each other, and I never understood a word of it. This made the job very stressful.

So did the fact that most of the customers I served were not criminals at all. At the stolen property house on North Mississippi, I knew that everyone I did business with was a criminal. Here in Old Town, I was dealing with people who just came into the store to purchase stuff. I didn't know, straight out, who the bad guys were.

I didn't enjoy that assignment much. But all the undercover work was good for me, on a lot of levels. It may have delayed my understanding of how the police department worked, and it certainly caused me to advance less quickly within the department, but it also taught me how to work and think independently, how to make smart decisions in a hurry, how to behave responsibly and compassionately in even the worst of situations.

I am also lucky to have survived it. The numbers suggest that black officers working undercover get shot on the job far more often than white officers. Worse, black officers working undercover get shot by white police officers far more often than white police officers working undercover get shot by other police officers. When cops are going into a situation where they know there is an undercover officer working, they generally assume the officer is the white guy. It has been historically difficult for the officers to recognize immediately that the black guy with the gun might be the undercover officer. Sometimes they don't find out until they've shot him already.

That didn't happen to me. But knowing that it could have is one of the many things from that rough early time as a police officer that have made me a better police administrator.

I wasn't doing as well socially as I was professionally. It was difficult for me to meet women who were willing to date a police officer. This was a leftover from the 1960s, and it was also a reflection on the Portland Police Bureau and its relationship with the community at large. Most girls didn't want to have anything to do with a cop.

One day this female officer I worked with, a white woman whose sister worked in an insurance company, offered to set me up with a girl. Her sister had a friend, a black woman, who was having trouble finding people to date. Not because she was a police officer. She had gotten pregnant in high school and had made a bad marriage, and now she was a divorced woman with a young daughter. It was more difficult at that time than it would be today for a single woman with a child to find dates.

She shouldn't have had difficulty finding any dates at all. She was very beautiful. Her name was Linder. She was tall and slender, a kind of *Ebony* magazine beauty. In fact she had worked as a model.

From the start our relationship was probably not normal. For some of the first two years we dated, I was working undercover. I'd live this private, dangerous life all week, and then on a Monday night try to act like a normal guy taking his girl out for dinner and a show. I couldn't tell her what I was doing, except that I was working undercover. I couldn't tell her anything about what I was working on, or where, or with whom, or how I felt about it. There was a strange lack of re-

ality to the relationship, and an almost complete lack
of accountability. I went where I went when I had to
go there, and I didn't apologize or explain if I wasn't
around.

Another kind of woman would have objected to that.
Linder didn't. I am not sure whether it attracted her, or
whether she expected no better for herself, or what. But
when she became pregnant in 1979, she knew that she
wanted to have the child and that she wanted to be married when the child was born.

Linder and I were married in the fall of 1979. It was a
big church wedding, presided over by the police chap-
lain. We went to Canada for the honeymoon. My son
David was born February 19, 1980.

On the surface, it probably looked pretty good. We
moved into a bigger, better house, with the big backyard
and the big basement, and we bought a new car. It
looked like it was going to be the American dream, for
a while.

But it turned out I wasn't very good at being married
and being a dad. I don't know if I just wasn't mature
enough, or I hadn't done enough, or what. But I wasn't
ready to be that kind of husband and father. I wasn't
ready to stop drinking and gallivanting around with the
guys.

I tried. I stayed home when I could. Once I was transferred to a more normal schedule, working downtown
in personnel, Linder and I even did the ride-to-work-to-
gether thing. But inside I knew it wasn't working out.

Growing up the way I did, I didn't have much of a
frame of reference for happy marriages. I went about
the business of being a father and a husband like it was
my job. I participated as much as I could, but there
wasn't much joy in it.

Part of the problem was my other job. Police work
wrecks a lot of marriages. It wrecks a lot of lives. I don't
know if that's what happened to my marriage, but I was
certainly not the kind of husband and father that I could
have been. I knew within less than two years that this

marriage was not going to be a success. When that became clear to me, and that I was going to have to leave my son, it was the saddest thing that ever happened to me.

5. Dear Policeman, I Am God

"There's been another shooting. It's a middle school student."

It was Captain Nancy Demme speaking. She had come into my office with the bad news. The sniper had struck again, and the victim was a child.

It was Monday morning, October 7, at just after 9 A.M. I was in my office at Camp Rockville. I had been there for two long days Saturday and Sunday, overseeing the staff, organizing resources and attending to the media. My office faces the parking lot, from the second floor. Below me was a sea of reporters, media trucks and camera crews. So far, they'd been pretty nice to us. We were giving press briefings every few hours. The message was positive and forward-moving: We didn't have anything conclusive, but the case was coming together and we were confident. The media was receptive and supportive.

Now a child had been shot. We didn't know much. A student was shot at a middle school in Prince George's County, Maryland, at 8:09, just as school was opening. His aunt had driven him to a clinic.

It sounded at first like some kind of school fight. We thought that because the student had been taken to a clinic his injuries must not be serious.

Then, shortly after, we received some more information. The clinic was Bowie Health Center, and it was almost a full-service hospital. Then we learned that the child had been life-lifted by helicopter to Children's National Medical Center in Washington. That told us it was very serious.

As more information came in, it confirmed our fears that it was the same kind of shooting. No witnesses. No one ran up to the kid. There hadn't been any arguments or shouting. The boy, whose name was Iran (pronounced EYE-rehn) Brown, was walking toward the entrance of the school, carrying a backpack and waving good-bye to his aunt. One witness heard a "pow!" sound. The boy fell to the ground. He was thirteen years old. He was an eighth-grade student at Benjamin Tasker Middle School. He had been shot once in the upper chest.

Witnesses reported hearing a series of shots fired thirty minutes later at a nearby Wal-Mart. It wasn't clear whether this was related, but there had been no injuries reported. We found out later it was unrelated. But it was an indicator of how frightened the people in the community were. Every incident seemed like the beginning of another killing spree.

For now, the boy was alive. The bullet had damaged his pancreas, spleen, stomach and a lung, and was lodged near his heart, but there was a little ray of hope. The woman who'd been shot on Friday was still alive, too.

But the shooting of a child brought this to a new level. I was very, very upset. I knew I was going to have to face the media, and that through the media I was going to have to speak to the community—to the parents, to the other children. What was I going to say to them? What was there to say that might reassure them? Nothing. I had nothing.

I went back to my desk and took a deep breath and made a telephone call to Kevin Lewis, the assistant special agent in charge for the Baltimore field office of the

FBI. He was a guy I'd known for many years through NOBLE, the National Organization of Black Law Enforcement Executives. We'd never worked together, but we'd been to conferences together and sat on panels together, and I felt I could turn to him to find out what kind of help might be available to me.

Because I felt now that I needed help.

Up to now, we had been asking ourselves questions about the schools, and we had been answering a lot of questions from others about them. Should we close the schools? Are they safe? Is there something else we can do to make them safe? We had felt, up to now, that the schools were safe. There had been no shootings at school locations, or even near them. We'd had no reason to be worried about the schools.

That wasn't true anymore. I knew there was going to be an outcry over this new event. In Montgomery County, people are obsessive about their schools. They're very proud of them, and rightly so, and they are fiercely protective of their children. We see this in things like the budgeting of county money. No one complains, out loud. You can fight like hell for your own budget, but you're not allowed to say anything about the schools getting an unfair percentage. We joke around the police department that if we want money for something we have to paint it school-bus yellow first and then make the request.

So a school shooting now was disastrous, above and beyond the human tragedy to this young man and his family.

As it turned out, Kevin Lewis was en route to Rockville at that very moment. We had had several FBI people working with us on an informal basis through the weekend. On Friday, the bureau had sent us their Rapid Start program—which is a huge computer program that gives you access to databases that ordinary police departments don't get access to—and a clerical team to run it. They were helping us field the 911 calls and later the hot line calls. There were also investigators working in various unofficial capacities. Kevin was coming down to check on them. We agreed that we'd sit down and talk when he got there, about what kind of resources the bureau might be able to offer us, what kind of help I might be able to reach out for, what kind of approach I might be able to make.

I didn't expect much. The U.S. attorney general, John Ashcroft, and the FBI director, Robert Mueller, had been told by their president that the bureau's new mandate was terrorism. Since the events of September 11, the FBI's focus and commitment was changing. They weren't doing as much with bank robberies. They weren't doing as much with kidnappings. I wasn't clear on what they could do for us, how many resources they might commit, how many people they might be able to make available.

But I had to do something. I had to ramp up the investigation, right away. I had to show the community that our response was rising to meet the rising threat to the schoolchildren. I realized that I had at least sixty people available to me that I hadn't used yet. They were the recruits at the police academy. They were new, but they were police personnel of a sort. I arranged with the academy to have them all moved to the area around Benjamin Tasker Middle School, in the community of Bowie, Maryland, to search the crime scene.

I got a call, too, right away, from a man named Al Genetti, the head of the Montgomery County Department of Transportation. Without asking, he had dispatched a bunch of buses to the police academy to move the recruits to the crime scene at the middle school in Prince George's County. This was just a spontaneous decision on his part. He didn't ask anybody. He didn't call to offer. He just did it.

Finally, I had to go out to meet the media and tell them about the shooting of the little boy.

I said, "Now we're really stepping over the line. Our children do not deserve this. Shooting a kid. I guess it's getting to be really, really personal now."

And the cameras showed, quite clearly, that one fat tear was rolling down my cheek while I was saying this.

I was just as surprised as anyone else. I didn't expect to be crying. I didn't even know I was crying. But I was very, very upset about this shooting. I wasn't that upset when I went out there. But after the press briefing got going, and I had to tell them about the boy, something clicked. I hadn't planned to use any of that language— about stepping over the line, or getting really personal—but once I started talking I just went off script.

I'm not sure why I got so upset. I guess I feel like adults are sort of on their own. No one was asking to be shot by this sniper. No one was putting themselves in harm's way. But the victims, up until now, had been adults. They were making choices to be where they were, to be doing what they were doing. Whatever issues the sniper had, they had seemed like *adult* issues.

With children, there's a whole different level of innocence. I guess I think kids should get a pass. They should be protected at all costs. For a child to be shot now by this sniper seemed grossly unfair. It seemed evil in a whole new way.

When the mayor of Portland, Vera Katz, gave me the job of chief back in Portland, she said she liked the fact that I was "passionate" about police work and the people I encountered doing it. It goes back to Bill Renoud, who told me to get out of police work if I ever found I was losing my compassion for other people.

This was just an extension of that. Some people said that by showing so much emotion for the child, I was disrespecting the other victims. If killing a kid is "going over the line," then is killing an adult *not* going over the line? Of course that's not what I meant. But children are particularly innocent, and particularly defenseless. It hurt me in a different way to have that boy shot.

Maybe it's because I'm a father, and a father who hasn't always been able to be close to his son, to be able to protect his son. Or maybe it's just human to feel so hurt when a child is injured.

I wasn't the only one who was moved by the shooting of the boy. A complete stranger, with no ties to the Montgomery County area, donated $50,000 to the growing reward pool, immediately after Iran Brown was shot.

"I felt the person who pulled that trigger really raised the ante by shooting a child," said Tim Blixseth of California, who donated the money. "And somebody has to raise the ante in his face. Somebody knows that guy. Somebody sold him gas or shells."

By Tuesday, October 8, the reward pool had grown from an initial $50,000 to $237,000.

That same day there was a funeral service at St. Camillus Church in Silver Spring for Sarah Ramos, the woman who'd been shot outside the post office near Leisure World. The county executive, Doug Duncan, attended, though I did not. I heard later that one of the men who spoke at the service, a friend of Sarah's, was also a friend of James Martin, the first victim in the sniper's spree.

At the same time, there was a wake for Lori Ann Lewis-Rivera, the woman who was shot at the Shell station in Kensington, held at the Rinaldi Funeral Home in Silver Spring—the funeral home where I was supposed to go for the wake for the police officer who was buried on the day the shooting spree started. I didn't attend this woman's service, either.

Duncan did. He attended all of the services. At one the previous day, for the taxi driver Premkumar Walekar, Duncan spoke very eloquently about how the community was reacting to the crisis. He said, "We have to use our faith to sustain us. We have to rely on our loved ones. Because if we let the fear, the anxiety, overcome us, then we lose our generosity, we lose our caring, we lose our compassion, we lose our kindness, we lose our goodness. Then what will become of us? Evil will have ruled the day."

I don't know why the media turned on me at this point, but they did. Maybe they were upset like I was.

Maybe they were angry and frustrated, like I was, and didn't know where to go with that. It seemed like they came after me.

There were suggestions, later, that I manufactured the tear in order to get sympathy, or in order to send some kind of message to the sniper. Well, I'm sorry, that's not true. If it was true, then I should get the part in every TV movie that's ever made about the sniper—because I'd sure be one hell of an actor.

Some other spectators thought I was just out of control. An editorial in *USA Today* said, "Emotional outbursts by police chiefs don't inspire professional conduct among subordinates, or persuade citizens that cool-headed pros are doing their utmost to protect them from vicious random murders." The author was a former San Jose police chief—a lot of my more visible critics were these talking head former police chiefs, who didn't have jobs, who didn't have anything to lose by criticizing a fellow police officer in a time of crisis—who might have been using this forum as a way of hanging out his résumé.

All I could think was, what did my getting emotional about a child being shot have to do with my willingness to do my utmost to protect the citizens? The suggestion was that I spent the whole day crying or cowering in my office, too upset to go out and look for bad guys.

I didn't spend a lot of time watching TV news or reading newspaper coverage of the events as they unfolded. I didn't need to. I was in the middle of the events. But we did have media briefings. Every time we prepared a media update, we would quickly review the tone of the recent news articles and maybe look at some footage. We wanted to make sure that there was no misinformation out there that needed correcting, and we wanted to make sure we were using the media in the most effective way to get our message out.

For example, we had a great deal of success using the media to show people what a .223 rifle looked like. If you say you're looking for a .223 rifle, that doesn't mean much to most people. If you show them a .223 rifle on TV, they say, "Oh, yeah. My next-door neighbor has a gun like that." We wanted our citizens to be good witnesses, to be our eyes and ears on the case. So we used the media to get out the message about the rifle, about the white box truck, and so on.

Sometimes the direction of the media's interest, though, was difficult for me. There were suggestions in some of the reporters' questions that my police department and I had fallen down on the job. We had failed to protect the young people of Montgomery County. Why had we said the schools were safe when they were not? Why had we failed to protect schoolchildren? Why hadn't we ordered the schools closed?

There were questions, at that press briefing, that were very hard to take. Someone said, "Don't you think, since you insisted the schools were safe, that you caused this shooting to happen?" That certainly made me very angry. I thought it was a ridiculous question.

But later on, when I sat back and reflected, I wondered whether that could be true. How responsible was I for the shooting of that young man? Of course I realized the answer was that I was not responsible at all. I didn't cause anyone to shoot anyone. Up until that point, when I was asked questions about the schools— had there been any shootings at the schools, or had there been shootings near the schools, or did we have any evidence to suggest schoolchildren were in jeopardy?—the answer was no. The facts told us the answer was no. For me to have folded into the idea that I was somehow responsible for this turn of events would have been ridiculous.

There was an element of truth to what they were suggesting, however. I believe now that the sniper was sending the police and the community a message. We had been saying the schools and the children were safe. This shooting was a "fuck you" to that. It said, "You think your schools are safe? You think your kids are safe? Well, what are you going to say now? I'm going to show you that *I'm* the one who's running this thing."

I didn't tell the media that. I told the media there would be another briefing in an hour or so.

When Kevin Lewis arrived, he showed me something interesting. The FBI had a fairly new statute on the books that would qualify a local police agency for all kinds of federal help if the attorney general officially designated a series of crimes as a serial murder. Kevin had his office fax over a copy of the legislation on this.

This statute had grown out of the Protection of Children from Sexual Predators Act, enacted by Congress in 1998. One of its provisions said, "The Attorney General and the Director of the Federal Bureau of Investigations may investigate serial killings . . . if such investigation is requested by the head of a law enforcement agency with investigative or prospective jurisdiction over the offense." The statute described serial killing as any series of three or more murders "having common characteristics such as to suggest the reasonable possibility that the crimes were committed by the same actor or actors." Assistance could be granted only after a "formal written request," and that request would have to come from me.

To me, this was great news. The shooting of the boy had unnerved me. We didn't have the manpower or the resources to take care of this problem ourselves. And now I saw that we might not have to.

It was also complicated news. It was critical to me that my request for help from the federal government not be seen by my people as a vote of no confidence in their abilities. I was really worried about offending them or hurting their feelings—these people who had been hit so hard emotionally by the sniper, whose families had been jeopardized, who had been working these crushing schedules, trying to bring this case to a close.

I asked Assistant Chief Dee Walker to sit down with Kevin Lewis and begin to draft the letter to Attorney General Ashcroft. I needed them to wordsmith it just right, to make sure we used exactly the right language and established exactly the right criteria to qualify for this statute.

I had to go out and present the press briefing about the shooting of Iran Brown. I told Assistant Chief Walker, "I want that letter finished when I get back."

I went out and cried on TV. Then I came back in, reviewed the letter to Ashcroft and asked to sit down with all my assistant chiefs. I had to let them know my intentions. I had to make sure they were on board in this request for federal assistance. They were.

Then I went downstairs to meet with the major crimes officers. I wanted to let them know that I was reaching out for help. I wanted them to know what that meant—and what it didn't mean. I told them I had every confidence in their abilities, that I fully expected that they would be the ones to solve this case, the ones to make the arrest. But I also told them that I thought we needed all the resources we could get, and that this was a way of getting a lot of resources right away.

This was, in some ways, the toughest decision I would have to make through this whole ordeal. There is a long history of local law enforcement not working well with the federal agencies, of mistrust between the local police and the FBI, or the local police and the ATF, or the ATF and the FBI. I had no reason to expect that there would be any harmonious "task force" teamwork ahead. I had every reason to think the case would be taken away from me, and that I would be accused by my own people of not having the courage to go it alone, of letting go of the biggest case ever to hit Montgomery County.

I also knew that my first responsibility was to the citizens, and my first job was to protect them. I knew that without federal assistance I was not going to be able to do the best job possible of protecting them.

It was still not an easy decision.

To my delight, and to my surprise, everyone I spoke with agreed that reaching out for federal help was the right thing to do. I didn't hear any quibbling. No one expressed any fear that the case would be taken over by the federal agency. No one complained. They gave me their support. This was a great relief to me. I needed for them to have the chance to tell me they didn't like this idea if they didn't—to say it was the wrong thing to do, or to tell me they felt insulted by the decision I had made. They didn't tell me any of those things.

An hour or so later, we had drafted the letter and faxed it to John Ashcroft at the attorney general's office. That was Monday, October 7.

We had also started a new line of defensive thinking about our next move. We asked ourselves whether we should close the schools. How could we protect the schoolchildren better? We made new plans about deploying officers to school areas for the following morning. We moved some people around to respond to this new development. It wasn't a matter so much of being able to prevent more shootings of students—because we understood that from a practical standpoint we probably couldn't do that—but a matter of getting enough visibility that it would serve as a deterrent to the sniper and as a reassurance to the community that we were doing all we could.

Then we found the tarot card.

This was the first piece of hard evidence in the whole case. This was the first communication we had with the sniper. This was the first real break in a case that up until now had had very little chance of being solved.

As they had for the shootings the previous Thursday and Friday, investigators had hit the crime scene Monday as quickly as possible with the canine units. Dogs trained to pick up traces of explosives, including gunpowder, began sniffing out the location. A dog pretty quickly found its way to a shell casing. This might have been nothing. It might have been left there by some person not connected to the shooting. It might have been a shell casing fired from a different gun and left there by the sniper to throw us off. But its location helped us focus and narrow our search. Combing the area around the shell casing turned up the bigger prize, the first real piece of evidence of a sniper at work.

The tarot card was found by one of the Prince George's County officers, who along with the sixty recruits from the police academy was combing the fields and streets around Benjamin Tasker Middle School.

The card itself featured a skeleton, on horseback, wearing a helmet and swinging a scythe. The Roman number XIII was at the top, and the word "Death" was at the bottom.

There was a message on it.

The message was handwritten, in ink, in a shaky, uneducated-looking hand. It had only a few lines to it, and they didn't say much. The words were "Dear Policeman, I am God," and "Do not release to media." That was it.

I had copies of the card made and handed out all over the Rockville headquarters. It was widely distributed to all members of the task force.

I wanted to keep this out of the media altogether. I didn't even want to acknowledge that the sniper had contacted us. I certainly didn't want the media to know what the sniper had said in his communication. I gave very explicit orders to the people who had seen the original card, complete with the message, that no one was to be told what the entire message was.

This wasn't out of any mistrust for the media. It was simply a matter of wanting to honor the request the sniper had made. This was the first communication, and the first attempt to open a dialogue. I was very interested in having that dialogue, and in doing whatever was necessary to make sure the communication continued.

In my experience, as a police officer and as a human being, communication, at whatever level, cannot start until there is some degree of trust. I know there are people who say you should never give in to a criminal's demands, that you can never agree to play by the criminal's rules. I disagree. This was a very important moment, a very important time to tell this person,

"We're here. We're listening. We want to know what you have to say."

So at the briefing on Monday when I spoke about the child and had that tear rolling down my cheek, I also started the effort to communicate with the person who was responsible for the killing.

No one in the media noticed it. Maybe they were still so stunned to see the chief of police crying on national TV, but no one noticed that I spoke directly to the sniper. I said, "I hope to God"—and I paused there, and took a deep breath, and looked right into the camera—"I hope to *God* that someday we'll know why all this has occurred."

I was hoping to give the impression that I was talking to him—and calling him "God." I was also asking him, in effect, to explain. I wanted him to hear me asking him, "Why *has* all of this occurred? What do you want?"

I believed that some kind of communication would begin, or that what had already begun with the tarot card would continue. This was a very significant break, and I was optimistic about it.

For the first time, I had a sense that there was a person out there doing these killings, and now this person was talking to us. I was very upset about the child, but I was very pumped up about the tarot card. I felt this was the beginning of the end of the killings, the first really solid step toward catching the person who was doing them.

There was nothing we could do with the card. It was established pretty quickly that there was nothing to be obtained from it in the way of fingerprints or DNA material. I was assured that the card was of such a common variety that there was no way of establishing where it was sold or where it was manufactured. There were no special identifying marks on it. There wasn't anything like a serial number. I don't know anything about tarot cards, but I was assured that there was nothing special about this one. We did, however, conduct some analysis on the ink.

We would later establish a connection between the ink used in the handwriting on the tarot card and the ink used on other notes written by the suspects. At the time, though, it was just a card with words on it.

Despite all these developments in the case, I went that Monday night to Montgomery College and taught my usual class in criminology. For two years I had been going on Monday evenings to teach undergraduates a few things about law enforcement. I think it was that night that some of the students, having seen what was going on with the sniper case, asked me why I was showing up when I must be busy with the investigation. I said, "I've been up from six A.M. I needed a couple of hours of fresh air."

The class took my mind off of things for a while. But when I went home that night, I was about as depressed as I've ever been. I couldn't get the idea of the injured boy out of my head. I sat down in the big rocking chair we have in our living room, and I was just numb. My son, David, was in his room, sleeping or maybe studying. I didn't speak with him. I just sat down and tried to rest.

I told Sandy a little about the day and what had happened. She knew most of it, from listening to the news and watching TV, so I didn't have to tell her much. I just kept asking why. Why would anyone shoot a child? What kind of evil person hurts a child?

I felt enormously sad, and worried that the boy would die. And then, on the other hand, I felt scared for the community, and worried that schoolchildren across the county would have to be afraid now.

I was a little worried, too, about what people would think of their police chief crying on national TV. I worried that they'd think I was falling apart, or that I couldn't do my job.

Mostly I felt angry. I had said at the press briefing that this was getting "personal." Well, it felt that way now. I don't usually get emotionally involved in the solving of crimes. I might feel sympathy for the victim, or frustration with the process, but I don't usually feel I have an emotional stake in the outcome.

That's because you can't, if you want to continue being a police officer. If you got wiped out every time a citizen got killed or injured, you'd never make it. It's like being a doctor, maybe. They do their best, but sometimes they lose a patient. They don't quit when that happens. They keep on being doctors. It's the same with police officers. You can't get too invested emotionally. Otherwise, what happens when you have to arrest someone who's beaten or killed a child? You'd want to be judge, jury and executioner and kill them right there. So you try to remain professional and not get too personal.

Now, though, I felt a much bigger personal stake in the outcome. And it made me almost physically sick that night. Sandy had cooked something for dinner. I couldn't eat it.

Sometimes, when things got tough at the office, I'd call home and Sandy and I would talk for a minute. Sometimes I wouldn't even tell her much about what was going on. I'd just say, "Pray, Sandy." I joke with her that she has a special connection—a hot line to God. So I just tell her, "Start praying." That night, we were both praying.

One of the prayers had already been answered. That afternoon, we had gotten a positive response from the attorney general's office. The case had officially become a serial murder case. We could rely on federal help.

I found out the next morning that the news about the tarot card had been leaked to the media. There it was, on Channel 9 and in the *Washington Post*. They were the only two that had it. I was told that a reporter named Mike Buchanan, who had been a police reporter and was very proud of his sources on the police, had been the one who broke it. By late the next morning, the whole world knew about the tarot card.

I was livid. That's an understatement. I was furious. That's an understatement, too. Let's just say I was very angry.

I didn't believe that the existence of the tarot card would never be leaked. We had made copies of it and posted them all over the place. We had distributed copies of it pretty widely. If I had thought about it, I would have been able to guess that the media would get a copy of it, too, sooner or later.

But I thought that I might have a little more time than overnight. I thought we would have an opportunity to establish some kind of communication with the person who had left the tarot card for us to find.

Now that was shot. The person had asked us not to contact the media, and it looked like that was the first thing we had done.

At first I was angry at the media. They didn't have to run with this. They especially didn't have to run with it without telling us they were going to. Later on, I would find myself getting even more angry at the person who leaked it to them. I realized I had two problems, two areas to worry about. The media can't go with something like this unless someone on the inside is giving it to them. I had my suspicions right away about who did it. I have my suspicions now. In fact, I'm about 90 percent sure I know who did it.

But at the time I had more anger than anything else, anger and a determination to get the investigation back on track and not let it be derailed by the media.

I went out to face the media and I blasted them. I said, "I have not received any message that the citizens of Montgomery County want Channel 9 or the *Washington Post* or any other media outlet to solve this case. If they do, then let me know. We will go and do other police work, and we will turn this case over to the media. And you can solve it."

It got worse. It was a real tirade. I raised my voice. I lost my temper. I said things that I had always wanted to say to the media, to tell the truth. Because when the media acts like that, I don't like the media. They have a habit of acting like they are the only ones in the world who know anything worth knowing, and that everyone else is basically stupid. I've been exposed to their ridicule for a lot of years. I was very disappointed that they had broken this piece of information out there, without asking, without warning, without checking with us on whether this was appropriate. I thought it was incredibly irresponsible. I thought it was going to jeopardize our ability to find the person doing the shooting, and our ability to prevent other people from being killed.

And I was right about that.

And I was wrong about losing my temper.

There is no way of knowing what the next communication was going to be, if the media had not broken this story. There is no way to know how much more quickly we might have been able to find out who was doing this killing, and stop it.

Today I am absolutely certain that the leak of the tarot card, on the morning of October 8, was a contributing factor in the five shootings that were still to come. I am also certain that the leak of the tarot card slowed down the investigation. From almost the next day, we started getting phone calls and faxes from people saying, "I am God." The knowledge that the sniper had written those specific words on the tarot card brought out every nut in the county. We had to wade through all these false leads. That contributed to our difficulty later in knowing which communications were from the sniper and which were from copycats and wanna-bes.

It seems weird, that anyone would pretend to be a serial killer, in the middle of a serial killing, but it happens. People who suffer from mental illnesses may see this as a chance to draw attention to themselves. So they make these phone calls, or write these letters.

This is one of the reasons we are careful with the information we release to the media. It helps us eliminate false suspects. If someone has been murdered with a knife to the throat, and we get some person calling in and saying, "Yeah, it's me. I stabbed him eight times in the back with a butcher knife," we know we can ignore the person, because we know the victim's throat was cut. If all of the information pertinent to the death is in the newspapers, anyone can call in and claim to have intimate knowledge of how the death occurred. That makes our job harder.

After my tirade, after I had completely yarded out the media, I called my wife. I told her, "It's over. I just yelled at the media. And they're going to eat me alive."

Assistant Chief Walker told me later that after my outburst at the media, she said to herself, "Check the date. Sometime within the next six months, the *Washington Post* is going to be calling for the chief's resignation. They're going to start grinding the axe now, and they'll start swinging the axe when this case is over."

And she was right. She also told me, though, that she thought this was one of the hallmarks of good leadership—that I was willing to stick my neck out and get my head chopped off simply because the situation called for that, that I was willing to alienate the media in order to get back some of the sniper's trust.

I expected complete retaliation. I thought losing my temper in front of the media was stupid and self-destructive. I've been a policeman for almost twenty-eight years. I've seen twenty-eight years of the relationship between the police and the press. And I know you don't pick a fight with someone that buys ink by the barrel. They can just write and write and write.

But I told Sandy, "I just had to do it. If there is any chance of reestablishing communication with the person that's doing this, what the media does to me doesn't matter. We have to have some communication that increases our chance of solving the case. Maybe seeing me attack the media will serve some purpose."

Sandy told me she understood and she thought I had done the right thing—for the case. She told me not to worry about what effect it had on my career, because that wasn't the important thing. She said, "I didn't fall in love with you because you were the police chief, so I'm not going to stop loving you if you stop being the police chief. Whatever happens, we'll be fine."

The truth is, I wasn't really hamming it up for the sniper. I wasn't pretending to be angry at the media as a way of sending him some sort of message. I didn't need to pretend. I was furious. Once I started, I couldn't stop. I was trying to speak directly to the sniper, to convince him that it was not the police that betrayed his confidence. I wanted the sniper to hear me saying, "I hear you. I want to talk to you. I did not violate your trust." But once I got started, it looked more like I was just blowing off steam.

I know that later on some people theorized that I wasn't angry at the media at all, that this was just an act I was performing for the benefit of the sniper.

Sorry. I am not that good an actor.

The immediate fallout was interesting. First we started getting calls and emails from all over the world, from people who said they could find the killer by studying the tarot card. I remember one from a person who said, "If you will fly me to America immediately . . ." You can't just dismiss all these things, but there wasn't much to follow up on.

Then we started getting phone calls and faxes from people wanting to show us their support or wanting to cheer me on for yarding out the media.

The media started asking questions about whether I was going to open an investigation into who leaked the tarot card. I guess this was their way of suggesting that the leak wasn't their fault—that it had come from my task force, and therefore repairing the damage was my job. They wanted to know how many investigators I was going to put on this new investigation.

I said I didn't think it was a good idea to waste valuable time, energy and resources opening a second investigation. We had our hands full already trying to find out who was killing citizens. We were not going to spend any effort at all to find out who was leaking information to the media.

Besides that, I thought, if I'm going to start expending resources going after members of my own team, how am I going to run the team?

Strangely, after that, the media started asking me—despite my tirade—when I was going to release the tarot card to them. They had this idea that if I would release the card, they could put it on television and solve the crime. They were convinced that if we gave them the card, and they put it on TV, someone would recognize the handwriting on the card and come forward with the identification of the sniper.

This must have been because of the Unabomber case. In that case there was a series of letter bombs and a series of threatening letters, and there was a composite sketch, and the police released all of that to the media. A man recognized the language and ideas of the letters, and then the handwriting, and then the sketch—and turned in his brother.

We didn't have a series of notes. We didn't have a composite sketch. We had a two-sentence note. Which the suspect had told us not to give the media. We didn't see any percentage in giving anyone the card.

On Monday we had been given the green light from the attorney general's office. I had a phone call from John Ashcroft himself. He told me, "We want to make sure we are doing everything we can to solve this" and promised me I would have the full support of the FBI.

I was surprised to hear from him in person. It showed me, first of all, that the case might be bigger than I thought it was. I was right in the middle of it, and so I didn't understand that it was getting national attention. The fact that the attorney general called me personally was impressive. I told him I appreciated the support and the prompt personal response.

I meant that, too. There was a lot of speculation that at this point we were risking having the case taken over by the federal agencies, that the federal agencies were going to "big-foot" us out of the case. That's not what happened.

What happened is that right away this took us to a whole new level of law enforcement capability.

Now the special agent in charge of the FBI field office in Baltimore showed up and was told this was his assignment for the duration. He was Gary M. Bald, a career FBI man who would, for the next three weeks, form the third leg of the task force triangle, along with Michael Bouchard of the ATF and me.

Bald impressed me immediately as a studious, low-key, nonconfrontational guy with a real eye for efficiency. He wore a dark suit and white shirt and dark tie, like almost every other FBI man I've ever encountered, and had small, metal-rimmed glasses over his pale eyes. He looked like a guy who knew how to get things done.

He started getting things done. His bureau started putting people on airplanes and sending them to Montgomery County to become part of the task force. We needed office space. There was a building right next door to police headquarters. We had started negotiations with the owner about what we were able to pay, and how much he was going to charge. Now the FBI credit card showed up. It's a big credit card. We started moving in two hours later.

Within a day, the FBI was there in force. The ATF was already there in force. We had assets from the Secret Service. We had assets from the U.S. Marshals. Department of Defense made things available to us—things like helicopters and pilots. They have technical equipment that we don't have—like a plane that can fly over the Montgomery County area, outfitted with a scanning device that can pick up the exact location of muzzle blasts if there is another shooting.

My police department didn't have one of those.

It's not just equipment and manpower, either. It's access to information. Now we were going to get access to information about credit card usage and telephone usage. These are all things you can request, and receive, as a local police department, but it can be days or weeks of convincing someone you need them before you can get an affidavit approving it.

Suddenly none of that took any time at all.

The infrastructure we created was dubbed the Joint Operation Center (forever after known as the JOC, which was unfortunately pronounced "jock"). We knew we were involved in a case that was bigger than anything we had ever handled. We knew it was going to strain our resources at every level—physical, financial, jurisdictional, mental, psychological and otherwise. So we decided to create some new procedural architecture to handle this. We took the structure we had started building over the previous weekend—the Intelligence Table, for example, and the Investigations Table—and added to it. At the head of these tables were the Command Table and the Operations Table. The Command Table was staffed by the primary decision makers of the FBI, ATF and Montgomery County Police Department. The Operations Table was responsible for keeping the JOC running smoothly.

Things also moved fast. The design of the JOC gave rapid decision-making capability to the commanders at the level below Bouchard, Bald and me. This was intentional. Because the killings were ongoing, we knew that the investigative team, if it needed a search warrant, or additional resources, might not have time to run that by the top task force officers. So we gave decision-making authority to people like Captain Forsythe, the director of the major crimes unit. He knew he didn't have to come to us. He didn't have to engage in the usual "mother may I" exercise.

On the other side, people in the command seat understood there was a risk attached to this. The key to success in the JOC was going to be the flow of information and the ability to make instant decisions. This might mean mistakes were made in the absence of the usual oversight. It was necessary for us to accept this risk, in order to assure that people like Captain Forsythe could command their teams effectively.

Mostly, we figured relations in the JOC were going to be pretty harmonious. There wasn't a lot of ego, or a lot of jockeying for position. No one was hogging the limelight, or trying to show off. Maybe it was because it was such an ongoing thing, and there was such a sense of urgency about solving the crime. Or maybe it was because such a high percentage of people working the case were personally involved. Whether it was one of my officers, or someone from the ATF, or someone from the FBI, or Maryland State Police, or Prince George's County Police, or Washington, D.C.,'s Metropolitan Police Department—we all had wives and husbands and children and parents and siblings living in the target area. We were all victims, or potential victims. That united us as much as anything else.

People have speculated that I somehow resented having these federal agencies involved. That just couldn't be less true. Their association with us made the odds of catching the killer much higher. I felt at once that we were that much closer to bringing this to some resolution. There was this much more talent. There was this much more brainpower. There was this much more experience. There was this much more equipment and access to information.

We needed all of that. The job we had ahead was enormous. Without more evidence, something to help us focus our investigation, we had a very, very wide field to study.

For example, there was the .223 ammunition and the gun that fired it. We had already started, once we got the first ballistics reports, pulling files from Maryland and Virginia on every person we could find who owned the kind of rifle that shoots this kind of bullet. We discovered right away that there were a lot of people in those two states who owned that kind of rifle, and the person we were looking for, of course, might not even live in either of those two states, or might not have bought the gun in either of them. There I was, a person who'd moved from Portland, Oregon. If it had been me, I could have brought in a rifle that I bought in Oregon, and there would be no local record of it at all.

Some people would say this was a pointless task. We were never going to find the person who did the shooting by interviewing everyone who owned a .223.

But that's what we started doing anyway. We had been getting tips, on the 911 line and then on the hot line. People called in to say, "My brother-in-law has a gun like that." Or it was the husband, or the stepson, or the neighbor, or the employee. Plus we had a "geoprofile," which suggested to us that the person responsible for this killing was familiar with the area around southern Maryland and northern Virginia.

Then we crossed that with people who had or drove white vans. When we found a match, we sent an investigator out to interview the people. If possible, the investigator looked at the weapon. If the weapon matched, the investigator brought it in for a ballistics test, to see if rounds fired from it matched the marks on the rounds taken from the bodies of the victims.

Mike Bouchard of the ATF later told me he figured we had brought in and ballistics-tested more than one hundred weapons. Most of them were from people who gave them up willingly. Some of them were from people we had gotten tips on.

There was a lot of that. A lot of times we got calls from people who were trying to settle a score, or maybe trying to get even, or who were scared of someone and wanted them put away. We'd get calls from people saying, "I always wanted to drop a dime on this guy, because I don't like him." We got calls identifying people who were felons and in possession of a weapon, which is not legal. So we seized a lot of guns. Or we did what's called an "abandonment." We said, "Give us the gun, and we'll destroy it," in exchange for not prosecuting the person for possession of the firearm. Some of the cases went to prosecutors, who mostly turned them down—the felonies were too old, the evidence was too weak, or whatever. But we got a lot of weapons off the streets, and out of the hands of people who legally shouldn't have had them.

Many of the gun owners were terrific. They volunteered. They called in. They said, "Here, take the gun. Do the test. Keep it as long as you like."

Other people had trouble. Some of them were treated roughly. Some were treated rudely. One guy I found out about wasn't home when the ATF came looking for him because he was working at the police station as a 911 operator. These ATF agents went to his house, scared the hell out of his wife, got kind of aggressive with her and took the gun. They found out it wasn't the right gun, and he wasn't the right guy, but no one ever said anything to this man about being sorry. No one from the police department ever said anything to him about why this had happened. I had to prepare a personal apology to deliver myself. I felt rotten about it. This man was an excellent employee, and the machinery of the investigation abused him, and his wife. Luckily, he stayed with the department, and accepted the apology.

With other people, we were amazed at the number of guns they had, and the number of criminal records and what you might call "lifestyle" problems—guns and drugs, guns and criminal activity, and so on.

We actually created a gun task force as a result of this. We found so many people with guns, and so much information about them and their guns, that we eventually went back and made a huge number of cases out of it.

Before the sniper started shooting, Dee Walker had been working up a gun task force out of the Wheaton station. We had begun working with federal agencies to help us prosecute our gun violation cases more effectively. Before that, we were getting sentences of a year, say, on violations where we could have gotten ten years if the federal gun violations had been considered. The sniper investigation accelerated this cooperation with the federal agencies. And we had so many people working so hard to turn up illegal guns. We had one case that netted seventy weapons from a single suspect. We had another that was a great example of interdepartmental cooperation. A man's neighbors started complaining about the amount of junk stored at this property. They said it was a fire hazard. So the fire department code enforcement people came out. They noticed that the man had an unusual amount of ammunition stored at his place, and they notified the local police. The police came out and saw the evidence, and they notified the task force. The task force came out and seized two hundred weapons, many of them illegal, and more than one hundred thousand rounds of ammunition.

We haven't brought anyone to trial yet on these charges, but we will. We are going to get a number of convictions as a result.

We also were getting reports, from police in Prince George's County, and from the media, that the middle school boy who'd been shot might pull through. He wasn't out of danger yet, but it looked like he might survive.

That was the good news.

In the meantime, there was plenty of bad news.

On October 9, at 8:15 in the evening, a man was shot dead while pumping gas into his car at a Sunoco gas station in Manassas, Virginia. Once again, it was one shot, to the head, from a distance. The victim was a white male in his fifties. We would learn later that he was a Vietnam veteran, and a recipient of the Purple Heart, named Dean Harold Meyers.

Every new killing hit the people on the task force hard, and hit different people in different ways. This one was especially difficult for Mike Bouchard.

Bouchard had been asked in a press conference earlier that week, or maybe the week before, why we weren't concentrating on suspects with a military marksman background—on the theory that these sniper shootings were obviously the work of an extremely skilled shooter.

Bouchard had answered by saying that this notion was misguided. The assault rifles available on the market were so accurate, he said, that it didn't really take an expert shot to do the kind of shootings we were seeing in this case. There was no reason to be looking for a marksman, or some SWAT team or weapons specialist. Any reasonably skilled hunter could shoot the way this killer was shooting.

The very next killing was the shooting of Dean Harold Meyers. It was a head shot. Bouchard later told me that he struggled badly with the idea that the sniper had been watching him on that news conference, and somehow felt insulted at the suggestion that anyone could shoot the way he was shooting. So he stepped up and made sure the next victim was shot in the head. Bouchard lost some sleep on that, before he realized it didn't necessarily make any sense. The sniper was just continuing to kill. I don't believe the head shot was anything more than coincidence, or luck.

But Bouchard's concern about it did help us to step up the task force in another way. After this incident, we went about setting up a Joint Information Center—which started to be called "JIC," or "jick"—to help us become more aware of what we were saying, before we said it, and what impact it might have. The JIC was composed of public information officers from ATF, FBI and the state police and one person from the Howard County Police Department. These people, together, had years of experience. They had good sources, too. They knew producers from the networks and the cable news shows. So while one of their jobs was to help us monitor the message we were putting out when we spoke to the press, another was to keep us aware of what the media was thinking and saying. We'd find out, for example, whether the media was onto something we wanted to keep quiet, or if they were getting close. If we had been doing surveillance on a suspect, and the media started asking questions about why we had people watching a certain house, then we knew it was time for us to move in on that suspect or abandon the surveillance—because it was about to be blown.

None of this helped us with something that was increasingly troublesome to me, which was the appearance of these "talking head" experts that were showing up on all the TV news shows. It seemed like each network had a collection of these people, and the people all seemed to have profoundly insightful ideas about who was doing the killing, and what the task force *wasn't* doing to catch them. I found it very upsetting that many of the experts were people from my own line of work. In answer to a reporter's question about this phenomenon, at a press briefing, I said, "It is very insulting when there are retired police professionals [commenting on the TV shows], because we know that they've not been briefed. They have not seen any of the evidence. They have not talked to any of the investigators. If they're putting people in this community at risk so that they can have the pleasure of being on TV, it is so sad."

There was no new evidence available at the Sunoco station crime scene, and very little in the way of new information. But an eyewitness said that a white Dodge Caravan was seen leaving the area.

At the task force level, we decided to plan a dragnet. We would coordinate the police agencies of Maryland, Virginia and the District of Columbia. If there was another shooting, we could shut down the freeways in all three jurisdictions, and close down the entire Washington area if necessary, with a series of strategic roadblocks. There wouldn't be any white van leaving the scene of the shooting and getting away in the future.

By sometime in the middle of that October 9, a week after the first shooting death, the Federal Bureau of Investigation had completed its "Criminal Investigative Analysis—Serial Murder" document. FBI Supervisory Special Agents Stephen E. Etter, Mark A. Hilts and Frederick C. Kingston of the FBI's Behavioral Analysis Unit issued this ten-page report that essentially "profiled" the criminal and his crime spree. These agents analyzed all the known facts of the case and created what they called "probabilities." The agents warned, in their report, that "no two criminal acts or criminal personalities are exactly alike" and said that the person responsible for the sniper attacks might not exactly resemble the person in their "profile."

By the time they compiled the facts, there had been eight shootings in the greater D.C. area. Six of the victims had died. Ballistics tests had definitively linked most of the shootings. The FBI agents made these conclusions:

- "There is likely only one offender."
- "The offender is a male."
- "Historically, cases similar to this series have been perpetrated primarily by white males."
- "The offender is not likely to have a lengthy criminal history of past offenses."
- "The offender will have a definite fascination/interest in weapons."
- "The offender will be fascinated with themes of violence."
- "The offender will also be competent in the operation of his firearms."
- "The offender will not likely be involved in a long-term successful relationship."
- "The offender will likely be known to others as an angry person."
- "The offender has an inflated sense of self-worth."

The report contained many other similar "probabilities." It assumed that the offender was employable, and might be committing his killings while on the clock. It assumed he was of average or above intelligence, was personally familiar with the areas in which his killings were committed, that he was a "risk-taker." The report said the offender probably collected books or magazines that dealt with assassins and snipers, probably frequented gun shows and owned as many guns "as his socio-economic level will allow."

Psychologically, they said, the offender would appear to be unstable. "He may regularly express frustration over minor inconveniences," the report said. "He may complain about how he has been mistreated by others, and how other people don't recognize or appreciate his talents and abilities." Further, the offender "is concerned only with himself, and devalues the lives of others. He is hypersensitive to criticism, and is suspicious of other people. He would display a lack of empathy and understanding of the suffering of others."

The FBI report concluded there was no pattern to the choice of victims. "The victims' individual personalities and characteristics appear to have had little to do with the selection as victims. [They] were targets of opportunity from within a previously selected hunting site."

The exception to this pattern was the shooting of "Victim Nine," Iran Brown, the thirteen-year-old middle school boy shot on October 7. The FBI reached no conclusion as to why a child had been selected, or why this child.

The report concluded with observations on "post-offense behavior," suggesting that the way a criminal acts after he's done his crime can be a useful investigative tool in evaluating or identifying suspects.

In this case, the report advised investigators to keep an eye out for someone whose normal routine had suddenly changed, or someone who exhibited an intense interest in the investigation of the killings, who expressed "admiration/understanding of the killer." The suspect might be more withdrawn or isolated than usual, or might be more extroverted and talkative. The suspect might be driving a white box-type vehicle, or might be hiding it in a garage or painting it to alter its appearance. If he drove such a vehicle on his job, he might be looking for reasons to avoid driving it. He might be observed trying to "sanitize" it.

The FBI guys were doing the best they could with the limited information available, but if we had been waiting on them to create a blueprint for our investigation, or a crystal-clear portrait of our killer, we would have been disappointed.

Instead, we just kept working

On television, the talking heads were working overtime. They had theories. They had ideas. They had profiles. They were armed with facts, from this study and that study.

The facts said there was a more than 90 percent chance that the sniper was male and under forty, and an 80 percent chance that the sniper was white. There was a 70 percent chance he was working alone. But the talking heads don't talk in percentages. They talk in absolutes. They said the serial sniper *had to be* a white male in his thirties, working alone.

I appreciated the work being done by the professional profilers at the FBI, but I did not encourage my team to treat the report as gospel. I encouraged the opposite. I encouraged them to keep their minds and their eyes open. If we were looking too hard for something that wasn't true, we might overlook something that was true. I didn't want the profiling, which was designed to help us focus our vision, to put us in blinders.

I didn't want the profiling to put the public in blinders, either. That's why none of the task force's profile work was ever released. The talking head experts shared their thoughts and theories, and pronounced the sniper work the work of a white man. We on the task force paid no attention to that. We were not interested in pursuing the racial angle. It's bad policing, for a start. And we couldn't afford to have any tunnel vision at all on the investigation.

There was another reason I resisted the profiling—or rather a personal side to the same reason. I had been subjected to so much racial profiling myself, over the years, that I had a personal understanding of how counterproductive, and how painful, it can be.

Over the years I have been stopped, questioned, detained and harassed many times by police officers who, I know, were only seeing the color of my skin. In most cases, I didn't fit any profile for any suspect. In most cases, there hadn't even been a crime committed. Nobody was looking for anybody that might have looked like me. I was just a black man who was in a place he shouldn't be, in these police officers' eyes, and I needed to be stopped or questioned.

Sometimes it was kind of funny. My wife and I were on a horseback ride in Hawaii one time. The guide was sort of flirting with Sandy. He asked her where we were from. She said we were from Portland. Then he asked her what we did. She said she was a law student and I was the chief of police. The guide asked her what I was the chief of police of. She said I was the chief of police of Portland. He asked her whether she meant I was a police *officer* in Portland. She repeated that I was the chief of police of Portland. Later she heard him telling one of the other riders that I was the police chief for some town near Portland.

It was not possible for him to understand, I guess, that a black man could actually be what I was. So he didn't spend any time believing it.

Other times it wasn't so funny. Sandy and I were in Phoenix one time for a football game. It was one of the bowl games. We were in a hotel filled with tourists who'd come into town for the game. We were on our way up to our room when we were stopped by the hotel security staff. They wanted to know where we were going. They wanted to see our room key. They wanted to see our identification. They wanted to escort us to the lobby. They wanted to call the police. Apparently they thought Sandy was a prostitute and I was a john, and that she was taking me upstairs to her room for sex.

All of this, of course, came out of a form of racial profiling. Prejudice, rather than facts or experience, had taught all of these people to see one thing instead of another thing—instead of the truth. They saw a black man and a white woman together, and could only imagine one thing—that one of them was a criminal. They saw a black man who said he was a police chief and could only imagine one thing—that he was lying.

I didn't want that kind of profiling, or any kind of profiling, to contaminate the thinking of the men and women on the task force.

I didn't even want anyone to profile the tarot card, or what they'd read on the tarot card. The person who left that piece of evidence obviously left it on purpose. Unless he was brain-dead, he understood we were going to be analyzing it. So perhaps the handwriting wasn't the person's real handwriting. Perhaps the note was written in a certain way, with certain writing, using certain words, or certain misspellings, or certain weird phrases, just to throw the investigators off the scent. I didn't want anyone to take that specific evidence too seriously.

By the end of that day, when we received the news about the Manassas shooting, we had officially become the joint task force. The building next door to police headquarters in Rockville had been officially dubbed the Joint Operations Center. The team was growing. It would shortly be four thousand strong, and composed of officers from more than a dozen police agencies. It would be twice the size of any team I had ever supervised, with ten times the resources.

I might have felt like a kid in a candy store. I didn't. I felt reassured that we would have every tool available to help us solve this crime. But I also felt concerned about how it would look to our community if we failed to solve the crime. If a criminal outsmarts a local police department, that looks pretty bad. If a criminal outsmarts the combined forces of the FBI, the ATF, the DOD, the Secret Service, the U.S. Marshals and representatives of ten police departments, that looks very bad. I worried what effect that would have on the people of Montgomery County—how victimized they would feel if this army of investigators could not make their community safe.

And I worried about the fact that I was increasingly becoming the face of that task force. If this investigation failed, it was going to have my name on it.

6. A Life in Portland, a Death in the Family

The education of a young policeman is a fast education. Once you're on the streets, you have to learn quickly or you wash out. In my first five years as a policeman I learned fast, and I learned a lot.

I was very successful as a police officer in Portland, right from the start. I made a lot of arrests. I covered a lot of crimes. I covered robberies and rapes. I learned that my childhood belief that cops made stuff up to get their cases to stick was ill founded. I never had to make anything up. There was plenty of crime to go around.

Some of it was pretty rough. I remember clearly the first time I saw a suicide victim. This was the first dead person I'd seen on the job. We were called to a house. The victim was in his garage, behind a parked car, which was running. He actually had his mouth placed around the tailpipe. He was very, very messed up—terrible burns on his mouth and face. He died sucking that tailpipe. I was freaked out. I kept thinking, *How could it be that bad, whatever was going on with him? How could there be no other choice for him but this?*

I was never a homicide detective, so I never saw a lot of the terrible things those officers see. I saw a lot of bad things, but my job was usually just to secure the crime scene. I didn't have to wade in the way the homicide people do. I didn't see a lot of murders.

But I did a lot of police work.

After I had done my undercover jobs, I got assigned to work in Northeast Portland, in the black section of town known as Albina. I was in what we called an "avenue car"—a car assigned to the Union Avenue area. If you wanted to learn how to be a cop, this was the place to be. If you were serious about the work, this was a great assignment. This was where all the crime was. The police officers assigned there were dedicated, hard-working guys who thought that by working Albina they were going to get more drugs and more guns and more bad guys off the street in a week than you could get in another district in a year. I was assigned to Avenue Car 561, and partnered with Bill MacDonald.

It was serious police work. No one was hanging out. We hardly even took a lunch break. It was exciting work, and exhilarating work. In order to do it right, you had to learn a lot and know a lot. You had to know everything about everybody on the streets. You had to know who the bad guys were, and where they lived, and what kinds of cars they drove, and what their aliases were, and who they hung out with, what they did when they hung out, and which family member they'd run to if they were in trouble. You'd have a whole trunk full of mug shots and these notebooks where you kept all this information.

When something broke, you'd start looking for the person that you knew from all your studying matched the crime. You'd show up and start showing mug shots right away, right out of the trunk of your car. You'd try to get a warrant for the arrest right away, and try to make the arrest right away.

The term we used in Portland at that time was "jackpot." You wanted to be able to make an arrest, or "go jackpot," at least once a shift. You'd hope to go jackpot several times a shift—arrest several people on several different things. Going jackpot three times a night was perfect.

I had to learn all kinds of things to get good at this. I had to learn how to talk to people, how to talk people into doing things they didn't want to do. I had to learn ways to make people let me search them, or their cars, when they really didn't want me to.

There were lots of little tricks. I used to tell suspects, for example, that for reasons of police officer safety I had to make sure they were not carrying any bazookas or hand grenades, and ask them if I could pat them down for that. They'd always laugh—because who the hell could conceal a bazooka? So they'd usually say yes. So I'm patting them down. Then I might find something that feels like a gun. I'd say, "Would you mind taking that out of your pocket?" And they'd usually say yes, and take it out.

It's amazing what people will do when they're trying to act cool and be nonchalant in front of a police officer. They're afraid that if they say no you'll think they're doing something illegal. So they go and show you they *are* doing something illegal. You find the guns, or the drugs, and you can go jackpot.

I almost never, during that time, was afraid anything bad was going to happen to me as a police officer working the street. I'm not sure why that is. I guess I never had the sense, if there was a fight of some kind, that we weren't going to win. We were the good guys. We had to win.

There was a certain Albina family that fought with the police for years—literally fought with the police, and literally for years. We might get a call about a disturbance, and arrive at the Garfield Street address to find a brawl in progress. Soon it was a complete street brawl. The heavy breathing, cuts, bumps and bruises would end with the street blocked off, a dozen people in custody and the entire neighborhood offering to fight the police to free the offenders. The whole mess would wind up in District Court, with a series of misdemeanors, and most everyone would be fined and released and thus be free to fight some more. It seemed like every week, or every month, the fight got bigger and there were more bad guys involved. Our injuries just encouraged us to work out more, get stronger, learn better fighting techniques and be better prepared for the next brawl.

On some level I'm sorry those days are gone. We all had such a feeling of confidence and invincibility. The game of good guy–bad guy that we played, and so thoroughly enjoyed, isn't the game that's being played today. At that time, there was a sense that the bad guys didn't have to play by the rules, but the good guys did. If you played by the rules, and you caught the bad guys, that was fair play. They might stare at you in the courtroom, but you didn't have to worry they were going to firebomb your house or shoot you down in the grocery store.

Now I think a lot of policeman legitimately worry that those things will happen to them. The likelihood that you will be killed in the line of duty has gone up.

I stayed in that avenue car, working Albina, for two years. Then I was sent to the special investigations division. That was the drugs unit.

It was similar work to what I'd already been doing. I was well prepared for it. I developed sources, worked up relationships with informants and began to get them to make drug buys for me. This worked better than buying the drugs yourself. You could do that, and make one arrest at a time, and run the risk of getting known all over the drug community as a police officer who was making arrests. It worked better to have several informants, making several buys, all around the community. You could make a lot of arrests that way, make a lot of good cases, take a lot of drugs and drug dealers off the streets, and stay anonymous.

Working with the informants was a matter, again, of having some compassion. These informants had their problems and their issues. You were banking on them to help you make your cases, so you had to be careful not to do anything to burn them. You couldn't reveal their identities in any way. You had to remember they were people. You had to treat them with respect and dignity, even though you might not have all that much respect for the way they lived or the things they'd done. They had their own philosophy of how the world worked. Your success depended on whether they would trust you, and be willing to work with you. You had to show them respect to earn their trust.

One of my best informants during that time was a man whose street name was "Mouse." He was a skinny little guy who really loved being an informant. Unlike some of our people, who became informants as part of a deal they made to avoid jail time or a conviction, Mouse was an informant because he liked hanging out with cops and he liked making money. He'd get $30 or $40 or $100 per tip, sometimes getting paid several times in one day, mostly for information on drug cases. He was pretty brave, too. He'd go into really bad places, in some cases three or four times, to make drug buys. We'd give him the money, and he'd come back with the drugs, and after three times we'd get the D.A. to issue a search warrant and we'd go make the arrest. Mouse would be our "confidential and reliable informant" to justify the warrant. Mouse was a whiner—the money was never enough for him—but we made a lot of mid-level cases behind his information.

Unlike Mouse, most informants became informants because the police offered them a deal. They were in trouble, and they wanted to get out of trouble. As a result, they might not tell the truth. This is part of the problem with informants generally. Everything they tell you has to be checked and double-checked. This is a proven bad guy, after all. So you have to be careful. You have to search an informant before he makes a drug buy, and then after he makes a drug buy, and make sure it all adds up. He might go in to buy $100 worth of drugs, with your $100, and come back with only $50 worth of drugs. He'll say, "That guy sells short," when really he's already done half the drugs himself or he's trying to steal half the drugs to sell them himself.

You also have to worry that, at some point, the informant is going to stop trading information and start trading *you*. You have to wonder whether he's going to burn you by telling some drug dealer that you're a cop.

There's also a worry, with informants, that spending too much time with the criminals can make a criminal out of a police officer. It does happen. We had an officer who started selling Dilaudid with his informant, to make money on the side. That kind of thing does happen.

I also learned a lot during that time about how to work the system. I learned about judges and warrants. I learned which judges you could go to, at 11 P.M., to get a warrant signed. Some were available, and some weren't. In a pinch, you had to know which ones were available.

When informants worked well, you'd get several of them making several buys, and you'd be doing the surveillance and the follow-up. You'd be working up the food chain, trying to move from the guy on the street, to the dealer, to the supplier and on up. You'd learn that on a certain day, at a certain time, a shipment of drugs was being delivered to a certain address. We made a lot of arrests off of situations like that.

Sometimes it was kind of comical. A partner and I were making a hand-to-hand buy one time. We were standing in this guy's living room. We had the drugs. We pulled out our badges and told the guy he was under arrest.

He didn't believe us. He thought we were crooks, pretending to be police officers, getting ready to rob him, or just not pay for the drugs. He said, "I'm going to put my pit bull on you."

He had this mean-looking pit bull. The dog started growling. He looked like a killer.

I said, "Okay. You go ahead and put the pit bull on us. But you have to know I'm going to shoot your dog, and then I'm going to shoot you, if you do that."

That got his attention. He didn't want us to shoot his dog. He said, "That's it. I'm calling the cops."

He reached for the phone. He started dialing 911.

This was perfect. My partner and I didn't have radios or walkie-talkies, because we were working undercover. We didn't have cell phones in those days. This was the only way we were going to get backup for this arrest. He called 911. We coached him. We told him what to ask for. We gave him the police codes to call for a backup unit—a Code Three. We made the arrest without any trouble.

By 1979, there were some problems developing with some police officers around me. We were all working narcotics. We had staked out this biker house, where we knew there was a lot of drug activity. We were going there to serve a warrant.

The house was the unofficial headquarters of a biker gang known as the Outsiders. They had a long-running feud with the Portland police. We'd follow them when they went on rides, trying to bust them on whatever we could. We had been working them, using informants, trying to make a drug arrest. Now we were ready.

The place was an old, broken-down two-story house in the St. Johns area of North Portland. It needed a coat of paint and had a patchy front yard that was filled with motorcycles and motorcycle parts. One section of the first floor was actually a motorcycle repair and parts shop. It might have been the only house on the block, and it was a bad block.

Going in, there were about twenty of us. When we got to the house, we found the front door had been hung backward. That is, it had been hung so that it opened *out*. This was true of the front doors of a lot of drug houses. It made it a little more difficult for someone to storm through the front door or kick the front door in.

We sent the biggest guy in our unit, an officer named David Crowther, to kick in the door. Gunfire erupted from behind the door. David took a bullet to the head and fell down on the porch. I was maybe three paces behind him. He almost hit me falling down.

We rushed the porch and got him out of the line of fire. But it was too late. He was dead already. Soon the place was crawling with cops. We flushed the bikers out of there. They later said they hadn't known it was cops outside. They thought they were being set upon by a bunch of robbers. This was easy to claim, because in those days we did not wear jackets with the big letters "POLICE" on them the way we do now, when we conduct a raid. We didn't bullhorn or broadcast our arrival, the way we do now. We snuck up and tried to get in.

David Crowther, it turned out, had drugs on him. He was part of a conspiracy to sneak drugs into the house, during the arrest, and plant them there, and then "find" them, in order to back up the arrest and secure a conviction.

As he lay dying, some of the other officers were trying to get his jacket off of him, to get ahold of the drugs and hide them. They could see he was in trouble, and they knew someone was going to inventory his possessions and start asking, "If he wasn't in the house yet when they shot him, why does he have drugs in his pocket?" So they were trying to get the stuff out of his pocket and hide it.

But David was a really big guy, like six-four and 250 pounds. And he was bleeding from the head. And we were trying to get him off the porch. So the plan to remove the drugs fell apart.

I was pretty upset about David's death. I had known him before he became a police officer. We lifted weights together. I had encouraged him in the lifting, and then I had encouraged him to consider working for the police department. I had helped him make the application, and then I had helped him when he became a police officer. In fact, I encouraged him to get into narcotics. To see him killed, in front of me, was painful.

This drug planting might not ever have come out, but there was another case developing. It had nothing to do with the bikers. There was a drug dealer, a black drug dealer, who'd gotten arrested and searched. The arresting officers had found drugs on him, and the drugs had been sent for analysis. This was just the routine. The analysis came back and the drugs tested out as China white heroin.

But this guy was a cocaine dealer. He kept telling his lawyer, as they were preparing his case, "I'm a *cocaine* dealer. I've never sold heroin. That's not my heroin."

Around the same time, some of the guys on the narcotics team were starting to behave strangely. One of them came to work one day in this brand-new truck, which everyone knew he could not afford. A few days later, two of the other guys on the team showed up riding brand-new matching motorcycles.

These three guys in particular had been doing real well. They were making tons of arrests and making tons of cases. They were all family men, and they all had wives and children, and they all made the same pay the rest of us made. When they started showing up driving all this new equipment, people started wondering: *How the hell are they doing that?*

All of this stuff started making sense. Somebody put two and two together and got four. We had crooked cops. They were making arrests, making the arrests stick by planting drugs, and stealing money—or drugs, and then selling the drugs for money—and getting rich on the side.

All of us in the narcotics unit automatically came under suspicion. Including me. We heard that internal affairs was coming after us. By then, I had figured out what was going on. I knew this was going to bust open and become a big, big scandal. I knew the internal affairs guys were going to have to take somebody down. I was afraid they were going to do me, or do the whole unit, as a way of vanquishing any suspicion that they hadn't taken care of the problem.

I was the only black guy on the unit. I thought that would matter. I was a natural profile for a drug cop gone wrong.

I did something aggressive. I got a lawyer. When it was my time to go see internal affairs, I went with a lawyer.

No one had ever come in with a lawyer. It wasn't *done*. The internal affairs guys were pissed off. The police management was pissed off. You just weren't supposed to do that. Maybe, if you were in real trouble, you'd bring in someone from the union. But you did not bring in outsiders, or lawyers.

I felt that I had to. I didn't trust them. I was determined not to go down with these crooked cops. I didn't know how else to make sure I was protected. So I brought the lawyer.

Other guys went down for it. One turned state's witness. Two quit the force, to avoid prosecution. One was prosecuted. One of them gave up his informant and was back on the street. He retired from the police and started dealing drugs with another of his informants. The police stayed on him and arrested him for dealing drugs.

I came out okay. I stayed clean.

But I was a little shaky for a while after that. The raid at the biker house was the first time I had ever seen a police officer killed. I had seen other victims of violence. I had seen dead bodies. But they weren't people I knew. Seeing someone I knew die, right in front of me, was hard. Making the next raid, after that, was also very hard. It was scary. It was difficult to get back into the saddle, after watching that officer killed.

David Crowther's death did result in some changes at the departmental level. At the time of his death it was common for us to conduct a drug raid dressed in T-shirts and leather jackets. At that time undercover officers wore their hair long and had mustaches and beards, and dressed only in street clothes. We'd pin a badge to our shirts, park our unmarked police cars two blocks from the house we were going to raid and go barging in. We just looked like a group of men, not a group of cops. Soon after this incident, though, it was determined that we should start wearing jackets that said "POLICE" on them, and soon after that that we should start wearing body armor. Then we started asking that more uniformed officers go with us, as backup, on these raids. Within a year, the entire approach had changed.

Much later, when my first son was born, I named him David—after my father. But the parents of David Crowther mistakenly guessed I had named him after their late son. I never had the heart to tell them otherwise.

Things at home were not getting any better for me. Things in my hometown were getting worse, too, with my father.

It seemed my father had taken up with a white girl when I was a junior or senior in college. This was something of a shock to me. My mother had been dead a few years. My dad was a single man. It wasn't his first relationship after my mother's death. Before this girl, there was a woman who had originally come to our house once a week as a cleaning woman. But after a while she was coming around more often, and I understood that there was more to the relationship than just housework.

But this was different. This was a white girl, and this was an underage female.

My father had always been popular with his female students. He seemed to have a special feeling for them. He always remembered their birthdays and was always buying them cards and gifts and things. He was popular with the boys, too, but he was especially popular with the girls.

After integration, as I've said, he was moved out of his position as a high school teacher and given a job in the junior high school. So he must have met this girl when she was that young, when she was a junior high school student.

I don't know how old she was when they became intimate. All I know is I came home for a visit one time, and she was there. And my father was there. They were in the bedroom. Then they came out. And it was like, here we all were, and I guess I understood pretty clearly what was going on.

This was 1973 or 1974, in Lexington, North Carolina.

This was very risky business, a black man his age with a white girl her age. I don't remember being outraged that my father was with a white girl. I don't even think I was upset that she was so young. But I was real concerned about what would happen to him if anyone found out. This was the sort of thing black men got murdered over. I thought of what would happen if the Klan knew what was going on. The only safe place for him would be in jail. He'd be lucky if they didn't come and get him and string him up.

My younger sister, Dorothy, was really upset. The girl was about her age, and she was getting all kinds of things that maybe Dorothy thought she ought to get—gifts and presents and money—and Dorothy believed the girl was taking advantage of the situation. Maybe there was more to it than that. Maybe Dorothy was jealous, or felt the girl was getting the love she should be getting. Years later, she would insist that our father was a pedophile, and that this relationship with the girl was one in a series of relationships he had with younger girls. If that's true, I wasn't aware of it.

I'm not sure how long that relationship lasted, or how it ended. It went on for at least two years, though. I was continually worried about what would happen if people found out about it. But I guess no one ever did. If there were similar relationships after that, I didn't know about them.

By the early 1980s, my father had begun to show signs of suffering from what we later understood was the early onset of Alzheimer's. He was having a difficult time.

I might have had some idea, at some point, about bringing him to live with us in Portland. That idea didn't survive his visit to the area, however, which didn't go all that well. He was very critical. He didn't seem to like the house where I lived. He hated the weather in Portland. I took him sightseeing, but he didn't seem all that impressed by any of the sights. He went back to North Carolina without any plan to visit me again.

By now his health was deteriorating. My sister,

Dorothy, was watching over him. She was working as a nurse in Greensboro, and she had an apartment there. But she'd come down to Lexington several times a week to take care of our father. He was still living in the house on Smith Avenue, but he wasn't living there very successfully. My sister would come to visit and find him doing crazy stuff—trying to light the furnace when it was already lit, for example. I remember her saying to me something like "He's going to blow that house up! I'm not going out that way. You got to do something."

It took us a long time to convince him to move into a retirement home. We finally did. But the end was near. He got deeper and deeper into the Alzheimer's. It seemed half the time like he didn't know who anyone was. The burden of caring for him on a day-to-day basis was off my sister, but it was very hard on both of us to see him falling apart that way.

I had a great reverence for my dad. I thought he was a great man. So it was very painful to watch him with the Alzheimer's. He didn't know who I was sometimes, and he didn't know who he was, and he was exhibiting this weird childlike behavior. Who was this person? What happened to the man I knew? He was such a strong, proud man, and now for him not to remember who he was, for him to be acting like a child . . .

I couldn't stand it. I just couldn't stand it. If there had been any such thing as assisted suicide back then, I would have applied for it for him, and done whatever needed to be done. Because the man that my father was—he was gone. He had already died. For the man I knew, life was over.

Within six months of his moving to the retirement home, I got a call from my sister. She had just heard from the home. He was gone.

I flew down to North Carolina at once. My father had died on June 30. We buried him in the same graveyard in Greensboro where my mother is buried, on July 2. My sister and I cleaned out the house, throwing out everything we didn't want and saving only the few things of sentimental value that mattered. We got the house listed with a realtor and put it on the market. On July 4, we were finished. Dorothy went back to work in Greensboro. I went back to work in Portland. Our life on Smith Avenue was over. Shortly after that, the house was sold.

Three months later, I had persuaded Dorothy to get out of North Carolina and come to Oregon. I had become aware by then that Dorothy was lesbian. It wasn't like we had a big conversation about it or anything, but I knew. So after my father died, and I had a clearer understanding of her lifestyle, I said, "Look, you *need* to come to Portland. I'm gong to come and get you. I'm going to put aside some money and get you a house. You can transfer from the VA hospital there to the VA hospital here. This is a much better place for you to be." I just knew, without being involved with it myself, that the climate in Portland was much friendlier to the gay and lesbian lifestyle than anything she was going to find in North Carolina.

I went and got her. I flew back home, and we rented a Ryder truck and filled it up with all of her stuff, and we began the drive to Portland. I don't remember how I calculated it exactly, but I decided this was a three-day trip. I told Dorothy I would be flying down on October 19. I wanted to be packed and driving by Monday morning. I had to be back in Portland for a 10 A.M. class on Thursday morning.

Dorothy says now that we did the trip with plenty of time to spare. She says I drove the whole way, until I couldn't stay awake anymore, and then I'd turn the wheel over to her. But it was a manual transmission truck, and Dorothy didn't know how to drive a stick shift. So she'd drive down the highway as long as she could without having to shift gears. When she had to get off the highway for gas, or she had to gear down to go up a big hill, she'd have to wake me up so I could take over and drive. Until we got going and she didn't need to shift again.

We drove so hard that the poor Ryder truck dropped dead on us in Medford, Oregon. We were only a couple of hours from our destination, having driven all the way across the entire country, but the truck engine just gave up. I think we just wore it out, because we hardly ever stopped for anything, the whole way. I remember Dorothy saying, "But that's the Grand Canyon! Can't we stop for a few minutes?" And I said, "No, we can't." We just drove and drove until the truck gave out. Then we got a new truck and drove on, into Portland.

Dorothy moved into the basement apartment I'd built into my house.

There was nothing in the stuff we cleaned out of our father's house to tell us what had become of our older brother, David. He had disappeared, once more, and it had been several years since we had heard anything from him or about him. There were no clues in my father's things.

After my father had arranged to have David returned from India, he was physically emaciated—110 or 120 pounds, on a six-foot-two frame—and obviously deranged. He moved back into my father's house, and my father nursed him back to health. He fed him, got him some menial work and tried to get him back on his feet. I was at the University of North Carolina at that time. When I came home to visit, I tried to reconnect with my older brother, but I wasn't very successful. He was still my big brother, but something fundamental had changed. He had no focus. He had no drive. He was spacey and out of it.

My father wasn't much more successful in building a new relationship with his son. David was irrational. He got a job in Lexington, at a glue factory, and continued to live at home. But he had wild fits of temper. He and my father fought all the time. One day they got into a serious fight, and David left the house. He never came back.

We don't know exactly what happened to him. Somehow, though, he got from North Carolina to California. He wound up living in Los Angeles. He worked as a security guard. He had other menial jobs. But he was more or less homeless for several years. When he wasn't homeless, he lived in residential hotels near Skid Row. When he lost his security job, he continued to wear the security guard uniform. He said it made him feel safe.

My sister, Dorothy, had meanwhile begun making a life for herself in Portland. She got a good job nursing. One morning in July 1985, just a year after our father's death, she was standing in her kitchen making breakfast when there was a knock at the door. A man had a message for her: Our older brother, David Moose, had died. His body had been found in a flea pit hotel room in Los Angeles.

I got the same message a couple of hours later. I called Dorothy at once to tell her. She said, "I know. I found out a while ago." I asked her whether she had been intending to call me and give me the news.

She said, "No. What for? He's gone."

This is a measure of how hurt and damaged Dorothy had been by my father's abusive behavior during the last period of his life. She wasn't even going to call me and tell me our brother had died.

The following day we flew down to Los Angeles to claim our brother's body. The room he died in was filthy. There was almost nothing to show what his life had been. Among his things was a diary. The writing was the work of someone who was clearly mentally disturbed. A lot of it didn't make any sense. It showed that he had been living a hard life, working hard jobs, living homeless most of the time, for years and years. It didn't tell us why he had died, but it certainly showed us the awful way in which he had lived, and how he had come to the place where he died.

We cleaned up what we could of his affairs and flew back to Portland. Everyone else was gone now. It was just Dorothy and me.

I had gradually become more ambitious about police work. I don't know when it was that I decided that I was definitely going to continue being a police officer. After working undercover and then being on the narcotics unit, I knew I wasn't leaving right away. I started thinking about how to move forward in the organization.

In order to advance, you took one test to become a detective or you took another test to become a sergeant. There are two tracks within the police department. One way, the detective way, was all about investigating crimes. The other way, the sergeant way, was about police administration and leadership. I knew, after the work I'd done, that I wanted to supervise. The police work was exciting, and the investigation side was fascinating, but I knew I was more interested in leadership.

Partly this was because I didn't like what I saw around me, and because of decisions I had made about what kind of police officer I was going to be. I knew I would never violate anyone's rights. I knew I would never lie, make up evidence, withhold evidence or abuse anyone. I also recognized that other officers might not do these things if they knew I was around. Obviously I couldn't be everywhere, at the scene on every arrest and investigation, but I could have influence over a higher number of arrests and investigations if I was a supervisor.

As a sergeant, I would have oversight of eight to ten officers. I would be able to assure that eight to ten officers were not violating anyone's rights when they arrested them.

As a lieutenant, I would have oversight of 25 to 40 people. As a captain, I would be responsible for 90 to 125 people, and would have an area of the city as my jurisdiction. Just as I was role-modeling my police personnel, I could begin to role-model the citizens. I believed that if the police were treating people decently, people would be more inclined to treat each other decently.

As a chief, I would have the opportunity to influence the behavior of an entire police department, maybe as many as 800 people, and be responsible for an entire city.

Obviously that was more fun and more interesting and more worthwhile, to me, than working one homicide or narcotics case at a time.

When I was a young police officer, I had thought my sergeant was a jerk. He thought he was a player. He'd show up whenever any of his officers arrested someone. He'd order his people to stand back and then search the suspect's car personally. He'd find the gun, or the drugs, or the evidence, and then *he* would go to court and claim the overtime that belonged to the officers who actually made the case.

Just getting even with that guy was motivation enough for me to take the sergeant's exam.

I took the examination for promotion, which was a multiple choice test on general orders, traffic codes, state statutes and laws. I passed. Of the sixty or so officers who took the test, maybe eighteen of them would pass and be eligible for promotion and then actually become sergeants within the next two years. When the scores were posted, I had finished sixth, which was well within the promotable range. I was promoted very quickly.

I was so proud of myself. I was excited about advancing. I had been on the street, assigned to a beat in the North Precinct—which was a very rough part of town—in a two-person patrol car. Now I was a sergeant, and I was responsible for scheduling and supervising. I was suddenly supervising my former partner, and a lot of my fellow officers.

This caused problems almost immediately. I was promoted, but I wasn't relocated. I was on the same shift, on the same days, in the same precinct, as I had been before the promotion. I had a run-in right away with Brian Duddy, an officer we called Doo Dah, who had been my partner for a year. There was a complaint against him, for doing or saying something inappropriate—something that I had probably witnessed him doing a hundred times when we were partners. But now I was his supervisor. I had to take him aside and speak to him about his behavior. This was very awkward, but it was my job. It didn't end our friendship, but it strained it, as all my friendships with other officers would be strained by my rise in the department.

That first promotion seemed like it had been a long time coming. I had been very frustrated prior to that. I felt like I couldn't get back to where the action was.

A lot of the action was on and around Union Avenue, in the Albina section of town, the black section of town. (In fact, Union Avenue was eventually renamed Martin Luther King Jr. Avenue, the name it has today.) That was the area in Northeast Portland where I had worked in an "avenue car."

Most of the officers that worked the avenue, and who ran the avenue cars, were white. And most of the criminals and suspects they arrested were black. This led to a natural hostility between the citizens and the police. There is no doubt in my mind that the police behavior exacerbated that hostility.

The mayor had made one dramatic move to reduce this racial tension. Portland had its first black city councilman, a guy named Charles Jordan. The mayor gave Jordan oversight of the police department. This was meant to be a signal to the black community that the city was sensitive to their needs and interested in their participation. Jordan was committed to change, too. He made several key decisions regarding leadership and policy and tried to address the style and the behavior of the police department toward the black community.

But then there were the dead possums.

One of the Union Avenue hot spots was a joint called The Burger Barn. It was black-owned, and its clientele was black, and it was a mess. There was all kinds of criminal activity there, night and day—drugs, illegal drinking, illegal gambling and all the violence that goes along with those activities. The police had been frustrated in their attempts to clean it up.

Someone began depositing bloody, dead possums on The Burger Barn's front doorstep.

There was an investigation. The officers dropping the dead possums—two white officers—were identified. They didn't take the charge seriously. The officers said they were dropping the possums there as a joke, to boost morale among their fellow officers, and that the dead animals were not meant as a racial slur.

This didn't wash. Charles Jordan called for the two officers to be dismissed. There was a huge protest march up Union Avenue. The police chief at the time, Bruce Baker, fired the two officers. The police union backed them, and filed appeals to get them their jobs back—and in fact hired them to work in the union organization for the duration of their appeal.

The officers got their jobs back. Chief Baker was let go. Between the possum incident and the drug scandal, and the fact that the mayor who had hired him had been replaced by a new mayor, and that fact that he himself had undergone heart bypass surgery, it was inevitable that he would be let go. It wasn't fair. These problems were not his fault. But he was the chief, and this was on his watch, and that's what happens to police chiefs.

The new mayor took police oversight away from Charles Jordan and installed a new police chief, named Ron Still. Still had the reputation coming in as a very tough, no-nonsense chief. The black community marched on city hall the day he got the job. They didn't even wait to see what kind of chief he'd make. They were fed up.

This was the atmosphere in which I made sergeant. In addition to the general instability of the department, it was an atmosphere of thinly veiled hostility to blacks.

When one new black officer was hired, for example, a certain captain and a certain lieutenant decided that someone had to test the level of this new officer's integrity. I don't know why they took it upon themselves to do this, but they put together this personal integrity plan and put it into effect.

Here's how it worked. Every afternoon, finishing your day shift, you were expected to return your police car, get it gassed up and get your personal belongings out of it. The new officer coming on for the night shift would attend roll call and then go pick up a car for his shift. He was expected to check the car for personal belongings and then pull out the backseat to make sure that on the previous shift no one had left anything or hidden anything back there. You had to check to make sure no suspect had hidden a gun or a knife or some drugs under the seat while he was being taken in, for example.

This captain and this lieutenant devised a plan in which they'd plant stuff under the backseat for this new black officer, to test him. They wanted to see if he'd check the car, like he was supposed to, and then see what he'd do if he found money, or a weapon, or drugs. Would he turn it in? Would he steal it?

Of course the officer did exactly what he was supposed to do. He found the stuff, and he turned the stuff in. But the talk around the department started. There was some question about his integrity. There must be, because the department had devised these tests for him. He'd passed the test, but . . .

That officer lasted a couple of years. Then he left the department.

This was the department I was working for. At the time of my promotion to sergeant, I had already reached the highest level ever reached by an African-American in the city of Portland. History did not offer me a lot of hope. I had no reason to believe I had a shot at serious advancement in this kind of department.

My behavior at the time was also not the behavior of a guy who thinks he's on track to becoming chief. Working nights, most of the time, I did a lot of early morning drinking. I'd get off duty and go someplace to chill out, to review the night's work, to try and calm down and get ready to get some rest before going back to the adrenaline rush of the job I was doing. There was always a group of us.

I was with about twenty of these guys the day Mt. St. Helens became an active volcano and erupted, May 18, 1980. We had taken over this bar. We'd pooled our money and laid it out. There were about thirty of us in all—twenty cops, mostly white cops, and some women, none of them wives or steady girlfriends—and we had $1,400. We told the bartender to start pouring and continue until all the money was gone. We started drinking at six in the morning. We drank until we couldn't drink any more.

The place was a dining, dancing and drinking place. It was only open at night. We had it opened special for us, and we didn't do any dining or dancing. This was power drinking. I was having Johnnie Walker Red, on the rocks—that way they couldn't mess it up. I drank my share, and probably someone else's share, too.

When we left the bar, we were shocked to discover it was dark outside. We figured we had somehow drunk all day and into the next night. It took us quite a while to figure out the dark sky was the ash cloud from Mt. St. Helens, and that it was still daytime. The volcano blew at about 8:30 A.M. Now it was only about two in the afternoon. Most of us didn't have to report for duty until eleven that night, so there was still some time for some more partying. Or more resting. I got some rest.

It was a strange night. We reported for work and were given these big raincoats to wear, and special masks to cover our mouths. We were told to stay off the streets and not drive the cars too much—maybe to prevent them from getting clogged up with ash.

That was fine. Most of us were very happy to be assigned to go park on a corner somewhere and not do anything. That was about all some of us *could* do.

It felt like a long shift. The city was covered in ash. For a while that night everything was quiet. But you can't stop crime. Eventually, the night people came out. They started to move around. They started to create the usual opportunities for police work. The city might have felt like something out of a science fiction movie, but we went back to the business of picking up the bad guys and taking them down.

Around the time I was promoted to sergeant, I became familiar with Captain Penny Harrington. I had been working as a shift sergeant, in the North division, and was assigned to supervising my old partners. I was pretty uncomfortable with this assignment. Penny Harrington asked me to join her in personnel, downtown, as her second in command.

Normally I would have declined. Most police officers agree with Clint Eastwood's *Dirty Harry* assessment of personnel: "Only assholes work in personnel." But I was eager to change my situation, so I agreed.

I don't remember whether I asked anyone's advice about taking the assignment. I probably didn't. During this period of my time in Portland, I didn't really have anyone mentoring me. I didn't have anyone I could talk to about my career, or my future.

In the beginning, that person had been Tony Newman, the police officer who took me in as a boarder and fed me and helped me figure my way around the police department. I hadn't had any friends in Portland when I got there. I didn't have role models, period. So this relationship with Tony was important to me.

Unfortunately, as time passed, Tony turned out to be not the best role model.

When I met him, he was already into the bodybuilding, and the drinking, and the pool playing. He was devoted to his kid, too, going to all his athletic events.

All these outside interests kind of distracted him. Or maybe they just interested him more than his career. In the beginning, he had been my mentor. But over the next several years, I found myself climbing the ladder at the police department and beginning to catch up with him. I was ambitious, and I was focused. I was moving forward, and Tony wasn't.

When I first got to Portland, I was on probation for eighteen months. That was standard. I didn't know for sure that I wanted to be a police officer for the rest of my life, but I sure as hell didn't want to flunk out.

I didn't. And pretty soon I was moving up. Tony had made detective before I made sergeant. But I made captain before he made lieutenant. Then I became an assistant chief, and he was still a detective. By then, Tony was already in some trouble.

One night, for reasons maybe only he knows, Tony got into a fight in a restaurant, in a town near Portland, with some woman. The fight got out of hand. You can't act like that if you're a policeman. The story made all the papers. Tony had to leave the police department.

By then, I was looking to other people for role models. If not, I guess I would have asked Tony what he thought about me going to work for Penny Harrington in personnel.

As I look back, making the shift to personnel now seems like pure genius to me. The shifts were now more regular. I was no longer working nights. I had my evenings to myself. Penny Harrington and her sister, Lieutenant Roberta Webber, encouraged me to make the most of myself and consider taking some night classes. I enrolled in Portland State University and began studying for a master's degree in public administration. I was spending time around the chief's office. I began to understand how the department really worked, from the top down. I began to understand the politics of the department, in ways that would prove essential to my ability, later, to move up through the ranks.

At the time, I was just trying to get out of a bad assignment. I had no idea this was the change that would change my entire life.

7. Your Children Are Not Safe Anywhere . . .

By the morning of Wednesday, October 9, the task force was in place. We were like an army, mobilizing. There had been no shootings since Monday morning, when the middle school boy was hurt. We had the tarot card clue working. We were ready for battle.

The team of commanders was composed of Michael R. Bouchard, Gary M. Bald and me. Bouchard ran the Baltimore office of the Bureau of Alcohol, Tobacco and Firearms. Bald ran the Baltimore office of the FBI.

On the surface, you couldn't have had three more different guys. Bouchard was broad and blunt physically, like a guy who might have played high school football. I'm somewhat the same, though maybe more muscular. Bald is tall and thin, almost professorial, and looks like he spends his free time reading academic journals.

Below the surface, though, we had very similar stories. We had all put in twenty-five years or more in law enforcement. We were all married. We were all parents. We were all pretty low-key guys. We had a similar, dry sense of humor.

Of the three of us, I had the most experience with violent crime. Gary Bald had only recently been named special agent in charge of the Baltimore FBI office. Mike Bouchard had done extensive work with arson

cases and explosives. He had also done some big, big
cases, working the logistics end of the Oklahoma City
Federal Building bombing case, for example, and working the Pentagon end of the 9/11 terrorist attacks.

But neither one had much experience with murder.
That's part of why I became the de facto head of the
task force. Some people might have thought I was just
this small-time county police chief who got lucky having
all this mayhem occur in his jurisdiction. But that wasn't
what happened. I just had more experience.

There was also the fact that they were there because
I had asked for help. If I had resisted getting help, if the
case had gotten out of hand and the federal government
had pushed in to try and save it, I doubt there would
have been much stability in this three-legged stool.
Maybe that's the reason this kind of task force, with this
kind of cooperation and power sharing, was so unprecedented. I have to remember that it started because I
reached out and asked for help, and these agencies responded.

We shared a strong feeling, from that first day, when I
sat down on October 7 with these two men, that it
would be a mistake to let the case turn into a federal
case, run by a federal agency.

I know that Gary Bald was under a certain amount of
pressure from people within his agency to take over, or
to let the FBI take over. He said, later, that his people
were pushing him to make this an FBI case.

Bouchard argued against that. He stressed that this
was a local homicide case, even though it now spread
over at least three police jurisdictions. He made the
point that if this became an FBI case, and control of it
was taken away from the local police, each police
agency involved would try and treat its own homicide as
a separate case. That would mean no cooperation between police agencies, no pooling of evidence, no sharing of evidence, no sharing of resources.

Gary Bald, Mike Bouchard and I agreed that the best
way to approach this case was as a team. Gary Bald had

to resist the pressure to turn it into an FBI case. After that, we were always united on this point. Somebody had to be the leader of the team, and we decided it should be the local guy, and so it ended up being me.

The real joke, of course, was that we were so far from arresting anyone, and the case had gotten so ugly so fast, that no one in his right mind would have wanted to take it over anyway. For the first six days, we had nine shootings—and not one good solid clue until we received the tarot card on October 7. Until then, it seemed entirely possible that we might never solve this crime. There were questions from the media about why this local police chief was still running things. There was pressure from certain politicians who wanted to know why the federal agencies hadn't taken over. But the reality was, who wanted it? This could have wound up being a huge embarrassment to the police agency that was responsible for it. The story was getting bigger, nationally and even internationally, and we were no closer to making any arrests. Maybe the reason we didn't feel any pressure from the federal agencies is that the federal agencies didn't want the case anyhow.

By that time, the entire task force was being assembled. We would shortly be engaged in what was later called the largest manhunt in the history of law enforcement. More than four thousand people were at work. I was told later that it was the largest investigative team ever assembled for a local murder case. We were surrounded by police. Also on our primary team were nine police chiefs or sheriffs, from nine different local police departments, aside from the MCPD. Among the other agencies assisting us were eighteen other local police agencies, a half dozen police agencies from other states, and such disparate federal investigative agencies as the U.S. Secret Service, the U.S. Marshal's Service, the Internal Revenue Service, the U.S. Customs Service, the U.S. Immigration and Naturalization Service, the U.S. Drug Enforcement Agency and the Department of Defense. We were assisted by the U.S. Postal Service, the

U.S. Park Police and the U.S. Army's 204 Military Intel Battalion. Before too long we would have a team of experienced profilers, composed of agents from the FBI, and a team of experienced negotiators, composed of agents from the FBI and the ATF.

Bald and Bouchard brought very different styles into the investigation, and the very different cultures from the agencies they represented. Bald gave the impression of being quiet and bookish, almost to the point of being impersonal. I knew he had a wife and family, that he lived over in Annapolis, Maryland, had a daughter who was into cheerleading and soccer—because later in the case he said something about all the games and practices he was missing. Over the course of the case, he'd sometimes stay overnight in Montgomery County, to avoid the one-hour commute he had in each direction. I knew he didn't like being away from home like that.

Bouchard lived down in Fairfax County, Virginia. He had a daughter he wanted to take to a Washington Wizards hockey game. I knew he had a son he felt he wasn't spending enough time with.

I could always tell which one of them was speaking, even if we were on speaker phones, because Gary had this little cough. About every ninety seconds or so, he'd have to clear his throat with this series of quick little coughs.

I never learned much about either man's private life beyond that. But each man had a very distinct way of working.

When Gary Bald took action on something, it was very deliberate. I have never worked for the FBI, so I don't know all the protocols and systems. But it seemed like everything had to go through lots of layers of management before it could get done. Gary had a cellular telephone going every minute of the day.

As a result, things happened slowly. At one point we decided we needed a composite drawing of the "white box truck" that witnesses said they had seen. We decided to turn this over to the FBI's graphic arts department. It seemed to take several hours, or even half a day, once we decided to take this action, for Gary to get this approved. Then, once it was approved, we thought we'd have the composite the next morning. It didn't look that complex. Draw a white box truck. But in fact it was almost two days before we got the drawing.

By contrast, Mike Bouchard was a little more casual. Not a lot. Both of these guys came to work every day wearing dark suits and dark ties and white shirts. They both wore a semiautomatic handgun under the suit coat, and they hardly ever took off that suit coat. They'd take it off, maybe, when they sat down to eat, but only when it was certain no one was going to be around. They never went out of the office, or to meet the press, without wearing that coat and tie. They were both very formal.

Bouchard was a little more "street" in his approach, a little more of a straight-shooter, a little quicker with his sense of humor. But he was still pretty buttoned up. One Saturday he came to work wearing a shirt without a tie, a polo shirt I think, and it happened that some people from *USA Today* were there. They took a picture of him. When it ran, he was so embarrassed to be in the newspaper as an ATF agent not wearing his coat and tie. I didn't think it was any big deal, and it's not like he got reprimanded for it or anything like that, but he was so embarrassed by it that we always kidded him about it after that.

Maybe the two different styles reflect the different culture of the two agencies. Things in the ATF seemed to move more quickly than with the FBI. When we decided it would be a good idea to do a presentation and describe for people what the suspect's gun might look like and what the ammunition might look like, Bouchard made it happen overnight. We made the decision, and the next morning we had four ATF gun experts there for a press conference. They had a collection of representative weapons and examples of the .223 shells, and they were ready to do the presentation.

The different agency cultures were visible in other ways, too. The head of the ATF, Bradley A. Buckles, visited the task force headquarters several times. He blended right in. He moved freely among his agents, who seemed pretty comfortable having him there. He seemed to fit in easily.

It was completely different when Robert Mueller, head of the FBI, visited. He came only once. There was a lead team and an advance team, and there was a complete agenda, approved ahead of time, showing exactly who he was going to meet, what he was going to say, where he was going to go and what he was going to do. He came and sat with me in my office, and the two of us had a friendly, professional talk about how the case was going. But the tone of his visit was very formal.

I'm not saying any of this is right or wrong. It's just different. The FBI seems more deliberate, with a tighter system of checks and balances. The ATF seems leaner, and quicker on its feet, with a less bureaucratic structure. It might be that now, since the ATF has moved out of the Treasury Department and under the control of Justice Department, its culture will become more like the FBI's.

The task force was coming together. We were now several thousand strong. We were on several floors of two buildings. We were not visibly any closer to solving the case, but the machinery was in place. The investigation was not yet a week old. There had been nine shootings, and nine victims. Two of the victims were still alive. No one knew when the sniper would begin shooting again. The county was extremely tense.

Camp Rockville had continued to grow, too. The media circus had started to get out of hand, because there were just so many reporters and news crews. We had already brought in portable toilets. We had already set up fencing. Now we had to set up credentialing checkpoints and entry checkpoints. We put up barriers to try and keep people from going places around the headquarters where they shouldn't go. We didn't want them interfering with investigators coming and going. We didn't want them putting their cameras through windows where sensitive work was being done. We also didn't want the media to be jeopardized. We had started to worry about whether members of the media would become targets.

I can admit now that it was very difficult meeting with the press as often as we did. With some of the reporters we were able to sit down and do little sidebar interviews, visit with them a little, make the relationship a little more personal. Most of the time, it was just people shouting out questions, screaming in order to be heard over the other questions that were being shouted out. At other times the questions were so weird, or so offensive. Reporters insisted on knowing what we were doing to keep the children safe, or when we were going to allow the children to start playing soccer games again, or whether I was getting enough sleep, or when we were going to release the tarot card so that someone might recognize the handwriting and turn the killer in.

All I could think afterward sometimes was *What the hell was* that *about?* Especially when the questions suggested that the police were responsible for the deaths of the victims.

We weren't responsible for their deaths, but we hadn't been able to produce the killer, either. We didn't know when he would strike again. We had failed to establish any pattern to the killings. There had been six people shot, all fatally, in the first thirty hours of the serial spree. Then the sniper had wounded a seventh victim the following day. There was no link between the victims. Then the sniper had taken a weekend off. Then the sniper had shot a child. Two days had passed since then, with no more shootings. The pattern was random, and unsettling. No one knew what to brace for, or when to brace for it.

Then there were more victims.

Dean Meyers had been shot down at the Sunoco station in Manassas, Virginia, on Wednesday, October 9.

Two days later, another middle-aged male was shot dead at an Exxon station in Fredericksburg, Virginia. He was exactly the same age as Meyers. His name was Kenneth Bridges. He was black. He was a Philadelphia resident, a married man with six children, who had to be in the Washington area on business. His wife, concerned about the sniper, had not wanted him to go. He was filling his tank when a single shot caught him in the upper back. A Virginia state trooper was parked fifty yards away, giving a traffic citation, when the fatal shot rang out. He rushed to assist Bridges, to no avail. The man died at the scene.

Then, three days later, on Monday, October 14—a Columbus Day holiday in some cities—a forty-seven-year-old white female was shot dead outside a Home Depot in Falls Church, Virginia. Her name was Linda Franklin, and she was an analyst for the FBI. She was married and had two children. She was shot once, in the head, while loading shelving material into the back of her car—her husband at her side.

The task force had already put in place plans for a series of roadblocks if and when there was another shooting in the area. Following the Franklin shooting, that went into effect. More than one thousand police officers rushed to checkpoints all over northern Virginia and southern Maryland. We closed Interstate 495, the Capitol Beltway. We closed the George Washington Parkway, the American Legion Bridge and the Woodrow Wilson Bridge. We shut down traffic while officers scanned the freeways for a white box truck, Astro van or Ford Econoline. We had helicopters from two police departments hovering overhead, looking for anyone trying to flee the area. One helicopter spotted a white van, in the middle of a miles-long stretch of automobiles, and instructed ground troops in riot gear to close in, shotguns and rifles ready.

Plainclothes detectives and undercover officers had already been given a special password to use to identify themselves in situations like these. The call-out was

"Bud," and the response was "Coors." Undercover and plainclothes vehicles had been given a special blue tag to place in the upper corner of their license plates, so they could move freely through roadblocks without being challenged.

It turned out the van we spotted wasn't the van we were looking for. The dragnet turned up nothing.

There was one very promising detail from the shooting at the Home Depot. We had an eyewitness who clearly saw the getaway car and the weapon—and the shooter.

A man named Matthew Dowdy said he had seen an olive-skinned man with an AK-47 point and shoot at the victim, and then drive off in a cream-colored Chevy Astro with a broken taillight.

This is good information—detailed, consistent with previous reports, potentially accurate. But there was a problem. Dowdy, who also went by the nickname of Slim, had a criminal record. Some of the task force people had a bad feeling about this. One of them especially didn't like the detail about the taillight. It was too easy. It sounded like a TV movie plot. When they asked me about the eyewitness, I told reporters, "We've been down this path before, and we'd like a little more discretion this time."

The media—which by now had given the person we were looking for inflammatory titles like the "Psycho Sniper" or the "Psycho Slayer"—reported the details as if they were the only active leads in the investigation.

In fact, we were chasing down all kinds of other leads. We were examining an abandoned box truck picked up by the Metropolitan Police Department, which had been recently repainted in a way that made the investigators suspicious. We were questioning an ex-Marine who had a gun collection and a white Chevrolet Astro van, and whose apartment, when we searched it, also contained a Marine manual on sniper training, a police radio scanner and a deck of tarot cards—similar enough to the one planted outside the middle school shooting to get our attention.

As it turned out, Dowdy was lying. He didn't see anything. Maybe he was after the reward money. Maybe he just wanted to be on TV. What he got was arrested, for making false statements to the police.

The ex-Marine's weapons didn't match up with the bullet fragments.

I started asking the members of the press to back off. Task force detectives and other investigators were complaining to me that they were being followed when they left the JOC to conduct interviews or surveillance. I thought the press was beginning to enjoy the manhunt a little too much—beginning to see it as a welcome boost to ratings and to readership—and getting a little carried away in its competitiveness. At a press briefing I said that we were going to start scheduling fewer meetings with the media and that we were going to be giving them briefings only when there were real developments in the case. I asked them not to do anything that might "put the investigation on edge" or "put people in danger," without specifically telling them to stop sending news crews out to chase the investigators. I said, "We have work that needs to be done, and don't want in any fashion to move into any arena that could be seen as entertainment." I didn't want the media circus to become any more of a circus than it already was.

For five days, there were no shootings. The task force continued to work the leads we had, putting suspects' names up on the big white board in the Joint Operations Center as the leads became solid, and then taking the names down as the leads disintegrated.

Sometimes a suspect would only be on the board for a matter of hours. Sometimes, when there were as many as a dozen names on the board, it would be a matter of days. Our investigation into these suspects was at different levels at different times. Some people we were looking for. Others we had under surveillance. They all came apart in different ways.

One guy had been under surveillance by the ATF for several days. We'd had a tip on him, and we knew he was a gun owner, and he was acting strange during the period he was under surveillance. Then, suddenly, he realized he was being watched. He blew out of his car and ran straight at the two agents who were tracking him. He charged their automobile and attacked them. Luckily they were able to subdue the guy without any serious damage being done. But I hate to think how it would have gone if he'd been armed at the time, or if the media had named him as the chief suspect.

There were two brothers from Virginia, too, who looked like especially good candidates. They matched up with a lot of the categories we were considering. They were reclusive. They owned a white van. They owned a lot of guns. They had a shooting range on their property. They had employment that brought them into the target area—they were contractors with Home Depot. We had some cell phone information that put them in the target area during the time of more than one of the shootings. Also, there had been a death in the family. That was another thing we looked for, an event that could have been the trigger for the killings.

These brothers were prime suspects. We figured maybe one was the shooter and one was the spotter. It made sense that a team with that kind of coordination could be more effective than a single person working alone, so this made them all the more attractive as suspects. We had them under surveillance when the next shooting took place. They came off the board.

There was another guy whose behavior was much more interesting than that. He lived in Montgomery County, in one of the more rural neighborhoods. His neighbors had seen him shooting long rifles or assault weapons. He had a white van. He also had a place out in the country in Spotsylvania County, which made him an interesting candidate. And he was acting kind of strange. While we had him under surveillance, he came out every morning in his robe and went to get his newspaper—on a full belly-crawl, creeping across his lawn like a guy dodging bullets. He had cinder-blocked up his windows. He had cinder-blocked up his basement. He looked like he was expecting a Waco, Texas-style siege. And for a while, during the period we were watching him, there were no shootings. He looked more and more like *the* prime suspect.

Then there was another shooting, while he was under direct surveillance. He came off the board.

Another suspect, an ex-Marine, came to our attention when he was shot by his girlfriend, in Baltimore, during a domestic dispute. In his apartment, after the suspect was taken to the hospital and his girlfriend was taken into custody, investigators found a high-powered rifle and a book on sniper techniques. Baltimore police also seized his vehicle—a white van.

None of the evidence matched up, though. The ex-Marine was off the board before he was even on it.

The white box truck continued to be of interest to us. A credible witness had come forward and volunteered this information from the first wave of shootings. A white box truck had been seen driving erratically, leaving the scene of a shooting. We wanted to know why that was. We kept looking for it. We had not been able to eliminate it as a useful piece of evidence, because we had not been able to find it. Other sightings of white trucks or white vans, at or near other crime scenes, all led to our finding the owner and the driver. We were able to interview each of them and eliminate them as suspects. But we never did find the owner or driver of the white box truck. Nor did we ever learn anything to think the witness was mistaken, or lying. We just never got to the bottom of it.

We had our hands full, though, with other leads. We weren't just driving around looking for white box trucks. There were multiple suspects who had their names, and the names of the teams who were investigating them, on the white board in the major crimes room almost every single day of the investigation— starting the Friday after the first wave of shootings and continuing right until the night the siege ended. I don't think there was ever a day after that first Friday when the white board was empty. We were always in the process of active investigation of suspects. I don't know how many of them didn't have anything to do with a white box truck, but I know that most of them did not.

Bill O'Toole remembered walking into the major crimes room one night when there were four names of suspects, and four teams of investigators, on the board. He stopped and read the investigative background on all four. He felt a great sense of confidence, because all four were strong, viable suspects. He felt confident that the case was coming to a close. He knew the surveillance teams watching these four suspects. There were three teams of investigators assigned to each suspect— each team working an eight-hour shift, then giving over to the next team. O'Toole knew, he just instinctively knew, that the sniper was among these four suspects. He felt certain that, very shortly, while they were under surveillance, one of them would be seen packing a rifle into his car, driving to a secluded clump of woods, setting up his rifle and tripod and scope and . . .

There were also, during this period, a number of false leads and bogus suspects picked up by the media. At one point we were contacted by a man from one of the national car rental chains, based in Loudoun County, Virginia. He had rented a white van to someone. When the car came back and was being cleaned, his employees found a spent shell casing. They called the task force at once. We had the van towed in to one of our labs. We had the shell casing taken to ATF for analysis. We were conducting the tests, and in the process of ruling out the evidence, when one of the newspapers called and said they were going with the story.

Captain Nancy Demme, in charge of the media division, took the call and started telling the newspaper reporters that they had the story wrong. The reporters insisted they had sources inside the task force who told them this was a certain kind of shell casing that came from a certain kind of gun, and they were running with it. Captain Demme said, "I don't know who your sources are, and I don't care, because they've got it wrong." She agreed to go on the record, in fact, telling them their tip was wrong.

The next morning, the newspaper had the story. They quoted their anonymous task force sources telling them this was a bullet from the sniper's gun. They did not quote Captain Demme telling them it was *not* a bullet from the sniper's gun.

This kind of interference didn't help morale much. Particularly on the days when we were losing suspects faster than we were gaining them.

O'Toole remembers the night when these four were under surveillance, and we had gone several days without a shooting, and then another occurred on Monday, October 14. Within an hour, while O'Toole watched, someone came into the major crimes room and walked up to the white board and started wiping it clean. All four names, and the names of all the investigators watching them, came down off the board. O'Toole remembers thinking this was the lowest time in the whole case. We were back at square one, with no suspects and a new victim.

O'Toole wasn't the only one feeling disappointment or outrage. President Bush, in a national address, spoke on Monday the 14th about the sniper and his victims.

"I'm just sick, sick to my stomach, to think that there is a cold-blooded killer at home taking innocent life," he said. "I weep for those who have lost their loved ones."

The reward money went up to $500,000.

O'Toole also remembers that I held an end-of-day briefing that day, as I did most days.

I had a pattern. It was a management tool I had developed in Portland and brought to Montgomery County. I'd tell everyone what I knew, and ask them what they knew, and then we'd go around the room. I'd make each of the senior people in the room answer four questions: What are your problems? What are your needs? What is a success story you experienced today?

And what does your self-check tell you about yourself right now?

This was my way of finding out what new difficulties had arisen, whether anyone needed any resources I didn't know about, what good thing had happened to each person during his or her shift and whether each person was getting enough food, enough sleep, seeing his or her family enough and so on.

Most of the time, I knew, everyone lied about the last part. Everyone was always doing fine on the self-check. No one would ever say, "Actually, Chief, I'm feeling a little worn down. I'd better take tomorrow off." Especially the managers, which is why I always ran this four-question check in the end-of-day meetings I'd have with Bouchard, Bald and my assistant chiefs. You can take care of all your people, and get burned out yourself, and fall down on the job—which is not the way to take care of your people.

But I learned things from the first two questions, and the third one was effective in getting people to focus on the positive—on some little piece of the positive, no matter how small it was.

Sometimes it was pretty small. Once, I remember, it was that someone had seen an ATF person and an FBI person and a Montgomery County Police person sitting down to lunch with each other.

These are all little things, but they add up. They contribute to the atmosphere, and can make it positive or negative. When I was in Portland, taking on the job of police chief, the outgoing chief, Tom Potter, told me his "elevator story." The chief's office was on the fifteenth floor of a sixteen-floor office building. You'd get on in the lobby and ride all the way up, or the other way around, and you'd see all these people riding with you. If you didn't smile, or say hello, or acknowledge your people, they'd go back to their desks wondering what they'd done wrong. They'd get on the phone or the email and start asking everyone what they had done to piss off the chief. They'd obsess over it. They'd lose a workday over it. They would have no way of knowing that the thing you were upset about was a toothache or a fight you had with your wife. They'd think it was something bad going on with them or with the police department. So a little smile and a kind word could do a lot to create a positive atmosphere, and a scowl or a harsh word could just as easily create a negative atmosphere.

That day the positive was we had eliminated four suspects from the white board. We were no longer going to be expending time and manpower keeping an eye on four suspects who we now knew were not the sniper.

It was kind of a stretch to see that as a positive, but those were the facts.

There was some frustration that it wasn't going faster. We were relieved at the end of every day that there were no new shootings reported. We got excited every time a new lead began to look promising. It had been a roller coaster ride up until this time, and the ride continued. Tips were still coming into the hot line. We were taking around a thousand calls an hour, after a shooting. We were getting up to a thousand actual tips a day. Most of them were nothing more than hysteria. Some of them were crazy—just a few inarticulate words and then a hang-up. But a lot of them were very earnest. There were sightings of the white van. There were reports of suspicious behavior. There were more reports from people who wanted you to know that their husband or brother or neighbor or employee owned a Bushmaster and was missing or behaving strangely.

One lead became very promising, one that hadn't come in on a tip line. Earlier in the investigation, when we had set up our first roadblock, a car was observed driving around the roadblock in a suspicious manner. Someone managed to get a description of the car, and someone got a partial on the license plate. We were able to put those together and go interview the owner.

At first it looked sort of innocent. There were two guys living together. The one who drove the car around the roadblock had some kind of driver's license issue, and maybe some kind of probation issue—he just didn't want to get stopped by the police. But there was also a .223 rifle in the house.

The guys were both from the area. They appeared to have had the time and the opportunity to be around to do the shootings. One of them also had a fairly serious criminal record. So the investigators thanked the two men and left, but they sat on them for a while.

Then there was another shooting, while the house was under surveillance.

They came off the board.

Then there was the media guy.

A week or more into the serial killings, right after one of the many press briefings we had during that week, a man walked through the crowd of media at Camp Rockville and approached the podium where I had just been speaking. He put a note on the podium. Then he melted back into the crowd.

The note was fairly generic. It just said, "Chief Moose, I've been watching you and I think you're doing a wonderful job," or something like that. I didn't make much of it.

But about twelve or fourteen hours later, one of the reporters came up to me with a videotape. He said, "I shot this tape of the guy that left the note on your podium. I don't know if you guys know who he is, but he isn't one of us. He's not a reporter anyone recognizes."

Suddenly it wasn't so generic. We looked at the video. It showed this very suspicious-looking guy, wearing sunglasses, carrying something in his hand, approaching the podium hesitantly, placing something on the podium and then slinking back into the crowd.

We suddenly realized, "It's the guy! It's the shooter! This is the guy that's out there doing all this killing. And he's coming to the press briefings. He watches us, then he goes out and does some more killing!"

We made copies of the guy's face from the video and distributed them all around. We didn't name him as a suspect. We only said we wanted to speak with him.

Shortly after, a woman who worked with the ATF spotted him. We swooped in and detained him.

It turned out to be completely innocent. He was just an office guy, who worked in a building half a block away from the JOC, and he really did think we were doing a wonderful job, and wanted to say so.

This event made it obvious to us that we had to do something to secure the press area. The psychology of this killer might be that he gets a kick from doing the killing and then watching us talk about it. If he was deranged, he was deranged in his own special way. Maybe that included wanting to hang around with the investigators when he wasn't busy shooting people.

We decided to enclose the press area, create a credentialing process, issue credentials and make sure we knew who was around us when we were out there exposed and making statements.

O'Toole told me later that he was concerned not so much about someone shooting someone in the press, as he was about someone shooting me. I was the figurehead of the investigation, as he put it. That might make me an attractive target for a certain kind of individual. It wasn't possible to put up bulletproof glass, but O'Toole felt strongly that we had to control access to the press area as a precaution against someone coming in and getting a clear shot at me.

I hadn't even started thinking about that prospect. Once it was in my mind, though, I agreed that we ought to take some precautions.

All of the hot-line leads had to be checked out. On the good side, we had the staff to run down a lot of these leads. On the bad side, no matter how many people you have, it all takes time. I was very aware of the ticking of the clock, the passing of the days.

Once again, I wondered on Friday if the sniper was done, and if it was over. If it was, it meant no more killings. But it also meant we might never find the person or persons who had killed nine people and seriously wounded two people already.

Then it was ten people.

On the night of Saturday, October 19, a thirty-seven-year-old white male was shot once in the stomach as he and his wife walked across the parking lot of the Ponderosa Steakhouse in Ashland, Virginia. They had just finished eating dinner. The wife heard a "pop" and her husband stumbled, took three steps forward and fell. His middle section was destroyed. Parts of his stomach, pancreas and spleen were scattered about him, along with the dinner he had just eaten. He was rushed to the hospital. Members of the task force rushed to the scene, sealed it and began combing the area for evidence.

It was a long search, conducted by over a hundred task force members and, as with the earlier shootings, more than one canine unit. The team fanned out from the shooting scene into the deep surrounding woods on this damp night. By the time the search began, it was raining, and within an hour the search team was soaking wet. Mike Bouchard, sitting inside the ATF's mobile lab truck, looked out at the weather and joked to one of his colleagues, "I'm the boss. I don't do the work anymore. I don't have to go out in the rain."

The Ponderosa sat by the interstate, bordered by a Burger King and a Wendy's, near some gas stations and low-priced motels, across the street from a Waffle House. Ashland is a town of only seven thousand, ninety miles south of Washington and fifteen miles south of Richmond. It's country. The Ponderosa and the other businesses were bordered by a wide parking lot, surrounded by woods. There weren't many roads and streets away from the location, so units first on the scene were optimistic that a dragnet might catch the shooter before he could escape. The interstate was shut down at once. On-ramps and off-ramps were sealed. Traffic on the highway was stopped. The area was locked down.

It might have taken investigators hours to figure out, in the dark and in the rain, the direction from which the shot was fired. The canine units, though, figured that out for them. As they had with the shootings of Iran Brown and Pascal Charlot, the dogs picked up the scent of the gunshots very quickly. That led investigators to a spent shell casing, on the ground, thirty feet off the parking lot, deep in the heavy underbrush.

From there, working in the pitch-black dark, investigators combed the area for more evidence. They realized quickly that the shooter had been closer to his victim than in most previous shootings—maybe as close as fifty yards. They worked the area around the shell casing.

Several hours later, they found the ransom note. Pinned to a tree with a thumbtack, protected from the rain in a plastic baggie, there was a four-page handwritten note. Investigators carefully removed the baggie from the tree. It was placed in the hands of an ATF investigator and taken by helicopter to the ATF lab in Rockville. From there, it was shipped that night to the FBI lab in Washington, D.C. It was determined by Bouchard and Bald and other task force experts that the FBI chemists would have to swab the baggie for possible DNA evidence—before anyone else touched it.

The team of investigators continued searching in the dark and the rain, well into the morning of Sunday, October 20. Late that night, Bouchard decided to drive home, into Virginia, rather than follow the note back to the lab. But the traffic jam resulting from the hours-long closure of the interstate was so dense that he spent an hour traveling the distance between one off-ramp and the next. He got off the freeway and checked into a motel. He knew the lab work would take all night. No one would know the contents of the note until at least Sunday morning.

Everyone on the task force went to bed that night not knowing that the sniper had finally shown his cards and told us his demands.

8. Cops, Community and Controversy

The road up is a hard road. I was rising in the Portland police department—slowly, and sometimes with a lot of frustration, but I was moving forward. I made sergeant in 1981. I made lieutenant in 1984. I was promoted to captain in 1991, and deputy chief in September 1992. Nine months later, in June of 1993, I was named chief.

Along the way, I was also building my education.

Part of the reason I wanted to be a sergeant was that I wanted to be a better sergeant than my sergeant had been. I realized that I didn't really know much about how to do that. I figured I could try to make sergeant, and then just pick it up along the way, and hope that I didn't make too many mistakes. Or I could try to get some training, and speed the whole process up. That seemed to make more sense. I wanted the people I was going to lead to get better leadership than I had gotten, so I decided to get some education in the leadership area.

Portland State University had a master's program in public administration. That looked like the way to go. The campus was right in town. The classes were for working professionals. They were held at night and on the weekends. I could take the classes without having to ask for time off from my job.

Initially I didn't think I could get in. My undergraduate GPA was not that strong. A counselor suggested that I take some classes at PSU first, and try to show my interest, and try to do well, and then apply to the master's program. I took four classes. I got four A's. I took the GRE, and I did pretty well. I applied and got in.

I was the only police officer in the program. I might have felt lonely, but I met Sandy.

It was March of 1982. She remembers it was the first week of the spring quarter. She had missed the first session, and arrived at the second session late, and eating a cheeseburger. She says now that I was staring at her. When we were introduced, I told her I was a policeman. She didn't believe me. She laughed and said, "Prove it!"

We went out for a date a little while later. We had lunch at a place called the Meat Market. It's a pretty nice place, despite the name. It was a humble beginning.

She had been married before and it hadn't worked out. I was still married and it hadn't worked out. She had a son. I had a son. I grew up middle-class black in eastern North Carolina. She was born into a dirt-poor white family in western North Carolina. We had both been subjected to a fair amount of abuse. I don't know why we were so trusting of each other. But we were.

I don't talk about stuff like this too much, but I guess I could say we fell in love.

Not at first, maybe, for me. At first, it was a physical thing. There was this major attraction. Also, I was still married. There was this unlawfulness about it. I was having an extramarital affair.

That may have prevented me from thinking very much, at first, about her being white. I don't think I worried too much about that in the beginning.

Other people started worrying about it for me, though. I heard from a lot of people. They seemed to think being with Sandy was a bad idea. A dangerous idea. An offensive idea.

There were the black men I worked with and the black men I knew, who were not very approving, but who were fairly quiet about it. There were the black women I knew, who were very disapproving and very vocal about it.

The men said, "Yeah, it looks like fun, but you can't really be thinking of leaving your wife and child over *that*." Having a relationship like this was something you did on the side, and then got over it and went back to your family.

The women said, "You have betrayed us." For them, I had turned my back on the community, on my race. It was a rejection. And they were twice as mad at Sandy as they were at me. It was like she'd come in and stolen something from them. I was a father! I was married! Who did she think she was?

Everyone seemed to have an opinion, judging from the remarks they made or the questions they asked. Some people warned me about the extra burden I was placing on myself, how I would be making myself a target for the racists, how life was hard enough without adding something like this.

There was, in time, a little extra ammunition for the people who didn't like the idea of me and Sandy together. Sandy got a job working for the city of Portland. She was asked to join a committee that was formed to conduct oversight reviews of the Portland Police Bureau's internal affairs division. Prior to that, Sandy had been a graduate student, finishing her master's in public administration. She had a job working as a counselor at the Rosemont School for Girls, an incarceration facility for teenaged girls in trouble. This was all admirable and nonthreatening.

When she became part of the internal affairs oversight committee, she became the enemy.

It turned out my wife's mother was part of the custodial staff at city hall. Eventually she put two and two together—from the fact that Sandy was working at city hall and I was spending a lot of time over there—and was able to report back to her daughter on what she knew. Which of course was very upsetting to her.

Linder had a litany of abuse for me. It hurt her badly, when she found out about it, that Sandy was white. It wasn't like I had permission to go and have an affair with a black woman. If I'd been discovered doing that, it would have been plenty bad. But this was much, much worse.

One of the first things she said, once she had learned of the affair, was that she would never allow my son to be around Sandy. She managed to make good on that threat for a long time. While she and I were in the process of getting divorced, and for a long time after we were divorced, this was the center of the custody battle I fought with her to spend time with my son. It was always that I left her for a white woman. The racial difference made it worse.

It wasn't clear to me for a long time whether it made things more difficult for me at the police department. I knew the hierarchy there was very white, very male, very conservative. I wasn't sure what impact my having a white girlfriend, or a white wife, would have on my advancement. Later on, when I was stuck in the lieutenant's job, and for nine years couldn't seem to make captain, it occurred to me many times that this was part of the problem. I was always sure that marrying Sandy had hurt my chances for advancement, but I could never prove that was the case. Like everything else, this increased my belief that I had to be better, and do better, than the other guys. If it came time for a promotion, and there were two candidates, and we had the same experience and the same ability, and one of us was white—then the white guy was going to get the job. I was convinced that I had to be better than the white guy, much better, in order to get picked for the job.

It never occurred to me not to be with Sandy, or to keep it a secret. We dated for a couple of years. Then it got serious and we started living together. We married in 1988. The judge who married us was Harl Haas, a circuit court judge for Multnomah County, who had been the district attorney during our big undercover stolen goods sting operation. His wife Mary Lou was one of Sandy's good friends. He didn't do weddings, but he agreed to do ours.

It was a very small ceremony, held in his offices. The only witnesses were his wife, Sandy's best friend Marcia Maple and her husband Bill Young, my son David and Sandy's son Lincoln. Somehow we had managed to get both kids for the afternoon. But we were not entirely ready to get married. When Judge Haas asked us if we had special vows we wanted him to read, we said we had forgotten about that part. Mary Lou happened to have a copy of the wedding vows she had said when she married Harl. We used those. Sandy, who had shopped forever for the right outfit to get married in, wore a fuchsia leather dress. I wore a blue suit.

Afterward, we all went out to the Charthouse, a fancy steakhouse in southwest Portland, with a great view overlooking the city. Marcia and Bill Maple presented us with a pair of silver candleholders.

We didn't have any kind of a honeymoon. We talked about it, and talked about maybe going away somewhere at the end of the year, for the Christmas and New Year break. But I had a tradition for that time of year: I worked, to give time off to the officers who needed to be with their loved ones.

The Christmas holidays were not my favorite time of year to start with, and during that period they were particularly painful. After my marriage ended, there were some years when I was not allowed to even see my son at Christmastime. Sandy and I would go visit her sisters, or her mother, and sometimes we would have her son Lincoln with us, but it was painful for me to be cut off from my own child. The parties, the store windows, the talk around the office, the TV commercials—all conspired to make me feel like a failure. I wasn't living the American dream the right way, and at Christmastime that was especially hard. Spending the holidays working always seemed to me to be a good way to get through them.

I told Sandy that we'd take a honeymoon some other time.

Sandy's still waiting.

I did well in school. Doing well in school helped me do well in other ways, too. Somewhere around the time I was finishing my degree, I took the promotion test to be a lieutenant, and I did very well. (I had finished sixth on the sergeant's exam, but that was in a field of lots of people going for sergeant, so it was also pretty good. For lieutenant, where there were fewer candidates, I finished first.) I made lieutenant in March 1984. A few months later, I got my master's degree.

By now, with a master's and a lieutenant's rank, I was beginning to realize that this was my career. I began to believe that I could succeed in the police department—despite the fact that, as a lieutenant, I was breaking completely new ground as a black man in the department. I figured with hard work and luck I might make it to captain. I had this ambition to one day be captain of the North Precinct. I did not have any idea, even any wild fantasy, that I could become the chief of police.

I decided to continue with the academic work. I took the summer of 1984 off, but that September I began my doctorate. I applied for and was accepted by the Portland State University's Ph.D. program in urban affairs, with an emphasis on criminology.

I had a lot of reasons to want to do this. One of them was for my dad. He had been called Doc Moose his whole adult life—but it was said in a kind of joking way. I would be able to earn this degree, maybe, and I could be called Dr. Moose if I wanted to be, and no one would be joking when they said it. I thought my dad would be proud of that.

I also thought it would be good for me as a police officer, and for after. I saw these ex-police guys working as teachers at PSU and other universities. I had the feeling that they got some respect from the academics because they had really been out there, on the front lines, doing the work they were teaching other people about. But I also had the feeling that they didn't get quite as much respect from the academics as the other academics got. I figured that with a police background and a Ph.D. I would be very employable at the university level, when I was done being a police officer.

I didn't get much official encouragement for this. Penny Harrington, who had been a captain working in personnel when I first got to know her well, thought it was a good idea for me to pursue my education. It was good that Penny knew about this, because she would later be named chief. She put something in my file about it, and mentioned that it would be a good idea for me to study public speaking and get comfortable with that.

This wasn't the last time the suggestion was made. Later, when I was chief, a lot of journalists and editorialists made the same observation—usually not being very nice about it. They didn't like my accent, or my inflection, or my choice of words. They didn't like the sound of the North Carolina way I speak—or whatever it is that makes me sound the way I sound—and several of them made fun of it.

I didn't know what to do about that except ignore it. I don't sound like a white guy, because I am not a white guy. Why should I try to sound different? People seem to understand what I'm saying. The only people that have a problem with how I talk are these newspaper commentators. How far do I need to go to please them and sound like something phony that I'm not? I decided I didn't need to change at all.

A lot of other stuff was changing for me, though, while I was beginning to work on my academic career. My father had died. My marriage had ended, and there was a lot of anger and bad feeling there. My brother had died. I was estranged from my son, David. My relationship with Sandy was rocky, and I had not yet developed any close feelings with her son, Lincoln. Coming up the ladder at the police department, I seemed to have fewer and fewer friends. I wasn't hanging out with the guys too much. I was working hard and studying hard.

There was a lot of frustration. I felt trapped a lot of the time, and impatient. The period between my making lieutenant and my making captain seemed endless to me. I felt like I was waiting, always waiting, trying to make something happen, but not being able to make it happen. Of course I didn't know, and had no way of knowing, that all the time I was a lieutenant I was learning things that would help me be a better captain. I didn't know I'd ever *become* a captain.

There wasn't any road map for me to follow. There had been so few blacks of any prominence in Portland city life that when I made lieutenant I got my picture in the newspaper.

It must have been a slow news day. There I was on page B6 of the *Portland Oregonian*, March 29, 1984, wearing a suit and tie and standing between two of my colleagues: Penny Harrington, who was then the bureau's only female captain and the first in Portland history, and her sister Roberta Webber, who had just become the bureau's second female captain.

The news story made a big deal out of these two historic events. Roberta was making history joining her sister in the captain's position. I was making history, again, by becoming the city's first-ever black lieutenant. When I was named sergeant, I was only the second black one in the Portland city police department. Now I was the first and only black lieutenant.

I told the *Oregonian* reporter that I was interested in advancement in the department because I wanted to change it. "You have to move up to get things done," I said. "If you work the street, you can affect your beat, but that's about it. I want to participate in the direction the bureau's going."

I also told the reporter, in response to a question I've forgotten, that I wasn't all that worried about other people's concerns that I might wash out as a lieutenant. "If

I do poorly," I said, "I'll be too upset at myself to worry about what anyone else thinks."

I did worry about what other people did to me, though. There were times when people didn't treat me right. On several occasions I became extremely vocal about that.

The first problem occurred at a Nordstrom department store. I was a sergeant at the time, but I wasn't in uniform. It must have been 1982 or 1983. I was trying to buy some shoes for my son. I was waiting in line, ready to pay for the shoes. Nobody would wait on me. I had been in Nordstrom before. I had a Nordstrom credit card. I had just bought this pretty expensive wool coat there. But now I couldn't get waited on. I saw other customers getting waited on. I saw they were white. I saw the salespeople were white. I was the only black guy there. I seemed to be the only one not getting waited on.

I lost my temper. I didn't go nuts or anything. But I lost my temper. I demanded to get some service. I accused the salespeople of disrespecting me and making me wait until all the white customers got waited on. One salesperson told me that wasn't true. I shouted something about how all the "honkies" were going to stick together and defend each other. I demanded to see a manager. They told me there was no manager on duty, and wouldn't be until the following morning. So I took out one of my business cards, from the Portland Police Bureau, and wrote my home telephone number on the back. I told them I wanted to hear from their manager, as soon as the manager came in, and I stormed out.

I never got a call from the manager. I did get a call from internal affairs. A complaint had been filed against me. The people at Nordstrom said I had threatened them, been abusive to them and was using my position as a police officer to bully them. I was told that I was under investigation. Nothing came of it.

But I didn't stay out of trouble. A couple of years later, I had a similar incident. I was waiting in line again, this time in the city employees' credit union. I can't remember what I was doing there—withdrawal, deposit, whatever—but I remember I was waiting in line for a long time. I am not very good at waiting in lines. I hate waiting in lines. And this day I got pretty disgusted when a guy who was waiting in line behind me, who had come in after I came in, got served before I did.

A woman behind the counter waved this guy up to the front ahead of me and started helping him with his credit union business. He was white. She was white. It was 1983 or 1984. I was the only black sergeant in the department. Obviously, I was the only black guy waiting in line that day.

I just went off. I started yelling at this white woman working the counter, and this white guy she was waiting on, about how long I'd been waiting and how pissed off I was that they were making a black man wait in line while they were serving all the white people first.

We had some words. The white woman and the white guy she was serving got all huffy. Then they apologized. It was all resolved. I left the credit union. I vowed never to go back, and I never did.

Someone from that office filed a complaint with internal affairs. So here I am being investigated, again. On the same kind of thing. Of course the investigators found there was nothing more to it than what happened. It took several months, again, but my name was cleared. There were no repercussions.

They say the third time is the charm. The third incident *did* have some repercussions.

I was a lieutenant by now. I was assigned to the North Precinct. One afternoon I came into the precinct wearing jeans and a T-shirt.

There was a woman there, an older white woman, who was a "crime prevention specialist" for the city of Portland. (The city employed these citizen experts, who were not police officers, or criminologists. They weren't in the police chain of command. This program worked the way the neighborhood watch programs did, and encouraged citizen involvement in police matters.) The woman took exception to the way I was dressed. She didn't like my jeans and T-shirt. She was very dismissive, and her tone was derogatory. She said I looked like a "gang banger." She was reprimanding me for not showing more respect to the police department, for not wearing a uniform or for not dressing better when I was out of uniform. She obviously wasn't joking.

I said, "I am not a fucking gang member, and you know it. You're wrong to call me that."

She was shocked. I was upset. I knew that what I'd said was offensive. I went to my captain, who at that time was Tom Potter—who later became chief of police—and told him what happened. He said, "You have to go and apologize to her."

I apologized. She accepted my apology. She apologized back. I worked with her again later when I was chief, and we had a good relationship. Our disagreement resolved itself.

A complaint was filed against me again, though, with internal affairs. I was never told who filed it. I know the woman I insulted didn't. Internal affairs finally told me that another police officer, a lieutenant, had filed the charges.

Well, I knew who that was. There was only one other lieutenant around the day this all happened. He was white. We were in the same academy class together. Maybe he saw me as the competition. Maybe he wanted to move his career along.

The internal affairs people didn't want to discuss who filed the complaint. They wanted to discuss whether I had said what the complaint alleged I said—especially my use of profanity.

I didn't deny it. I did argue that it was just an adjective. It wasn't like I said "fuck you" to her, or told her to "fuck off." I just used a rather aggressive adjective. I said that I was proud to be a police officer. I was proud not to be a gang member. I said she was wrong to call me that.

The internal affairs people didn't agree. They sent the

results of their investigation to my superiors. My superiors decided I needed a punishment. They docked my paycheck for the equivalent of two days' pay.

I thought this was an extreme punishment. Two days' pay was a lot of money to me then. I had an ex-wife. I had child support. I thought the punishment was unfair. This woman had been completely out of line with me. She had said something extremely insulting to me, that she would never, ever have said to a white police officer. It was a racist remark, delivered in a racist manner. I was the one getting punished.

I knew that any police officer had the right to appeal a punishment of this kind to the police chief or the police commissioner. In the structure of the Portland city government at that time, there was no police commissioner. The only person with oversight on the police department was the mayor. He hired and fired the police chief. I took my appeal to him.

The mayor at that time was Bud Clark. He'd been a tavern owner. He was a salty sort of fellow who'd been around plenty. I had a feeling he would agree that my punishment was excessive.

I was right. He said to me, "They docked you for two days' pay for using the F word?"

He backed me up. He went to the police chief and said, "Do you reprimand all your police officers this way for using the F word? Do you give all your officers two days off, without pay, for saying 'fucking'?"

The chief admitted that he didn't. The mayor overruled docking my pay for two days. The chief told me he was going to have to put something in my personnel file and that I was going to have to go see a counselor of some kind. We didn't call it "anger management" in those days, but that was the idea.

They gave me the name of a psychologist. I went to see him. It turned out he was the only black psychologist in Portland. We talked about what had happened. He understood. He told me, when I had explained everything, "You live in America, and you work for the police department. The police department is a racist organization. Every police department in America is a racist organization. You can't be surprised if you get exposed to racist behavior. You can't get angry. You either have to contain yourself when this happens, or you have to get out."

I wasn't willing to get out, so I decided I would learn to contain myself.

The psychologist sent a letter to the department saying I had fulfilled the obligation of my punishment. I never saw him again.

But here's another repercussion.

Years later, when I was police chief, we had a problem with a gay police officer. He was found to have been hiring male prostitutes. He was paying them with personal checks. It was a terrible embarrassment to the department. Not because he was gay. I didn't care about that, but I did care that he was hiring prostitutes.

I had to reprimand him. He was a police officer, and he was engaging in illegal behavior. Unfortunately, the officer filed a lawsuit against me, and the police department, and the city. He alleged that I was discriminating against him because he was gay.

As the case moved toward trial, lawyers from his side started making these remarks. They started saying things like "If you knew what was in the chief's personnel file, you'd see that he isn't in a position to be reprimanding *anyone*." They started insinuating to members of the press that there were things in my file, the results of internal affairs investigations, that would be embarrassing to me and that might disqualify me from being allowed to reprimand an officer on my staff.

Sandy and I talked about this. We believed in being up front and honest. We didn't think we had anything to hide. I wasn't ashamed of anything I had done or said, and I wasn't worried about how it would influence this case. On the other hand, I *was* worried about what conclusions people would draw from this inference that I had embarrassing things in my personnel file.

I had photocopies made of every single piece of paper in my personnel file: every promotion, every commendation, every letter of congratulation, every letter of recommendation, all my university degrees, and the papers pertinent to these three incidents in which I'd been subjected to racist behavior. I called a press conference and had someone help me carry this stuff over to city hall—two huge boxes of papers—and I dumped it on a table in front of all the reporters.

They had a field day. It was headline news. One newspaper reported that I'd called the people in Nordstrom "honkies." The TV stations replayed that story and showed the article on camera, but with the word "honkies" blacked out. They said I used a "racial slur." Which somehow sounded worse than saying "honkies."

You don't usually hear about black people using "racial slurs" when talking about white people, but there it was.

It was very painful to be subjected to the kind of front-page coverage that followed. The papers were full of it for a couple of days. No police chief had ever done anything like this before: I poured it all out there—no secrets. See for yourself! I had nothing to hide.

Looking back at all that drama, I wonder whether it was the right thing to do. Then I decide it *was*. No matter how much trouble it caused at the time, I still believe that openness and honesty are always better than keeping secrets. First of all, if you think you can keep the secret permanently, you're going to be disappointed. Second, if you're keeping a secret, you're giving a lot of power to the person who knows your secret. I have always believed that telling the truth is ultimately smarter, whether it's on the job or with your parents or with your spouse or whatever. It's sometimes painful, but it's always better in the long run.

This was a very long run. I had left Portland and had been the police chief of Montgomery County for eighteen months before this situation resolved itself.

It started a story that has never died. Some reporter

wrote that I had been forced to undergo psychiatric counseling as a result of my repeated temper tantrums. In fact, I had been to see one psychologist, one time.

Later on, the story got one more twist. It said that I had been forced to take anger management classes— did anger management classes even *exist* in 1986 or 1987?—as Portland's chief of police. I didn't become chief until six or seven years after this incident, but never mind that. This became the story.

When I got angry and yelled at the media for printing leaked material during the sniper shooting, this story would come back to haunt me. Once again, I became the hotheaded cop who'd been forced to attend anger management classes while he was chief of police in Portland, because he couldn't control his temper.

It's a lie, and it's wrong, and it's easy to prove that it's wrong, but I've stopped trying. This has become the fact. It will be in my obituary. Despite the fact that it's a lie and it's wrong.

In the mid-1980s, the Portland Police Bureau was in bad shape. It was demoralized, angry and dispirited. The police department was trying to clean up its act and the police union was trying to defend its officers. Neither of those things was helping bring the crime rate down, or giving the citizens much reason to expect anything to improve.

Officers fired by the police department were routinely reinstated after pressure and arbitration from the police union. For example, two officers were fired for producing and selling T-shirts that said, "Don't Smoke 'Em, Choke 'Em"—while the community was attending a funeral for a man who died in a police choke hold. The union lobbied to get those officers their jobs back, and succeeded.

Despite the strength of the union, it wasn't a great time to be a black police officer in Portland. For one thing, there weren't very many of us. The African-American population of Portland was under 10 percent.

The African-American population of the police force was under 5 percent. There were over eight hundred officers at that time. Just about forty of them were black police officers. The police department had made recruiting women a priority. There were about eighty female officers. The department hadn't done so well with minorities.

When the department stepped up its attempts to hire minority officers, there was dissension in the ranks over that, too. In 1990, the newspapers were full of stories about how the police department had lowered the requirements and test score standards for nonwhite applicants. White candidates had to score over 80 percent on a certain civil service exam to complete the application process; black candidates, for example, had to score over 70 percent.

Some white officers, and candidates, were outraged. Then Police Chief Richard D. Walker got letters of complaint.

I was a lieutenant at that time. I was the highest ranking black officer on the force. I determined that if I ever got the chance, I would do something about this.

It took longer than I thought. I have a clip from the *Portland Oregonian* that says, "Seven years after Charles Moose turned minority recruiting into a mandate, 10.3 percent of Portland's sworn officers are nonwhite." That clip is dated July 2, 2000.

All organizations resist change. Police departments *really* resist change.

Competition between officers doesn't help, either. When I was made captain, in 1991, there was a complaint filed by a Japanese-American officer on the force who felt that he had been passed over for promotion because he was the "wrong minority." There were twenty-two candidates among lieutenants who took the promotion exam for captain. This other officer, Lieutenant Glenn Miyamoto, I was told, held the first position on the eligibility list. I was in fifth position. I got the job.

What was left out of that story was how long it had

taken me to become captain. Leaving aside any question of which of us was the "right minority," I had been a lieutenant for nine years. For nine years I had been trying to get promoted. For nine years I had been taking that test. I'd tried hard, as I had on all the promotions test. When I tested for sergeant, I finished fifth. When I tested for lieutenant, I finished first. But when I tested for captain, I didn't score as high. There were fewer positions available for captains so I was stuck. I felt like my earlier ambitions were coming to nothing, and that I would probably end my police career as a lieutenant.

What changed—in the department, and in me—was the idea of community policing.

When I didn't get promoted to captain one more time, in 1988, I started changing the way I thought about what I was doing. I remember deciding at the time, *Maybe I should forget about helping me, and concentrate on helping other people.* We had people in the police organization at the time who cared much more about themselves than they did about the citizens. I decided to not be one of those people.

This decision would affect everything in my life— how I did my job, where my career would go and even where Sandy and I would live.

The change all started with a place called Iris Court.

Iris Court was a government housing project in North Portland. It was a two-square-block collection of two-story brick apartment buildings. I had been familiar with it as a patrolman in that district. It was a place filled with crime and violence. You never went in alone. If you had to make a call there, you went with two or three police cars. There was a lot of drug activity. There were constantly rapes and assaults. There were always people standing around drinking and fighting. It was rough and unsafe, and the violence and criminality of it was starting to bleed over into the surrounding neighborhoods. It was the worst kind of urban blight.

I was still a lieutenant, and still frustrated in my attempts to get promoted to captain. I was restless. I needed a project for my doctoral thesis. I needed something new to do in my job. Iris Court came along in the form of a job. There was a campaign under way to create an experiment with community policing. A job came open for "neighborhood revitalization coordinator." No one was applying for it. So I did, and I got it.

At first the job was simply to oversee a citizens group that was conducting a survey of the residents of Iris Court. We had gotten some grant money to study the problems of this microcosm, and it started with finding out all we could about who lived there. From the survey we developed a theory of how to correct some of the problems.

Over the next couple of years, we reoriented Iris Court. First we closed off some of the streets and made them into cul-de-sacs, so people would be less likely to try and drive through Iris Court to buy their drugs. Then we took an empty apartment and turned it into a police substation, so it would look like police were around all the time. Then we took another empty apartment and turned it into a laundry facility, to replace the filthy, drug-infested, dangerous laundry in the basement, so women could wash and dry their clothes without being assaulted. We got the various local agencies to give us the right to evict anyone who was not technically on the lease for an apartment, which gave us the chance to get rid of some of the more dangerous criminal element. We got the power to arrest people for trespassing. We created a jobs program, at first just by hiring women to "supervise" the laundry facility, and later by hiring women to do little clerical jobs for the police substation. Soon we had women who had real jobs on their résumés, and who listed me, a police lieutenant, as a reference.

We held all kinds of events. We had an Iris Court Day, where we barbecued ribs and burgers and brought in musical groups. We had an afternoon "Snack Attack" program, in which we gave the schoolchildren something healthy to eat, every day, after they came back to Iris Court. We had a huge Christmas party, and found this big black guy who was willing to wear the Santa suit. We borrowed a horse and carriage and had this guy roll up saying, "Ho ho ho!" It was the first time any of these kids had ever seen a black Santa Claus.

Little by little, things began to change. We started a day care center. We had a community health nurse come in, but no one would go see her. So she started offering to repair the children's bicycles. They'd stop by for that, and she'd fix their bikes, and talk to them, and maybe figure out which kids had head lice. Then she'd drop by their apartments and give their moms the special shampoo to treat that. Soon she was considered trustworthy. I kept trying, on the other hand, to get officers in the North Precinct to stop by and spend a little time in our substation. None of them ever did. I put in a request for a color TV and cable. I figured if I could get that, then the officers would stop by to watch football games. I was right. Soon I always had a couple of officers stopping by for their lunch breaks or dinner breaks. That made for more police presence in Iris Court, which meant more deterrence and made it possible for us to respond in force, right away, if there was a disturbance.

About seven months into this project, we had a homicide at Iris Court. A veteran homicide detective named Jim Bellah caught the case. He knew Iris Court well. He came out to begin investigating, and he couldn't believe what had happened there. He found people willing to talk to him. People were coming up to him, saying they were there the night the woman was killed, and they saw her boyfriend the night she was killed, and they'd be willing to go to court to identify him if necessary. They were participating in public safety in their own community. That was almost a first.

What I discovered was that poor people wanted safety just as much as rich people did—or even more. I discovered that it was wrong to think they were willing to live in a place that was all messed up, just because they had always lived in a place that was so messed up. Given a chance, they were eager to participate in an effort to make it better.

The Iris Court project became a nationally observed experiment in community policing. I became the guy in charge of turning this one neighborhood, in this one city, by going one citizen at a time, into a model of creative, responsible, solution-oriented police work. I'd wind up captain because of it. I'd wind up getting my Ph.D. because of it. I'd wind up on national television because of it. And a lot of citizens in Iris Court—and a thousand places like it, all over the country—would wind up having better lives because of it.

All these years later, the facilities we put in place at Iris Court are still functioning. There's even a Charles Moose Center there. I was very honored that they would name anything after me, and very proud that they did.

The city of Portland during the 1980s was a city without unity. The African-American community was disenfranchised. The gang problem, due to an influx of new violence from the Los Angeles Bloods and Crips, was becoming chronic. Hispanic immigrants, many of them poor and arriving in the city without proper work documentation, were living on the edge of poverty and outside the edge of the social fabric. The growing gay community was also outside the edge of things, too. Gay pride had become a reality, and the gay issue became a Portland issue.

Since it started in the 1980s, the annual gay pride parade had been a problem for many of Portland's more conservative citizens. It was a problem for many in the police department, too. For some of the old-guard officers, this was an affront to propriety.

When Police Chief Tom Potter started marching in the parade, in uniform, it was a real affront to some of his police officers.

Potter had several reasons to march. One of them was his daughter. She was a police officer, and she was gay. To support her, and to show his support for the gay community in general, Potter began marching. By himself. There were no other uniformed police officers with him.

The next year, he asked if anyone would go with him. By then, I was captain at the North Precinct. I didn't have any problem with the parade, or with walking in it. I thought it was important for the police to show they supported civil rights—everyone's civil rights. I wasn't making any announcements. I wasn't saying I was gay. I just knew that people of all persuasions had been victimized and subjected to violence in my city, and I thought it was important that the police department show them we would not accept their victimization. So I told Tom Potter I would march with him.

Why wouldn't I? My sister, Dorothy, had come out as a lesbian many years before. I wanted her to feel welcome in Portland, in a way that she might not ever have been welcome as an African-American lesbian living in North Carolina.

We began marching together, Dorothy in her civvies, Tom Potter and I in our uniforms.

I had no way of knowing that my decision to march in the annual gay pride parade would have any bearing on my career—except possibly a negative one—or play such an important part in my advancement within the ranks of the police department.

But it did.

Chief Potter was an immensely popular guy. He was popular within the ranks. He was very popular within the community. When he announced in late 1992 that he was going to retire, it was the end of an era.

Just as it had been a time of divisiveness in the community, the time prior to Potter's tenure had also been a time of disruptiveness in the police department. The life expectancy of the chief had been very short. I was hired onto the force in 1975, when Bruce Baker was chief.

Over the next fifteen years, I served under nine chiefs. Not one of them left the police in the usual, traditional way. None of them lasted until retirement, until Potter.

Vera Katz is a round, bubbly woman with beet red hair and bright blue eyes. She's New York Jewish and chatty—the kind of woman you wouldn't be surprised to meet running a reading group at the local library or baking pumpernickel rye bread at the local bakery. You might be surprised to find her running a city, but that's her job. She's the mayor of Portland, and she's the woman who decided, in 1993, to make me the chief of police.

She had started looking around and sizing up the candidates to replace Potter once he made his retirement announcement. It was well known that Chief Potter was pulling for Dave Williams, who was his assistant chief and whom he was clearly grooming to be his successor.

Williams and I had already crossed swords. Potter made me deputy chief, one of four deputy chiefs, which was a rank just below assistant chief, in September 1992. I was very pleased, because I would be working hand-in-hand and shoulder-to-shoulder with the chief. But suddenly I wasn't. I was taking orders from the assistant chief. I went to see Potter and complained to him that I hadn't taken the job in order to take orders from Dave Williams. I handed Potter my resignation. I had done the paperwork. I wanted to be knocked back down to captain and get another assignment. I don't like to think what would have had happened to my career if Potter had accepted my resignation. Instead, he told me to go home and cool off and come back the next day if I was still serious about this. I came back the next day and had a talk with Williams. We reorganized our relationship. I didn't resign.

There were other candidates besides Dave Williams and me. There was Joe Brand, who was chief of police in Hayward, California. There was an assistant chief from San Diego, California. It was a four-way race. Then the guy from San Diego pulled out, because he was going for the chief's job in his own department, and a guy from Spokane, Washington, was added to the mix. It was still a four-way race.

I had an edge over the other candidates, though I didn't know it at the time. Vera Katz told me, long after I became chief, that she had decided to look inside the police department for Potter's successor as a way of increasing harmony within the force. She told me she wanted a career police officer from within the force because she felt that kind of chief would have the respect of the rank-and-file officers—as previous chiefs, hired from outside the department, had not. She wanted someone who had experience with the kind of community policing that Potter had initiated in Portland. She wanted someone who had the respect of the minority communities around the city. She wanted someone who was young enough to have been a police officer, on the beat, in the not-too-distant past.

She said to me later, "I needed someone who understood the day-to-day operations of the police force, because I didn't—and I didn't intend to learn."

She also told me, later, that she was determined to try and advance African-American police officers within the department. This wasn't why she chose me, but it was an additional reason to choose me. She knew that by promoting me, the department would have better success recruiting more black officers, and she would also be making room in the upper ranks to promote younger black police officers, one of whom might be a future chief.

It became clear, within a short while, that Dave Williams and I were the two most serious candidates from within the force for the chief's job. I reckoned it was probably a dead even competition.

I knew Mayor Katz respected us both. I felt she liked us both. I felt she knew that both of us had the respect of the officers. We both had strong careers on the force.

I heard Mayor Katz was doing research. I heard she was going around, holding public forums and asking community groups—PTA groups, social organizations, fraternal organizations and business groups—what they needed to see in a police chief. She started getting a sense of what the public needed, and what they would support—and wouldn't.

I also heard she was doing research on me. I learned that she had been getting calls. Citizens were complaining. Citizens were telling the mayor to take a look inside Charles Moose's personnel files. They told her she would find things there that would convince her not to make me chief. So she pulled my files.

She found the three complaints that had been filed against me, from the three incidents in which I had lost my temper and said something in public that I shouldn't have—something that would stay in my personnel files and come back, time and time again, to haunt me.

I had no way of knowing how Mayor Katz would react to these incidents. I had no way of knowing, especially, that they would inspire in her a kind of grudging respect. What she told me later was that, as a Jew, and as a woman, she understood what had driven me to lose my temper. She told me she understood that, as a black man and a black police officer in a town like Portland, I experienced this kind of disrespect on a daily basis. She told me she understood why, from time to time, the weight of being disrespected that way would become too much for me to bear.

Years later, Mayor Katz's deputy chief of staff Elise Marshall, the liaison between the mayor's office and the police force, said to me, "The mayor was Jewish and a woman. That allowed her to see things in you that another person wouldn't have been able to see. It encouraged her to tolerate things that another person wouldn't have been able to tolerate."

I don't know if she tolerated it, but she understood it. The incidents she found in the personnel file did not influence her judgment in choosing the next police chief.

But the gay pride parade did.

Mayor Katz told me, years after the fact, that this was

the "litmus test" she used, in the end, to choose between me and Dave Williams. She took each of us aside. She asked each of us whether we'd feel comfortable marching in the annual gay pride parade, as Chief Potter had done, and whether we'd feel comfortable marching in uniform.

I told her I had already been marching, in uniform, for years. I didn't have any problem with it at all. To me, marching in the parade didn't have that much to do with gay pride or gay rights, or whether I did or didn't support gay people. To me, it was about showing my support for civil rights for all the citizens of Portland—irrespective of their sexual, racial, religious or economic orientation.

Dave Williams answered differently. He was a deeply religious man, and conservative. He told the mayor that he would not be willing to march in uniform in the parade.

This cast the deciding vote. The mayor weighed the two answers. She felt that the answers indicated one candidate who might promote more unity in her city, and one candidate who might promote more divisiveness.

One evening I got a call from the mayor's assistant. She said the mayor wanted to see me, and that I should come to this house where there was some sort of party or function. When I arrived, the mayor took me aside and we talked about one thing and another and then, very suddenly, she told me she'd made up her mind. I got the job. She had decided to name me the new police chief. She congratulated me and told me we'd make the official announcement at city hall the following morning.

I drove home. I was stunned. I wasn't even happy, really. I just couldn't believe it. I felt good, of course, but more than anything I think I felt a sense of relief. It was over. The horse race was over. This public scrutiny, this measuring up of the candidates, was over. I probably would have felt almost as much relief if she'd told me she was picking Dave Williams. At least it would have been over.

The following day we had the little ceremony at city hall. I was named chief on June 28, 1993.

One of my first acts of business, which I announced at city hall, was to ask Dave Williams to stay on as assistant chief. To his great credit, after the decision, he agreed to stay on. We were able to settle our differences and go back to work.

Having made the grade, I probably could have forgotten about completing my Ph.D. It could no longer help my career as a police officer, but I had invested too much to let it go. Even though I wasn't exactly swamped with free time after being named chief—in fact, I had zero free time, so I don't know how I did this—I continued and finished the work and presented and defended the dissertation. I received the Ph.D. in October 1993.

As police chief, I was able to start making a difference right away. I had thought about being the chief for a long time. I had a thousand ideas about how to use the job to improve the police department, how to make it more effective, how to make it more fair on the officers and the community.

I raised the entry-level hiring requirement to a four-year degree. I wanted educated men and women on the street.

I created a Crisis Intervention Team, to improve my officers' ability to recognize and respond to someone who was having a mental health breakdown. Prior to that, police officers were shooting people like this. I thought it might be better to restrain them and get them treatment than to shoot them.

Similarly, I created an awards program, called the Nathan Thomas Award—named after a young man who'd been shot by the police in a case of mistaken identity—for officers who solved crisis events with conversation instead of bullets.

I started mandating the use of beanbag shotguns, for use in situations where less lethal force was required.

I tried also to improve the situation for the police officers generally. I put a day care center on the first floor of the Justice Center downtown, to help working police personnel who had children to tend to.

I also redesigned the structure of the department. Other chiefs had fattened up the police organization at the upper levels, creating more jobs for upper management. I went the other way. I made more positions for assistant chiefs and raised the pay scale for these officers, as a way of *flattening* the organization. I wanted more responsibility, and more accountability, at a lower level.

This was part of the community policing idea. So was creating "community response teams," which I instituted to respond to community crisis events. Officer Victoria Wade had been pushing this idea for a number of years. As chief, I was able to listen to her and then help make her dream a reality.

I also moved into the community myself. I was determined to show people how to walk the walk—and not just talk the talk. To make a point, Sandy and I decided to go and live in the darkest heart of the community I was trying to serve and protect.

We had lived for two years in the "Hollywood" area, in a little frame house on Schuyler Street. Prior to that, we had lived in the suburbs, out of town, in an area called Aloha. We had bought a townhouse there, and we were facing this huge balloon payment on the mortgage, and we didn't think we could afford it. We thought we were going to have to default, when the developer offered us the chance to use our mortgage to move into a new house he was building in the development. We stayed in that new house for almost four years, until Sandy decided she hated it.

It was a nice house, but a difficult neighborhood. I was the only black guy, it felt like, for miles around. No one was unpleasant to us, but it was still weird. I remember at Christmas a neighbor who was welcoming us to the community said, "I'm so glad my son is going to grow up with diversity." I thought, "My God! Now I'm diversity!" Sandy found it stifling, she said, to be in that environment. We started looking for someplace else to call home.

We moved back into the city, into the Schuyler house, and then later into a nice one-bedroom apartment in lower Northeast Portland. Sandy was going to law school. I was trying to finish my Ph.D. We were spending a lot of time at the university. We needed fewer distractions. The apartment seemed to help us scale down and focus. I didn't need to be mowing any lawns or fixing any busted pipes.

After I made chief, we found the house at 422 N.E. Going Street. It was a two-story, 2,200-square-foot frame house built in 1911, with three bedrooms, a formal dining room with a working fireplace, a finished basement, hardwood floors and cove ceilings throughout and a wide wooden porch across the front. It had been the home of these old maid sisters, Ruth and Esther Halvorsen, who'd moved in as children, when the house was built in 1911, and lived there until they died, four days apart, in 1993.

By then, the neighborhood had turned bad. There were used hypodermic needles and condoms on the ground, and graffiti on most of the buildings. The house itself, which had sat empty for six months, was rat infested. It had an odd smell—the result, we were told, of a tenant-landlord dispute that ended with the tenant dumping over a ton of manure onto the hardwood floors in the living room.

Across the street was an elementary school and a community center, with lots of evidence of drug sales and drug use. The surrounding streets were filled with boarded-up old homes that had become crack houses.

It wasn't just drugs, either. The *Portland Oregonian* published a "Locations of Homicides in Portland" for 1993, not long after we moved in. The map identified the locations of sixty-three killings. Half of them were in Northeast Portland. A third of them were within a one-mile radius of the house we'd just moved into.

The neighborhood had, officially, the highest homicide rate in the city. It had the highest unemployment rate in the city, and the greatest number of empty and abandoned buildings.

Sandy and I decided this was the place for us to be. We wanted to make a point. We wanted to demonstrate our commitment, in a very real and physical and personal way, to the idea of community policing.

This was a neighborhood where there were black children who had literally never seen a man get up in the morning, put on his clothes and go to work, and then come home in the evening having done his job. I was Portland's first black police chief. This was a great chance for me to become a role model for these black children who had been given no positive role models at all.

We bought it for $65,000 in November 1993 and set about fixing it up. We added sixteen hundred square feet with an addition and then built a small house at the other end of the lot and rented that out.

We were pleased to be there, in that neighborhood, on that street. The whole area was so sad. It had been so depressed, for so long. We wanted to be part of the revival, to be part of the healing of the community. We wanted to set an example, and we hoped that other people would follow our example.

The example we were setting got a lot of attention. It was front-page news in the *New York Times*. There were news crews all over the street when we moved in, taking pictures of me and Sandy unloading our furniture. It created quite a stir.

But I didn't get the reaction I'd expected. I had hoped people would applaud the idea of the chief of police moving into a depressed neighborhood, as a way of showing solidarity with the community, as a way of becoming part of the solution to the problems in the community.

In fact, I got the opposite. There was graffiti in one of the precinct houses. It said, "The chief's moving in his ho' and turning her out."

A newspaper cartoon appeared, and copies of it were clipped out and hung up in precinct offices. The cartoon showed someone robbing a house, and two policemen standing by. "Look," one of them says. "There goes the chief's VCR."

Even a year later, the stigma was still there. Sandy got a telephone call early one morning. A voice said, "Nobody fucks niggers." Then the line went dead. I was out of town, at a chiefs' conference. When Sandy called the police department to file a complaint, the officer who came to the house and took the report said, "What did you expect, moving into that neighborhood like you did?"

It wasn't all easy. I had people coming to the house at all times of the night and day, asking me to fight crime for them. One lady came around several times to say her man was beating on her, and sometimes, to tell the truth, if it was the middle of the night, I didn't feel all that much like taking the case. Sandy got tired of all the work she had to do to keep the place up, too. Every two days or so she'd go into the street in front of our house with a big black trash bag and start picking up junk from the street. She'd fill a whole bag. Every once in a while, when I'd come home from work and pull my car up to the curb in front of my house, a prostitute from Martin Luther King Jr. Blvd., a block away, would come running up to the car, thinking I was pulling over for her. You could get tired of things like that after a while.

On the ground level the example we set was more successful. Neighborhood kids who never had anything to bring to show-and-tell, except that someone had been shot on their block, could now say they had the police chief living on their block. They could say they visited with the police chief.

A handful of other police officers followed my lead. One police officer I knew did buy a house not far from Going Street. He was a black officer, with a wife and five kids. The wife refused to move in, though, once she got a look at the street. She was scared. I think they sold the house without ever living in it.

*   *   *

In 1995 I was contacted by this little eleven-year-old boy who lived in my neighborhood. His name was Detrick Mans. He was a fifth-grader. His family was a nice, ordinary, working class family, struggling to get along. Detrick was a nice, ordinary kid. The thing he loved most in the world was his bike. He had a red-and-black ten-speed bike. His parents had worked hard to save the $130 to buy it. For Detrick, it was his ticket to the world. He ran around the neighborhood on it. He *ruled* the neighborhood on it.

Then it got stolen. He had parked the bike at the Matt Dishman Community Center, on N.E. Knott Street, and someone took it. He and his friends saw two boys running off with it.

Detrick was real upset. But he knew what to do. He came to me. I'd been living in the neighborhood for two years or so. Detrick later said he came to me because I was the only policeman he ever knew. I don't know if he knew I was the police chief, or if he just thought I was another cop. But he trusted me, and he came to me for help.

I told him I could help him if he had a serial number for the bike. He didn't. He and his parents still had an owner's manual, but they had no documentation. So, basically, I knew we weren't ever going to see this kid's bike again. I told Detrick there was nothing we could do.

I felt awful about it. I remembered being a kid in Lexington. I remembered how liberated I was when I got a bike. I went everywhere on it. It opened up the whole world for me and made me feel independent. My folks had been doing all right. They could have afforded to buy me a new bike if my bike had been stolen.

This kid's parents could not.

By coincidence, doing some other police work, I happened to meet with Detrick's fifth-grade teacher. I found out that seven other kids in Detrick's class didn't have bikes, either.

I got creative. I had received a $500 check from *Reader's Digest* because they had done this story about me living in a rough neighborhood in Portland, calling me a hero for moving into the heart of the community and making it my home. I didn't know what to do with the check. I didn't feel right cashing it. I hadn't done anything to earn the money. I didn't think it would be ethical for me to spend the money on myself.

But I thought I could spend it on someone else. I called these people I knew over at Fred Meyer, the big department store. I told them I'd be willing to spend my $500 on these kids at their store, if they'd be willing to match that amount in store credit. They agreed.

Detrick's teacher cooked up this idea to have a contest for the kids in her class to write essays about how they could use a bicycle to help with community policing. I visited the classroom, and I told them I wanted them to do their best, to write their essays in ink and in their best handwriting. I told them their essay should be the best work they could possibly do.

A little while later, we held an awards ceremony, and seven kids from Detrick's class—two girls and five boys, including Detrick—were presented with new bicycles.

The bike program became an annual event, held at the end of every school year. Many more children were given bicycles. When I left Portland, there was still money in the account and the program was still going strong. Community policing had opened many doors and affected many lives.

This is the kind of opportunity you have to be of service when you live in a community for a while. I had another opportunity around that time. There was a real good guy in my neighborhood, a white man named Jamie Partridge. He was my mailman, a tall, thin, pale man with an absolute passion for politics at the most basic, personal level. He was very involved with the labor movement—he was a union man, and a proud member of the National Association of Letter Carriers, AFL-CIO, Branch 82—and he was very involved with the black community. He'd lived in the Albina section for years, just a few blocks from where Sandy and I lived. He was a regular fixture at the local New Hope Missionary Baptist Church.

I'd see Jamie on his route. I'd see him at community meetings. He always had an armful of leaflets and literature. He was very involved in Jesse Jackson's Rainbow Coalition.

During this one period I started to notice that he was looking kind of worn down. His uniform, especially, was in terrible shape. The pants he was wearing were thin in the knees and there were sections around the pockets that were actually ripped and torn. So I said to him, "Jamie, you're looking kind of raggedy. What's the trouble?"

He looked sort of sheepish. He said, "We're supposed to get this clothing allowance, to pay for the uniforms, but I haven't got mine yet, and it's getting embarrassing."

I knew where Jamie bought his letter carrier pants. It was the same store that sold the police officers' uniforms. The city paid for my police uniforms whenever I needed them. But Jamie wasn't getting the same deal. So the next day, I went down there and bought Jamie a pair of letter carrier pants. They cost about $50. Next time I saw him, I pulled him aside and said, "I got you a new pair of pants. Now you don't have to look so raggedy." I knew Sandy and I wouldn't miss the money, and Jamie could spend his time doing something other than worrying about holes in his pants.

Jamie tells that story now, often enough that *I* end up being the one that's kind of embarrassed. But it's a good example of how I lived in Portland during the time I was chief. Things like that, making that kind of change, on the one-to-one, neighborhood level, were possible for me.

I wouldn't have been put in a position to do things like that if I hadn't been a police officer. I wouldn't have had the power to do things like that if I hadn't been the police chief. It's not a big thing. But they're both good examples of the kind of police work I was able to do as a result of the community policing idea, and as a result of how the community policing idea changed *my* idea of what a police officer could do.

Nobody does anything all on their own. I could not have succeeded in Portland, as a police officer, as a husband or as a human being, without the help and guidance I received from Edna Robertson.

Edna was born in Birmingham, Alabama, in 1929. She came to Portland in the 1950s and bought her house in Albina—right around the corner from where Sandy and I would live on North Going—in 1958. She raised all her children in that house. By the time I met her, she was a mother and a grandmother, and a fixture on the political scene in Northeast Portland. She was the director of the Northeast division of the Coalition of Neighborhoods. Nothing happened in Northeast without her involvement. If you were a political candidate, or a clergyman, or anyone who wanted to make anything happen in that community, you went through Edna. She was the heart and soul of Northeast.

She had been pushing for change for a long time when I met her. I was in the North Precinct. Albina was part of my territory. I started seeing Edna wherever I went. And she wasn't shy about telling me what she thought had to happen to bring about real change in her neighborhood. She wanted more black police officers. She knew that the kids who were in trouble and the kids who knew who was causing the trouble were not going to talk to white police officers. She knew they were scared of police officers. She knew that the drug dealing wouldn't stop as long as no one would talk to the police. She told me that people in her community were begging for more police involvement in these neighborhoods, but she said the kind of police involvement they got wasn't helpful. It was just cops sweeping in to arrest people or kick some ass and knock some heads. The drugs were out of control, and the gangs were out of control. Stable families were leaving. More houses were left empty, which made more territory for the gangs and the drug dealers.

When I started trying to bring the idea of community policing to bear on the Albina streets, Edna was a real supporter. And she was everywhere. When I went to any meeting, at any church or school or community center, Edna was there. She was totally committed. I guess I was pretty committed, too, because she used to say, afterward, that no police officers were ever at any of these meetings but after I started coming she never went to one that I wasn't already at. I guess we were working for exactly the same thing.

She once said to me, "When I was a little girl, I saw Klansmen with white sheets on. When I came to Portland, I saw a different racism, in the form of men with white collars on. They didn't want to hire you, didn't want to do business with you, didn't want to sell you a house. A lot of that has changed. But I never expected to live in a future where a white police chief would retire and a black police chief would get his job. Whatever else happens, I know my granddaughter will be able to say to her children, 'I knew the first black police chief in Portland. He lived on *my* street.' "

I don't believe that a police officer or a police chief or an entire police department can fight crime on their own. Most of what the police do is pick up the pieces *after* a crime has been committed. You can solve a crime. You can sometimes prevent a crime. But you can't ever have the manpower and the resources to end crime. To do that, you need the cooperation of all the city, county and federal agencies available, and you need the cooperation of all the citizens, too. Law enforcement is just one part of the formula. Part of law enforcement's job is to use the badge to inspire people to become involved in crime prevention themselves, to insist on safer streets, safer neighborhoods and a safer life for themselves and their children.

I spent a lot of time in the community working on that. I was at every community meeting I could get to. I sat in more church basements and more elementary school classrooms than I could even count. I met teachers and parents and working people. I spent an enormous amount of time meeting with kids—at-risk kids, kids in gangs, kids who'd escaped from gangs, kids who had nothing to do with gangs. And what I was trying to do with all of this was to inspire them to insist on a better and safer community—using the police force as a resource to make that happen.

There were lots of things about the department that I did not like. One of them was what I thought of as the "old boy" network of police officers who used their seniority and their relationship with other senior officers to skirt the legal or technical limits of acceptable behavior.

That was partly because of the times. Police officers were not held as accountable twenty years ago as they are today. They were not under the microscope they're under today. In the old days, an officer could get pulled over several times on suspicion of drunk driving and, unless he'd run over and killed someone, could be let off with nothing more than a warning. Officers in the old days got themselves into all kinds of trouble but were not required to pay the price that other citizens were expected to pay.

In Portland, this was evident in all kinds of ways. One of them was tragic.

There was a deputy chief at that time named Rob Aichele. He was a career police officer, an absolute straight-arrow guy—shoes always perfectly shined, short hair always perfectly combed, uniform always perfectly creased. He and I had crossed paths, unhappily, years before. During the investigation into the special investigations division (later called the drug and vice division), Aichele was very upset when I showed up for my interview with an outside lawyer. I knew I was within my rights, but he thought I should have come on my own.

Three years later, he retired. I subsequently became chief. And then tragedy struck his family.

His son, who was also a police officer, became distraught over a family matter. He was newly married and had a one-year-old child at home, and he believed his wife was about to leave him. It unhinged him. One day he shot his wife, and then shot himself, in front of the child.

The son had friends in the department. The father had friends in the department. I was brought a request that the son be buried with full honors—that the funeral be attended by the department's honor guard, with all the ceremony afforded an officer who had been killed in the line of duty.

I denied the request. I knew this was going to be an unpopular move within certain sectors of the department. But I denied the request. The man was a police officer, but the crime was murder-suicide. There was no way I could grant a request for a full honors funeral.

Word came back to me that Aichele was upset. I can understand that. I still feel I made the right decision. I had resisted the wrong kind of pressure, in order to make the right kind of decision.

Years later, I was myself on the receiving end of a similar kind of impersonal justice within the police department. When I was chief, and after I had married Sandy and begun living with her and her son, Lincoln, I was delighted to learn that Lincoln had applied for a position with the Portland police. I was so proud of him. I got all pumped up just thinking about the day I would swear him in. I was excited about all the things I could teach him, how I could help him learn to be a fine police officer. I let him know how pleased I was and how proud I would be to welcome him to the department.

Then he didn't make the cut. The decision was made not to hire him. As his stepfather, I was crushed. As the police chief, however, there was nothing I could do— not even make inquiries as to why he had been turned down, much less make any attempt to overrule the decision. I remember how tough it was that night at dinner, for both of us, for me to tell him that he was a great kid, and that it was okay for him to be something other than a police officer, and that not becoming a police officer didn't mean a thing about what kind of person he was or was going to become.

As it turned out, he ended up following more in his mother's footsteps. He went to law school, and graduated. At the time of this writing, he had taken the bar exams, and was anxiously waiting to find out whether he passed. And I'm just as proud of him now as I was the day I heard he wanted to be a police officer.

You can't find a solution without running the risk of making new problems. I learned that in Portland. I kept learning that in Montgomery County.

We had an area recently, in the community of Silver Spring, where there was a lot of money being spent on renovation. A section of the community was being restored. There was a lot of visibility on that. So I had to increase the visibility of my people there, to make it look like we were participating in the renovation, and to make the citizens feel safer about this area that was being restored.

That's fine. But moving the manpower there meant taking manpower away from somewhere else. In order to put officers there, I had to take them away from work they were already doing.

If there is a trouble spot, for example, you're going to want to concentrate some officers there until you make the trouble go away. You're going to need your narcotics people available. You may need your SWAT people. You may need to send in the DARE (Drug Abuse Resistance Education) team.

You run the risk that while they're on duty preventing crime, there will be actual crimes committed someplace else that they should have been.

Or something else can go wrong. In Portland, we made a strong effort to clean up crime in an area known as Old Town. We sent specialized units there, to make a really concerted effort to step up the numbers of arrests there, to become really aggressive about stopping crime in that area.

It worked. But six months after I left Portland, it became a scandal. It came out that a lot of the officers making all those arrests had actually not been working full shifts. They were making arrests, but they were getting paid for time they were not actually putting in. This all got into the newspapers and made everybody look real bad for a while. It didn't mean the policing plan was a bad one. In fact, the policing plan had been very successful. But at the command and control level, the exercise had been something of a failure.

What I've tried to institute, in Portland and in Montgomery County, is something like what's been called the "broken window" approach—the kind of holistic police approach that says everything that's wrong with a community needs to be addressed aggressively. The idea here is that you don't want to let anyone get the impression that law breaking of any kind is going to be tolerated. One broken window not repaired might give someone the impression that no one cares about broken windows in the community. That might make someone think no one cares about graffiti. If there's graffiti, that might make someone think no one cares about drug sales. And if there's drug sales, that might make someone think no one cares about burglary or robbery. And so on.

Addressing the problem requires a lot more than just cops. It requires the participation of every agency available. You can't just go in and start arresting everyone in sight and hope that every criminal or would-be criminal is going to suddenly go straight. This kind of holistic approach requires the participation of the entire community.

You have to get the Department of Sanitation to get all the garbage off the streets. You have to make sure the Bureau of Street Maintenance fills in the potholes and keeps the lines painted on the streets and replaces all the burned-out streetlights as soon as they're burned out.

You have to create after-school programs so that bored teenagers have someplace to go and something to do.

You have to send DARE teams into the schools so that at-risk kids learn what drugs and alcohol will really do to them.

You have to get police officers to attend PTA meetings, so the community knows the police are available to them.

You may need housing revitalization, to create more affordable housing for poor people in the community.

You may need the cooperation of local judges, to get them to understand that they're going to have to start sentencing people to maximum terms if they're going to keep them from creating more crime in the community.

You have to get the authorities to move in on the public housing areas, to make sure no one is living there that shouldn't be living there.

You have to get the probation department to move in on the area, too, to make sure there are no parole violators on the street.

You have to do everything you can do to counteract the problem of passive law enforcement—the kind of policing that only comes in after the fact, to clean up the problem that has already happened. You have to let the people in the community know that someone is watching, and that someone cares.

What we saw in Portland, and what I've seen in some neighborhoods in Montgomery County, is a kind of "halo effect." One neighborhood starts to clean up, and then the adjacent neighborhood starts to want to look like that, too. An entire area will change its expectations, and its tolerance. Soon there are whole sections of the city that are fundamentally unfriendly to criminals.

But you can't make changes without making enemies. I learned that, in Portland, coming up the ladder from police officer to police chief. It is not an exaggeration to say I had a lot of conflict coming up.

When I was a young officer, I felt I was not being given a fair chance at promotion. There were several of us in the department, all minorities, that felt that way. The problem was the promotion process. The decision to promote was made by people who had no training in the process, and who came from places that lacked any kind of diversity. They had worked on small-town police forces that had never had a black officer. So they were not inclined to recommend black officers for promotion.

I knew there was no one in the department for me to go to. I had become friends with Penny Harrington, the very strong woman who hired me to work in personnel and was a great mentor to me over the years. But Penny was fighting her own fight, as a female officer trying to get ahead.

So I went outside the department. A group of us took our complaint to Ron Herndon.

At that time Ron was the head of the Black United Front. He disliked the police. No one was more vocal about disliking the police than he was. If you asked the citizens of Portland, "Who dislikes the police more than anyone alive?" they would all tell you it was Ron Herndon. So for us police officers to go to him for guidance was kind of outrageous. But it was the only place we could go to discuss racism in the police department.

Remember, I was trying at that time to become a lieutenant. There had never been a black lieutenant in the Portland police. I would become the first one—and the first black captain, and the first black deputy chief, and the first black chief. And there was no reason to believe at that time that I would ever become even a lieutenant.

The result was change. We didn't file lawsuits, but our complaints resulted in some promotions being thrown out and the promotion process getting overhauled. People who made promotion recommendations after that had to be trained in the process, and to come from backgrounds where there was some diversity. This gave everyone a much fairer chance.

But it also gave me the reputation for being a troublemaker.

The reputation continued.

When you became sergeant in Portland, they made you go for two weeks to the police academy at Monmouth, Oregon. Most of the education was very basic, because most of it was geared toward police officers from the more rural parts of the state. Very few of them had been to college. None of them had advanced degrees. So I knew if I wanted to learn about how to be a police administrator—to learn about budgets and supervising and management—I'd have to go somewhere else, which is why I started taking classes in public administration at Portland State University.

When you make lieutenant, you're supposed to go back to the academy for another two weeks. But I learned that because of the classes I was taking at Portland State, I could avoid this. I could file some paperwork and get a waiver. I could spend that two weeks doing police work in Portland, instead of getting paid to sit in a classroom in Monmouth being taught things I already knew. I thought this was a pretty smart plan.

My supervisor didn't. His name was Wayne Inman. When he found out what I'd done, and that I'd sent my paperwork directly to Monmouth without going through his office, he was furious. I thought he'd be happy to have me on the streets for those two weeks, but he was angry because I hadn't gone through proper channels. He called me on the carpet and chewed me out.

I got a lot of that.

After I made lieutenant, I was assigned to the North Precinct again, and I decided to do something about The Burger Barn, the place on Union Avenue where those white officers had gotten into trouble for laying the bodies of dead possums on the front door. It was a sensitive location, for that reason and many other reasons, all of them concerning race and crime.

But it was also a location where there was a lot of crime being committed. So I came up with a plan.

I went in there one night with another officer, Sergeant Larry Kanzler. There was drug activity and gambling and illegal alcohol sales. We were in uniform, so the folks there knew who we were. We asked to see the owner or the manager, whoever was in charge.

No one stepped up. No one would admit to being the owner or the manager. So I said, "If there is no owner or manager here, I have to assume you are all on the premises illegally. I am closing this location down."

I had everyone run out of there, and I had the place boarded up, pending notification of the owner or manager.

Captain Potter was outraged. He was convinced there would be an outcry from the black community. He thought there would be an uproar. I had gone and caused trouble in this sensitive area, and I hadn't asked his permission first. He called me in and chewed me out.

I told him I was sorry. I asked his forgiveness. I went back to doing my police work.

Two months later, The Burger Barn was open again. I went in there again, and I saw the same illegal activity going on, again. I asked to see the owner or the manager, and of course no one would admit to being the owner or the manager, so once again I had everyone thrown out and I got the place boarded up.

Tom Potter called me into his office again. He chewed me out again. I said, "I'm a police officer. I'm a police lieutenant. This is the area I'm supposed to be policing. I went in there. I saw all that illegal activity. What am I supposed to do, if I'm not supposed to stop that illegal activity?"

He was very angry. He didn't understand, maybe, that the climate in the North Precinct was changing, and that the expectations of the black community were changing, too. The residents of Albina wanted this place closed. He may not have understood that.

A couple of months earlier I had been accepted at the

national police academy, run by the Federal Bureau of Investigation. This was very prestigious, and it was a big honor to be invited to attend. This was a program designed for police officers with a big future. The department only sent the officers it wanted to promote and encourage—the best of the best.

I was due to leave in a couple of weeks. Tom Potter told me, "Just stay home. Don't bother coming in. Go do your thing at the FBI. But when you come back, you don't have a job. I don't want you in my precinct."

Most of the guys I met at the national academy had exciting things waiting for them back home. They were all due for promotions and interesting assignments when they got back. They'd say, "My chief's got me doing this. My captain's got me doing that." Me, I didn't even have a captain. All I could say was "I don't know if I've even got a job when I get back."

Not too long after that, Tom Potter was named police chief. I figured my future as a Portland police officer was pretty much over.

But all of this stuff was ultimately helpful to me. Wayne Inman, later on, asked me to join him in his precinct. And Tom Potter, later on, made me a captain and a deputy chief. I succeeded him as chief of police. The difficulties I had with these two men only made me focus more on my police work. They made me work harder to be a better police officer. And the experiences taught me a lot about managing talent, about being a boss. They taught me that you put your personal feelings aside, and you go to the bench for the best material when you need help, regardless of whether you like someone or not.

For several years, during the time I was a lieutenant and a captain, I was convinced that I had no real future in the Portland Police Bureau. I started looking for work somewhere else. I knew I was going to stay in law enforcement. I knew I wanted to be a police chief. But I couldn't seem to get a police chief's job.

I tried, though. I went up for a job as chief of police

in Gresham, Oregon. I didn't get it. Then I went up for a job as chief of police in Jackson, Mississippi. I almost got it. I looked at other jobs, and made inquiries, and tried to figure out what my future was. Then Chief Potter resigned and I was named chief of police in Portland.

I was chief for just over six years. I wasn't looking to get out. I wasn't really looking to move. But I was looking, as I had always been looking, to get ahead. I was in a weird financial bind in Portland. The city government had a rule about salaries. The head of the police department couldn't be paid more than the head of the fire department. I don't know who makes up rules like that, but this one seemed ridiculous to me. I don't want to take anything away from the fire department—the men and women of the fire department are real-life heroes—but running the fire department is not the same as running the police department. I felt strongly that I deserved more money. I made it clear to the mayor that I was willing to change jobs to get more money, if that's what it took. This wasn't a hollow threat. I was serious. I was making $103,000 a year. I knew what my colleagues were making in other cities the size of Portland. I thought I deserved what they were getting.

I also had this idea, for several years, that one day I might want to try being a police chief in an east coast city. Law enforcement is handled differently from one place to another. I knew what the west coast was like. I wanted to see what the other side was like. I wanted that on my résumé, too. I felt that if I was ever going to be in line for the big police chief jobs—Los Angeles, say, and New York—I'd look like a better candidate if I hadn't been the police chief of only one city.

I also had a weird notion that somehow I'd lucked into the breaks I'd gotten in Portland, and I wondered if I could cut it in a different environment. I wondered if I'd be good enough to make it in another city, if I'd be ready to be chief in Los Angeles or New York, if I was ever offered a job like that.

When the people from Montgomery County came

calling, they got my attention pretty fast. For one thing, they had deep pockets. In Portland I was stuck at $103,000. I was told there was no more money for me there, period. In Montgomery County, I would start at $120,000. Within two years, if I stayed on the job, my salary would rise to $160,000. This was quite an inducement.

I sat down with Sandy. We weighed the pros and the cons. We looked at all the angles we could think of. And then we made the decision. I said yes.

We put our house on Going Street up for rent. We packed everything up and made the move. There were some going-away parties. There was an event at Iris Court that I found very moving. You couldn't park your car for three blocks in any direction, there were so many people there. I felt really appreciated, and loved, and for a minute or two I was sorry to go.

Later I found out my successor as chief of police in Portland started at a salary of $130,000—$27,000 a year more than the top dollar that was ever going to be available to me. Funny how that works.

By then I was living in Maryland.

9. We're Just One Tip Away

The sniper had left a clue—a four-page, handwritten note, inside a plastic bag, tacked to a tree outside the Ponderosa shooting location. Investigators found it more than sixteen hours after the shooting at the restaurant. Following strict guidelines for evidence, they had it bagged up and taken immediately to the FBI lab in Richmond, Virginia.

I was in my office all that Sunday morning, waiting. Gary Bald was in the JOC. John King, who was covering the weekend shift for Barney Forsythe, was the one who took the call from the FBI lab. He told the lab to hold while he got Gary Bald on the line. The two of them listened as the contents of the note were read to them. John King took notes. He later remembered thinking that, since the incident with the tarot card had turned out so ugly, he would probably have to commit the contents of the note to memory and destroy his own notes, in order to prevent any leak of the sniper's message.

When they'd heard the entire message, John King asked Gary Bald to meet him in my office. King got there first. He told me they'd heard from the FBI lab. He didn't tell me what the note said. He only told me, "We have the news from the lab," and added that Gary

Bald was coming directly over. He waited until we were together before telling me anything about the note itself. This is how careful and methodical we were in our behavior concerning evidence. We didn't want to mess anything up in the slightest way. Everything had to be done strictly by the book.

King said later that I sat poker-faced while he read the contents of the sniper's message from the notes he'd written down.

The note began as the previous one had: "For you, Mr. Police, Call me God." It continued with a complaint: "We have tried to contact you to start negotiation." The sniper, speaking to us through his note, indicated he had made several attempts to reach the task force by telephone, to begin a negotiation. He made reference to having spoken with an Officer Derick and a "Priest at Ashland." The note said the police dismissed these calls as "a hoax or a joke."

The sniper backed up his offer of a "negotiation" with a threat: "If stopping the killing is more important than catching us now, you will accept our demand which are non-negotiable."

The sniper's non-negotiable demand was for money. The sniper wanted $10 million. He included in the note the number for a Bank of America Platinum Visa account credit card, and its PIN code, expiration date and name and "Member Since . . ." information. (We would discover shortly that the card had been stolen from some people on a bus trip in Arizona.) The sniper wanted the card activated, and he wanted $10 million issued to it, so he could withdraw the money from ATMs.

The note also contained several threats. It said, "Try to catch us withdrawing at least you will have less body bags," which I found a little unclear. Then it said, "If trying to catch us now more important then prepare you body bags."

The note added, "If we give you our word that is what takes place. 'Word is Bond.' "

There was a P.S. The final note, written on a page dotted with bright stars, said, "Do not release to Press" and "Your children are not safe anywhere at any time."

There were several references in the note to "us" and "we." For the first time, we had some evidence to support our suspicions that the sniper killings had been the work of more than one person. We had considered it likely for some time that one person was doing the shooting and another the driving. We thought that might explain how the killer was able to so consistently hit a target and then escape the area quickly, without being detected.

The discovery of the note was a very dramatic and exciting development. For the first time, we had a motive. We knew what the killing was about. We knew what the killer wanted. We had the beginning of a real negotiation.

We also had some problems. The note insisted that we comply by 9:00 Monday morning. We were to wait for further instructions. The snipers would call us, at a pay phone located inside the Ponderosa Steakhouse, at 6:00 the next morning. They gave us the number for the pay phone.

That presented several problems. First, the Ponderosa wasn't open at 6 A.M. on a Sunday. Second, the phone number they gave us was the wrong number—it was one digit off, so it wasn't going to ring at the pay phone in the Ponderosa anyway. Third, it was already after 6 A.M. on Sunday by the time the note was found, handled and properly secured, brought back to the JOC and analyzed.

There was no avoiding the last part. It would have been the worst kind of police work to rip the bag open and read the note and try to comply with the snipers' demands. Everything had moved according to proper procedures. By the time we located the phone and figured out it was the wrong number and realized the Ponderosa was closed, it was after 8:00 Sunday morning.

That wasn't so bad. I was not too worried about having missed the deadline. If they were communicating with us now, they would be ready to communicate some more. We could speak to them through the media. We could tell them that we wanted to talk to them, and that the number they gave us was no good, or something. That was all manageable.

The threat was manageable, too. The sniper wanted me to know the children were not safe. Maybe he'd seen me on TV, with a tear rolling down my cheek. He knew how powerful that was, killing a kid. So the sniper was repeating that threat.

Well, guess what? This wasn't new information. He had demonstrated already that no one was safe. He had shot women and children, old people and young people, black people and white people. I didn't think it was significant that he was telling me about children not being safe. I knew that. I knew that no one was safe.

But the money thing . . .

I have to admit it hit me hard. It really upset me that, after all, this was about money. I don't know what I'd expected, exactly. I don't know whether some other motive would have seemed better. But the fact that it was about money, that it was a demand for $10 million—it just disgusted me.

I mean, if we were going to give someone $10 million to stop killing people, we'd give it after one person was killed. They already had our attention after the first shooting, or the second. Certainly after the six people were murdered on October 2 and 3, they had our attention. They did not need to shoot twelve people. They did not need to shoot a kid.

I was really angry. It was so insulting, somehow, that they were doing this for money. To kill all these innocent people, for money? To terrify the entire area, and to ruin all of these lives, just for money? For no greater thing, even, than $10 million.

It also enraged me that the sniper said in the note that the "incompitence" of the task force, and our failure to respond to his earlier telephone calls, has resulted in the loss of five lives.

The note said, in part:

"We have tried to contact you to start negotiation. But the incompitence [sic] of your forces in (i) Montgomery Police 'Officer Derick' at 240-773-5000, (ii) Rockville Police Dept. 'female officer' at 301-309-3100, (iii) Task Force 'FBI' 'female' at 1888-324-8800 (four times), (iv) Priest at Ashland, (v) CNN Washington, D.C., at 202-898-7900. These people took of calls for a Hoax or Joke, so your failure to respond has cost you five lives."

I wondered whether that meant the sniper would have been happy to stop shooting at some point. Assuming that the sniper expected the victim at the Ponderosa to die, did that mean all of the shootings after October 3 were extra? Did it mean that the fatal shootings of Linda Franklin, Kenneth Bridges, Dean Harold Meyers and Pascal Charlot, and perhaps the nonfatal shootings of the woman outside the Michael's store and the thirteen-year-old boy outside the school, were the result of the sniper's impatience to issue his demand?

Maybe he couldn't count any better than he spelled. Maybe he meant something different.

Despite these feelings, the note gave us some extremely positive leads to chase down. The note did not lead us directly to the sniper. But it certainly led us to some very strong investigative leads. We now had work to do.

The first job was to find "Officer Derick." Then we'd try to find out what we could about a "Priest at Ashland."

Finding "Derick" was easy. Because of all the work I had done with the media office, I was able to identify this person as Derek Baliles, one of Montgomery County's own police officers. We found him right away and found out what he'd been told.

A call had come through on the hot line, or maybe directly into the media office, two days earlier, on October 18—the day before the Ponderosa shooting. Officer Baliles had listened while a man talked about how he'd been trying to get through, how frustrated he was that the police wouldn't talk to him. The call lasted more than three minutes. The caller said he'd been required to shoot extra people because the police wouldn't talk to him. He said something about events that had taken place in Montgomery, Alabama. He yelled at Baliles about the incompetence of the investigators and said, "Don't you know who you're dealing with?" He said more people were going to die if the police wouldn't talk to him.

Baliles made notes. He followed procedure. He wrote up an extensive report. He didn't necessarily dismiss the call as a hoax, as the snipers had said in their note. But he didn't assign it top priority, either.

The load of calls had been overwhelming. As of October 18, according to an FBI log, the FBI tip line had received 59,997 calls. According to the same memo, the Rapid Start computer program used to cross-reference and tabulate leads had chewed through 15,293 solid leads. These had been broken down, as per the Rapid Start program, into "Routine," "Priority" and "Immediate" categories. More than 60 percent of them, by category, had been cleared—which meant, as a practical matter, that as of October 18 the task force was still investigating more than seven thousand active leads. Of those, about five thousand were classified as "Routine." That meant close to two thousand of them were considered either "Priority" or "Immediate" in urgency.

We had been getting lots of hoax calls. We had people calling who were clearly mentally ill. We had people calling to confess on an almost daily basis. Sometimes they sounded drunk or high. Sometimes they sounded like they were joking. Sometimes they'd call and say they'd just seen a white van driven suspiciously by a guy with a Bushmaster rifle in his hand. Then they'd say they were calling from California. With the volume of calls, and the wild nature of so many of the calls, I'm not surprised that Officer Baliles didn't realize he had the sniper on the line.

There was another call that I wish we had been clearer on, too. Earlier in the week, a dispatcher at the Rockville City Police Department—not the Montgomery County Police Department, and not the task force, but the tiny Rockville PD—got a call from someone who was talking very cryptically about the sniper killings.

The dispatcher listened for a minute. Then she said, "I am not able to help you, sir. I need to forward your call to the hot line."

She was just a one-person shop at the switchboard. She took all the calls, and routed all the calls, and did all the dispatching of the police units. She was doing exactly what she should have been doing—referring this call to the task force's hot line.

But the person on the other end of the line got frustrated and hung up. Maybe the person suspected a trap, or thought we were going to be able to trace the call. It wasn't anything like that. It was just an overworked, understaffed dispatcher trying to forward the call to someone who could adequately handle it.

It was gone before it ever got to that kind of person.

The information contained in the note about a priest in Ashland wasn't much to go on, but it was a good place to start. We dispatched investigators to start working that. We figured the sniper was probably referring to Ashland, Virginia—not Ashland, Oregon, or any other of the dozens of Ashlands there are around the country—because the Ponderosa shooting, where we had found the note, had taken place near that city. We figured there couldn't be that many priests in Ashland, Virginia. I don't remember how many investigators we assigned.

It wasn't long before they turned up something solid. They found the priest.

Monsignor William Sullivan, the pastor of St. Ann's Church in Ashland, told investigators that he had received this strange, garbled telephone call from someone who identified himself as "God" and claimed to be the sniper. The investigators, who arrived at St. Ann's during morning mass on Sunday, had to wait for the monsignor to finish conducting the service. Then the priest told them what he knew. The call had come in on Friday, the day before the Ponderosa shooting. The caller said to the priest, "I am God," and told the priest to write down a message for the police. He repeatedly mentioned Montgomery, Alabama.

The monsignor had not called police, as the caller had instructed. He dismissed the call as a hoax, or the work of a deranged person. Now, two days after the call had come in, he was telling the investigators everything he remembered about the conversation.

Back at the JOC, Gary Bald and Mike Bouchard and I were trying to figure out how we could communicate with the snipers again, and what we were going to say. Obviously a big piece of the puzzle was the money piece.

On one hand, the fact that the snipers had made a ransom demand was a good thing. I was disgusted that it was just a money thing, but it cleared up some of my concerns about why someone would be doing these killings. Now I knew I was dealing with a criminal. That was better than some of the other alternatives I had considered. There were moments when I thought the shooting would turn out to be the work of terrorists. Now I knew it was one person, or two, and that they had killed for money. That meant we had a chance to catch them.

But the ransom money had problems. By the end of the day on Sunday we had determined that the sixteen-digit Bank Of America credit card and the pin number mentioned in the Ponderosa note belonged to a stolen credit card. When it was reported stolen, it was deactivated. For several hours on Sunday we were told that the card could not be reactivated. Then, much later, we were told that the card *could* be reactivated, but that once it was reactivated there would be no way of instantaneously tracing where and when it was being used.

This didn't make any sense to me. But the experts were sure about it. We could conceivably put $10 million into that credit card account, and the money could conceivably be withdrawn from ATMs around the country—or maybe around the world—without our knowing for at least a couple of minutes. This was what the sniper had requested in the Ponderosa note. "We will have unlimited withdrawal at any ATM worldwide," the note had said. By the time we would find out where, they could be long gone with the money.

Giving them the money that way was not an option.

The surprising thing, to me, was that raising the money was an option at all. At the local police level, it could not have been considered. We would never have had access to that sum of money. Even pretending to discuss it with a criminal as a ransom amount wouldn't begin to happen. With the federal assistance we were getting in Montgomery County, though, no one ever said, "We can't do that." Everything continued to be possible. Everyone continued to have an open mind.

It wasn't immediately clear how we were to continue. We considered putting the $10 million into the account as requested. Then we'd monitor all the ATMs in the area by stationing detectives nearby. As soon as the card popped up electronically, we'd swoop down and the posse would grab the person using it. Maybe we could be sure to limit the amount that could be withdrawn at any given time, the way it is for most ATM cards. That would give us more than one chance to get the posse on them. It would take several tries for them to get any substantial amount of money—unless of course they had figured out some way to have multiple people withdraw smaller amounts all at the same time, at multiple locations. We didn't think we were dealing with someone as sophisticated as that, with that kind of systematic teamwork approach, but for now we weren't ruling that out, either.

Depositing any amount of money now looked less possible. If we couldn't track the card within seconds of the withdrawal, we couldn't go forward with the deposit. We had to find a way to communicate with the sniper, without telling the media what we were doing—because we were still sensitive to the sniper's insistence that we not inform the media of the communication we had received. "Do not release to Press," the sniper had written on his note.

But we knew we needed the media, in order to communicate with the sniper and in order to continue to ask the public for help. As Mike Bouchard repeatedly reminded me and the other members of the task force, "We're just one tip away here. Just one call, from just one citizen, could be the one that leads us directly to the person responsible for this."

We started by putting out the message that we had not been able to receive calls at the number the sniper suggested, at the time the sniper suggested. I went out to do a press briefing, and I said, "To the person who left us a message at the Ponderosa Saturday night, you gave us a telephone number. We do want to talk to you. Call us at the number you provided."

On Sunday we had determined that we could get the telephone company to reroute the number we'd been given, for the pay phone inside the Ponderosa Steakhouse, to a location within police headquarters or the JOC. (Actually, we had to fix that, sort of. The number the snipers had given us wasn't even the number of the Ponderosa pay phone. They had gotten it wrong by one digit.)

There were two reasons for this. One of them was *not*, as was later suggested, that I could answer the call personally without having to leave my desk. I had no intention of answering any calls from the snipers.

The reasons were to prevent any of our officers from becoming targets—and getting shot while answering a pay phone at a predetermined location—and to make sure that the person who answered the phone and took that call was a trained negotiator who had knowledge and experience of how to talk to someone who was demanding $10 million and threatening to kill more people if he didn't get it.

So we made that electronic arrangement. We wired it so the phone would ring in the JOC. We had negotiators standing by.

This was one of the few areas where we found friction on the task force. The negotiators and the profilers did not agree on how we should communicate with the snipers. The negotiators, who were a mix of FBI and ATF people, were hard-liners. They wanted us to be very firm, very tough and very strict with the snipers. They encouraged us to be much more confrontational, to call the snipers out. The profilers, who were all FBI people, took the opposite approach. They thought we should be gentler, and smoother, and more approachable, and encourage more communication. They wanted to message to be "Let's talk, let's keep talking, we can talk about this . . ."

At one point, the negotiators had prepared a memo detailing exactly how we were supposed to talk to the snipers in the next communication. It had been reviewed and signed off on by the profilers—which surprised me, because the language was very tough. So, for some reason, someone called the lead profiler to double-check. It turned out the profilers had gone home for the day, hours before they were supposed to have signed off on the memo. They hadn't even seen it.

I mention this only because it's a very rare example of disharmony on the task force. It wasn't a big deal, and I'm sure it was the result of some innocent miscommunication, but it stood out as an unusual moment.

By Monday morning, we felt like we were in a position to respond quickly when the snipers called again. And we did. And it blew up in our faces.

We did not have sufficient manpower to stake out every public telephone in the target area. First of all, we didn't know how big the target area was. The snipers had shown an ability to move about very freely. Nevertheless, we figured they would want to call from somewhere in the general Ashland, Virginia, area. We pinpointed the location of all the pay phones and mapped them out. We had a huge number of police officers and task force members standing by. They weren't exactly staking out the telephones. They were waiting in places where they could swoop in on a location once it had been determined that the call was coming in to the special number we had set up.

We had experienced some uneasy relations with the Richmond area police already. As this event began to unfold, the people down there indicated that they were going to make this part of the investigation happen alone, without our assistance. They said we had talked to the media too much. Now that the action had moved into their jurisdiction, they were going to take care of this thing on their own, and solve it on their own.

It wasn't because they were glory seekers, or snobs. I don't know if it was because of the North-South, white-black thing either. Some people have suggested that— that this was a bunch of good ol' boy white Southern police who didn't trust a black Northern police chief to solve a crime on his own.

I don't know about that. I think they were just feeling confident and convinced that they were good enough to handle this on their own and bring the case to a close. This happens because police officers are good people, who are serious about what they do for a living, and who want to do the right thing.

I was in my office in Rockville, Maryland, when we got the call that an arrest was about to take place. The Virginia branch coming in to the task force, operating out of Richmond, had locked down the number and pinpointed the location of a call coming in to the special 800 number. They were moving in.

But the Rockville branch of the task force, operating out of the JOC, had somehow *not* locked down the number or pinpointed the call. Something was wrong.

The dragnet closed. At an Exxon gas station in Richmond, police officers armed with assault rifles descended upon a pay phone and a white Plymouth Voyager van parked beside it. They apprehended two men and took them into custody.

It had taken long enough to set up that the media was on it, too. The scene ran on TV over and over as a massive show of force descending on these two confused-looking men in a white van.

I watched this play out from my office, and I said, "It's not them."

I don't know why I knew, but it just didn't feel right. It was too easy, and there had been the problem of the two task forces not agreeing about whether the sniper was on the phone to the hot line, and the time frame was wrong. It had taken a while to get the assault team to the phone booth. Would these guys still be chatting away? It didn't make sense.

I later found out that there were several phone booths at the location. It appears that one of the snipers made a phone call to the hot line, then hung up and walked away.

The assault team arrived on the scene, saw the white van, saw a man talking on a phone next to the white van, and put two and two together. They came down with both feet and got the wrong guy—while the right guy, the sniper, watched from across the street.

The assault team, meanwhile, carted these two suspects off and towed away their white van for study. In Rockville, we were getting word that the suspect in the phone booth had been on that call for quite a while and had been talking to a woman. We knew for sure that he hadn't been talking to anyone from the negotiators team in the JOC.

So even as the media was reporting that the sniper might have been caught, we knew they were the wrong guys.

The two men caught in this ambush were illegal immigrants, it turned out. One was from Mexico and one was from Guatemala. They were turned over to the Immigration and Naturalization Service. They were later deported.

I didn't sit in on the decision to deport these guys. I would have argued against it, if only because we were asking people to help us with this case. Some of the people who knew about it, maybe the person who knew the most about it, might be illegal aliens. How could we ask them to come forward with information if they knew they might get deported? We had to send out a special message that said we would not deport anyone who came forward with information. In fact, as damage control, we promised we would help speed up the green card and other naturalization paperwork for anyone who came forward with helpful information—as a kind of reward for any hesistant illegals.

I am not sure exactly what happened with the phone call. I wasn't on the scene. I am not sure whether we responded too quickly, too slowly or with too great a show of force. But we missed.

Much later, we learned that the snipers were actually within spitting distance of the Exxon station. They watched the swoop of squad cars, uniformed officers and the SWAT team come down on the two laborers. They had made their phone call and slipped into the shadows before we were able to get there. One report I heard said that one of the snipers had made the telephone call, hung up, stepped across the street to buy a candy bar and was standing on the sidewalk eating it when the task force arrived. He stood and watched as the two unfortunate illegal aliens were arrested.

Worse, they had not been clear in the very brief telephone communication they'd had with the negotiators on our end just before all the activity in Richmond had gone down. Once again we were frustrated in our attempt to converse with the snipers.

Later that day, I had to go back out in front of the media and issue another cryptic message to the sniper, via the press. I said, "The person you called could not hear everything that you said . . . The audio was unclear and we want to get everything right. Call us back so that we can clearly understand."

We felt we were getting closer to a resolution, but as I recall that Monday it was an exhausting day. It had been, at this point, almost three weeks of a very intense manhunt. The first Montgomery County victim had been gunned down on the night of Wednesday, October 2. Now it was the evening of Monday, October 21.

We had all been running on adrenaline, but we were all running ragged by now. I was only averaging four hours of sleep a night. I wasn't eating right. I wasn't getting any exercise, of course. I imagine the same was true for everyone else on the task force. We had tried hard to make sure the police officers were all being rotated in the most humane way possible, so that all of them were getting plenty of time to rest, to see their families, to blow off steam, or whatever. But everyone was worn and beat by now.

With every day that passed—and some days with every hour that passed—I could feel the weight of the case a little heavier. I could feel the county, and after a while the entire district and even the entire country, looking for a resolution.

We had seen the growing impatience. We had felt it. Sergeant Tony Emanuel was one of the people answering the phone calls from citizens who wanted to get a message to the chief of police. Early on, he had said to me, "This county is full of constituents that only experience life on the TV miniseries time frame. If this case isn't solved in two hours, with time out for commercials, it's going to take too long."

The first week the overall tone of the messages he received was "You're doing a great job" and "We love Chief Moose." The second week, the message was "Hang in there" and "You can do it, Chief Moose." The third week, the message was "What the hell is going on?" and "Why can't you catch this guy, Chief Moose?"

I figured we had one more week before people started saying, "Dump Chief Moose."

As the days passed, though, I kept on not having anything of real substance to say to them. I often thought during this period, *This is probably the last job I'll have in law enforcement.*

My personal life during this time was—I didn't have any personal life. I just stopped doing everything. Sandy and I didn't socialize. We didn't go to any movies. We didn't go to any restaurants. When I got home each night, it was too late and I was too tired to participate in anything. I didn't pay any bills, or wash any laundry, or buy any groceries. I usually had the energy for a brief recap of the day's events. Sandy would give me a brief recap of her day, and sometimes summarize for me things she had seen on the news or read in the papers.

She was very good about not asking me to say more than I wanted to say. She understands the job of the police officer's wife. I was not under any pressure from her, because I know she knows this is the deal she bought into when we got married.

When something happens, whether it's twenty-two days or twenty-two months, it means we don't go on vacation, or we come home early from vacation, or we stop going out and we stop doing things. She just doesn't see me. That's part of the contract.

For my side of the deal, I never come home wearing my uniform. I leave the house wearing street clothes, and I come home that way. This is my way of saying that I might be the boss when I'm at work but I am a partner when I'm at home.

It's damned inconvenient, too, sometimes. Even if I finish the day right by my house, I have to drive back to the station and change before I come home. This can add twenty or thirty minutes to my day some days. But that's the deal.

In Portland, when we established this rule, it was easier. Portland didn't have take-home cars. You had to go back to the station at the end of the shift to turn in the vehicle. In Montgomery County, though, officers drive home the cars they drive at work. Especially the chief. So there's no reason many days for me to go back to the station at all. But I go back, no matter what hour it is, and I make sure I come back through the door wearing street clothes.

Sandy did have a lot of useful advice for me during that time, especially as regarding my relations with the media. She could see me in the press briefings. She could hear what I wasn't saying, and she knew how frustrated and angry I was getting. She told me, "They have a job to do, and they're not going to stop doing it. You can't make them go away. Be respectful. Take your time. Answer their questions. Don't get frustrated. Remember that you're talking to the media, but you're also talking to the perpetrators, and you're talking to your police officers, and you're talking to the community at the same time. Think about them."

This was very helpful. I like to think I don't need advice, or guidance, or support. But of course I do. I lose my perspective when things are tough. I remember once telling my friend Bob Lamb, when I was frustrated with things in Portland, that I was going to tell my employers to take their job and shove it. I was going to quit. He said, "You're not going to quit. You're not going to tell them to shove it. Because if you did that, you'd be saying 'screw you' to everyone who sacrificed to make it possible for you to have the job you have today. There's a lot of people that came before you. Do you want to tell all of them to shove it, too?" Sandy helped me remember where I was and who I was and what I was really trying to do during this crisis.

She was also my substitute teacher in the classroom. I think it might have been that Monday, October 21, that she went out to Montgomery County to administer the midterm exam to the criminology class I teach there. It was the first week I missed—the only class I missed—and that night I felt like I could have her there and take the evening off to stay on top of the sniper investigation. This is only one more example of how she sacrificed, along with everyone else, during the siege.

I saw even less of my son, David. He was busy with his schoolwork and his classes at Howard University. We talked only briefly, if we talked at all. One night he shared with me his own personal plan for not getting shot while filling up at the gas station. It had something to do with putting the nozzle in the tank, then running in a zigzag pattern to the cashier, and then running in a zigzag pattern back and crouching beside the car. I didn't want to tell him this wasn't going to protect him. The sniper, with a scope, even at a distance, didn't need all that much time for target acquisition. He didn't need his victims to be standing perfectly still in order to hurt them. But I was proud of David that he cooked up this plan and implemented it—rather than be paralyzed with fear and stay home, or start talking about moving back to Portland to live with his mother. He was going on with his life, which took some nerve.

I didn't have any sleepless nights. When the time came for sleep, I went unconscious. Often I would only get three or four or five hours a night. I never got more than six, I don't think, during the whole crisis. Somewhere in there, I stopped dreaming. I'd just sort of pass out, and then I'd be awake, with no consciousness of what happened in between.

On balance, I was probably pretty difficult to live with. I'm more of a quiet person to start with. Opening up, saying what's going on, talking about myself—I don't do too much of that even when things are normal.

But in Sandy I've had a good teacher. Back when we lived in Portland, Sandy and I started teaching classes together. She was teaching a class called "Street Law," for the Multnomah County juvenile justice department. (That's the county that surrounds Portland.) She'd get these juvenile delinquents and teach them things about how the police operate. We'd teach the class together. I'd come dressed in a suit and tie. Then, according to the curriculum, in week five the class would be visited by a police officer. So, in week five, I'd show up wearing my police officer's uniform. The kids would freak out. They'd be thinking, *We hate the police, but we already know this guy—and he* is *the police!* They'd want to hate me, too, but they'd already started liking me. It was a very effective teaching tool.

Later, Sandy started teaching a class at Portland Community College in conflict resolution. Sometimes we taught that together, too. And we brought home a lot of what we learned there about how to communicate. Sandy helped me learn a lot about telling the truth, and about saying what's really on your mind, about telling the other person what you need, instead of just hoping he or she is going to guess and give you what you need, or else getting mad at the other person for not guessing right.

We needed all the communication skills we could find getting through this period.

The following morning, on Tuesday, October 22, at the 10 A.M. press briefing, I said, "We are going to respond to a message that we have received. We will respond later. We are preparing that response at this time."

We were partly, with these messages, playing for time. We did want to speak with the sniper. We did want to keep the communication alive. We did hope that the sniper would stop shooting as long as we could keep him talking.

But we also had leads now that we believed were going to crack the case open shortly.

The interview with Monsignor Sullivan, the priest in Ashland, combined with the sniper's notes and the telephone conversation he'd had with Officer Baliles, had put us on the phone with the Montgomery, Alabama, Police Department.

They had an unsolved murder. In fact, it was a double. On the night of Saturday, September 21, two weeks before the shooting started in Montgomery County, Maryland, an unknown assailant had fired multiple rounds at two women as they walked out of the Alcoholic Beverage Control Board's Store No. 5 in Montgomery, Alabama. One of the victims, a liquor store employee who was black, was shot in the back and died. The other victim, a liquor store employee who was white, was shot in the back of the neck and survived. Fleeing the scene, the suspect had dropped a copy of a firearms magazine. On a single page was a single fingerprint.

By Tuesday evening, we had received the file on that case from the Montgomery, Alabama, authorities. Copies of the fingerprint on the catalogue went to the FBI lab in Quantico, Virginia. The bureau's latent fingerprint examiners ran it through the FBI's Integrated Automated Identification System. Having access to a larger database than the authorities in Montgomery, Alabama, had—one of the benefits of federal involvement in our task force was access to information from all federal agencies, including the INS—we were able to pull up an identification on the fingerprint.

This required working through the night. We did not have a solid I.D. until very early on the morning of Tuesday, October 22. The computer database said it belonged to a juvenile named Lee Boyd Malvo, a seventeen-year-old Jamaican who had been detained by the INS in Seattle, Washington, almost a year earlier. INS notes said that Malvo had entered the United States through Florida, via Haiti, with the help of smugglers, and that he had lived in the Northwest with a man named John Allen Muhammad, whom he identified as his stepfather.

Not long after, we determined who Muhammad was—a veteran, aged forty-one, who was wanted on an outstanding firearms charge. Muhammad, who at that time of the charge was called John Allen Williams, was from Baton Rouge, Louisiana. He had served in the Louisiana National Guard from 1978 to 1985, at which time he had enlisted in the U.S. Army. He served at Fort Lewis, in Washington State, then in Germany, then at Fort Ord, in California, before being transferred back to Fort Lewis.

Along the way, he had earned his Marksmanship Badge with an "expert" rating—which is the highest of the three grades given by the Army. When he was discharged in 1994, he entered the Oregon National Guard.

Muhammad had been in legal trouble several times. He was disciplined twice in the Army and was convicted of striking an officer while on duty. He fought a bitter custody dispute with his first wife, Carol Williams, who in 1994 sought court protection to keep her ex-husband away from their son. Muhammad later faced a restraining order, filed against him in 2000 by his second wife, Mildred Muhammad, after he threatened to harm her.

Muhammad also had an arrest warrant out in Tacoma, Washington, on a shoplifting charge.

We also gradually got more information about his companion. Lee Boyd Malvo was a seventeen-year-old Jamaican national. He and his mother, Una James, had been detained by immigration authorities in December 2001, in Bellingham, Washington. She had apparently smuggled herself and her son into the United States a year earlier. Malvo and his mother were held for a month before being released on $1,500 bail. We would later learn that Muhammad had met Malvo's mother on the Caribbean island of Antigua sometime in the 1990s.

We may have been moving closer to the suspects, but we had not stopped the killing.

On Tuesday morning there was another shooting. At 5:55 A.M. a single shot hit a bus driver named Conrad Johnson in the abdomen. Johnson was getting ready to go out on his route, standing in the stairwell of blue Montgomery County "Ride On" bus #5705.

As had been the case outside the Ponderosa, and outside Benjamin Tasker Middle School, the sniper had staked out a wooded area for his shooting. He had drawn aim and fired from a clump of trees near the bus depot in the Aspen Hill section of Rockville, where the drivers prepare their buses before going out on their routes, or where they relax for a few minutes between circuits. Johnson, who was 35, black and a Montgomery County resident, had been a bus driver for ten years. He had a wife and two children. He was rushed to the hospital, where he was worked on by the same trauma surgeon who had struggled to save the lives of James Buchanan and Lori Ann Lewis-Rivera. Johnson died after two hours of emergency surgery failed to revive him.

The surgeon, James W. Robey, later said, "This is just the face of evil."

As he had done with the shooting of the thirteen-year-old middle school student, the sniper left us a note, in a clump of woods where investigators think he stood to do the shooting.

As with the previous note, this one told us not to reveal its contents to the media. It contained more demands about money, including a demand that we set up a toll-free 800 number for the sniper to call us on.

The note also told us, again, that the children were not safe. Maybe I was becoming numb, but I paid almost no attention to this. Of course the children were not safe. The sniper had told us that already, and he had proved it—firing on a school and injuring a child.

Virginia jurisdictions had already issued an order to have some schools closed. I knew this information would become public, and that citizens from other areas would start demanding to know why that had happened—and why schools in their areas were *not* being closed. I thought they had a right to know what was going on.

So I quoted from the note, saying on television what the sniper had written: "Your children are not safe anywhere at any time."

I don't know if I did the right thing. I think I did. I hoped that, whatever the media might make of it, the people of Montgomery County would know I was not lying to them, or leaving out information they could use to protect themselves and their families. I thought that telling them less than I did would have been dishonorable, and irresponsible. But I knew that telling them more, or releasing the contents of the letter to the media, would endanger more lives.

The note concluded with this other weird demand. The sniper told us we had to read a message, over the airwaves, so he would know we were cooperating. We were to say, loud and clear, "We have caught the sniper like a duck in a noose."

At first, we didn't have any idea what that meant. We assigned some people to research it and report back. Before we heard from them, though, my wife, Sandy, recognized it as a reference to a Native American story. Sandy comes from the mountains of western North Carolina and has some Cherokee Indian in her roots, and she recognized this as a story from Cherokee or other Native American folklore. In the story, a prideful rabbit concocts a plan to catch a duck using a rope with a noose in it. He slips the noose over the duck's head—but the duck flies away, carrying the rabbit with him. The rabbit cannot let go, or he will fall and die. So he hangs on, until the duck slips free of the noose, and drops the rabbit into a hollow tree stump, where now he is trapped.

This didn't make any sense to me. Were we going to catch the sniper, but be the ones who were truly caught? We were going to lay a trap for the sniper, and catch him, but then no one would go to jail? We were going to make an arrest, and then go to jail ourselves? It was a kind of taunt, but an illogical taunt.

Just the same, I decided to do what he asked us to do. Once more I would go in front of the cameras and speak to the sniper. I knew it was important to him to hear me say it, and I thought it would prompt some further action on his part.

All we were hoping for, by then, was more time. We wanted to stall. We wanted to confuse the sniper. We wanted him to think we were doing all we could to arrange for the money to be delivered—although by that time I think it was clear to us that we were not going to actually deliver anything.

"In the past several days you have attempted to communicate with us. Call us at the same number you used before to obtain the 800 number you have requested. If you would feel more comfortable, a private P.O. box number or other secure method can be provided. You indicated that this is about more than violence. We are waiting to hear from you."

The toll-free 800 number part was important. The sniper had complained, in one of his earlier messages, about running out of quarters at a pay phone. We didn't want that to be an obstacle to any further communication.

There was, that Tuesday, October 22, an enormous amount of other investigative work going on all around us.

The priest in Ashland was listening to tapes of 911 calls, to try and make a voice match.

A man who witnessed the October 14 shooting of Linda Franklin was being interviewed extensively. This witness and another man were certain they had seen a "pearl white metallic colored station wagon, with an individual in the back of the vehicle in the prone position. This individual was holding a black rifle with a scope on it. There was another individual driving the station wagon." The witness could even describe the driver, as a Hispanic male, in his thirties or forties, wearing a dark shirt with a hood. The individual aiming the rifle was a Hispanic of roughly the same age. The witness said he could identify the suspects if he saw photographs of them.

Subsequent to that, the DMV offices were searching their records for stolen station wagons in the Maryland, Virginia and Washington, D.C., areas.

Videotapes from the crime scenes, such as the gas stations, were being studied once more, with a special view to finding that cream colored station wagon.

In addition, four pay telephones considered likely to have been used by the snipers were removed from their locations and taken to an FBI laboratory for examination.

Also, all telephones in the general vicinity of the Ponderosa Steakhouse were disabled so they could only be used to call 911.

A review that afternoon of the "aerial assets" available to the JOC showed that we were getting up to six hours' service a day from an Army RC-7, an Army Cessna 208 Caravan and an Army U21 Beechcraft Air King. The FBI had available or in the air two C-182s, one C-210 and several helicopters. All of these aircraft were conducting surveillance flyovers or patrols.

Later that Tuesday, maybe because I was feeling more confident, my communication to the sniper was more direct. At 7:15 that evening I said, "It is not possible electronically to comply with your demand. However, we remain open and ready to talk to you about the options you have mentioned. It is important that we do this without anyone else getting hurt."

I went even further. I think I was frustrated at that moment at the idea of how many people had *already* been hurt. I said, "We have not been able to assure anyone, any age, any gender, any race—we've not been able to assure anyone their safety, in regards to this situation."

The reason for this change in tone, I think, was that I knew we were getting closer to closing the case. I didn't want there to be any more killing before we did.

The pieces of the puzzle began to fall into place. The priest in Ashland and the notes from Office Derek Baliles's telephone call led us to Montgomery, Alabama. Police there told us about their double shooting. From that we got the fingerprint off the gun catalogue. From that we got an identification on Lee Boyd Malvo. That led us, through the INS files, to John Allen Muhammad.

We were also looking for a blue Chevrolet Caprice. Department of Motor Vehicle records had turned up a 1990 model, New Jersey license plate number NDA21Z, registered to a John Muhammad. The registration listed a Camden, New Jersey, address, right across the Delaware River from Philadelphia.

We meanwhile had gotten a tip, through the FBI, out of Tacoma, Washington. A man living in the Tacoma area had reported having visited recently with a man known as John Muhammad, a former Army buddy with whom he served at Fort Lewis. He had told investigators that Muhammad had been target shooting with assault rifles, fitted with scopes, and talked about how to attach silencers to weapons like that. He told the investigators that Muhammad had a companion, whom he referred to as his son, and who went by the nickname "Sniper."

This directed investigators to an area in Tacoma, a lower-middle-class community that was home to a lot of the soldiers, fifteen miles away from Fort Lewis, where Muhammad once served.

Investigators from the FBI's Seattle office swarmed over the blue wood-frame duplex at the Tacoma location. They determined, among other things, that Muhammad had done a lot of target practice in his backyard. A neighbor described listening to Muhammad firing rifle shots—always three shots in a row—into a thick, wide tree stump.

Fearful of damaging, destroying or compromising any evidence that might be inside the stump—bullets or bullet fragments, for example—FBI agents took X-ray pictures of the tree stump, developed the pictures and determined from their readings that the stump contained bullets and fragments. The agents had the tree stump removed—sawed off at just above the ground and shipped to the FBI lab in Maryland.

This is further illustration of the wisdom of reaching out to the federal government for help on a serial murder case. If it had been just the police department of Montgomery County, it would have taken us forever to do this—get the budget approved, send someone to Tacoma, have them hire a crew to remove the stump, hire a rental van to drive it back to Maryland ... It would have taken days, or longer, to get it done. You can't just ask FedEx to pick up a tree stump. But the FBI handled this in a matter of hours.

Unfortunately, they were not able to handle it quietly. Before we could get a good lid on the information coming from the Northwest, the whole Tacoma scene was on CNN. The senior members of the task force were sitting in my office in Rockville planning our next move, and the Tacoma location was all over the TV. There were neighbors being interviewed, talking about the nice guy that used to live there. The FBI people were forced to give a press conference. They did a good job, and didn't say anything except that they'd been asked to come to the location by the task force in Maryland.

As the news broke, sitting in my office watching the reports on TV, all I could think was, *If the snipers are watching this, they are going to rabbit. They will figure out we're closing in, and they'll get rid of the gun and go underground.* We figured these guys were probably watching TV, because that's the principal way we had been communicating with them, with messages we sent them through the media. If they had been watching that report from Tacoma, wouldn't they have realized we were getting close and taken off?

That would be fine from one standpoint—because the killing would probably stop. But it would not be fine from another standpoint—because we might all still be sitting in the JOC, working the case, with no one in custody, and the entire Washington area wondering when and where the next shooting would occur.

Another possibility that occurred to me was that, feeling we were closing in, the snipers would go on some kind of final, insane shooting spree—and that our having released the name and ID on the suspect would have caused this.

The other possibility, of course, was that we would find this man Muhammad and discover he was just another set of coincidences. When we finally had an arrest warrant issued, it was not for murder. We didn't refer to him as a suspect. We said we wanted to speak to him in connection to the shootings.

This was not about keeping secrets, or keeping the

media out of it or—and this was the most preposterous suggestion I heard—about keeping the patrol officers ignorant so that the detectives could make the arrest. (Actually, that was the second-most preposterous suggestion I heard. The prize-winning stupidest suggestion was one made by a magazine writer on a radio talk show. He said that I had withheld information, and let the sniper keep shooting longer than necessary, because I was collecting information for a book I was hoping to write. This doesn't even deserve a response. It's insane.)

In the next press briefing, on Wednesday, October 23, I announced that we were interested in talking to Muhammad and a "juvenile companion," whom I did not identify. I said, "We believe that Mr. Muhammad may have information material to our investigation." I did say Muhammad was considered armed and dangerous, but I added what I called "a strong word of caution." I said, "Do not assume from this allegation that John Allen Muhammad . . . is involved in any of the shootings we are investigating."

By the late afternoon on Wednesday we had asked the ATF branch of the task force to try and have a warrant issued for Muhammad's arrest on an outstanding weapons charge out of Seattle. Since that charge existed, we had a convenient, legal way to bring him in— better than simply picking him up and trying to detain him as a suspect. From a strictly legal standpoint, we didn't have much to go on. He had a gun. He was involved with a juvenile. The juvenile's fingerprints were on a gun magazine near a crime scene in Alabama. A priest in Maryland had a message from a man who claimed to be responsible for the crime in Alabama, and for the shootings in Maryland . . . It wasn't a very solid case. The weapons charge warrant was rock-solid.

We had also asked the FBI branch of the task force to try to obtain a material witness warrant issued for Lee Boyd Malvo.

The warrant gave us the legal right to pick up Muhammad. We had learned, later that afternoon, that he had a connection to the Maryland area: His ex-wife lived in Prince George's County. She worked, or had worked, at a Michael's craft store.

The fact that he and his accomplice were African-American was, or course, the very opposite of what the profilers and TV talking heads had predicted. I didn't spend much time thinking about this, but I was pleased that we on the task force had been able to ignore the tunnel vision the profilers were encouraging. This told us that our message, that people needed to keep their minds and their eyes open, was the right message. We hadn't been boxed in by any preconceptions about what kind of suspect we were looking for.

I also knew Muhammad might not be the right person. If the gun wasn't found, or the gun didn't match up with the ballistics on the bullet fragments we had, if this was just another promising-looking suspect who happened to have a rifle, he wouldn't be the first one.

Even as late as that Wednesday, we were investigating and eliminating other suspects.

Earlier in the investigation, members of the task force had visited and questioned two suspects from the Maryland area. They were very good suspects. There was a white station wagon. There was a .223 rifle. There was some criminal background. One of the suspects had driven recklessly in order to avoid a roadblock we had set up after one of the shootings. Some of the task force investigators were convinced these were the guys.

They came off the board after the October 19 shooting at the Ponderosa Steakhouse. We had them under surveillance, and they were nowhere near the crime scene. We eliminated them as suspects.

But now, after the Conrad Johnson shooting, they were suspects again. The same driver had been seen, once again, skirting a police roadblock, driving recklessly, trying not to get caught.

They went back on the board. We figured it was possible one of them had somehow slipped out without being seen for the October 19 shooting. Or maybe they had accomplices? Maybe they were part of a larger team? We didn't know. But the investigators returned to these two suspects and began considering some new way to snag them.

We still had surveillance going on the gentleman who had barricaded his doors and windows with cinder blocks. Was it possible he had slipped out in the night and been able to do the Conrad Johnson shooting? It didn't seem possible, but it had to be considered. He was still a viable suspect, as late as that afternoon and evening.

In the press briefings, I was trying my damnedest to make sure I didn't accidentally "charge" anybody with anything. I was trying to be as accurate and fair as possible and not accuse any innocent person of something he hadn't done—either by my statements or by their implications.

There was an investigative briefing at 4:00 Wednesday afternoon. We told the task force leaders everything we could about what we knew, as the Muhammad-Malvo connection got more interesting, and as the other suspects began to take shape. At my direction, members of the JOC had drawn up flyers for the investigators. They featured pictures, supplied to us by the federal agencies, of Muhammad and Malvo. The investigators were going to begin right away visiting hotels, gun stores, gas stations and other likely locations, looking for anyone who might have seen either of these two men and might know more about them. Shift supervisors were shown copies of the flyers and instructed to have all their officers look at them, too—though we did not distribute copies, out of concern for media leaks and a desire to keep the information off the police radios. There was also some concern about the legal implications of showing photographs of Malvo, because he was a juvenile.

We also wanted to be careful about the language that we used. We were still upset about the earlier suspect having been so publicly identified. We did not want another Richard Jewell situation. Initially the flyers said,

"Wanted—Persons of Interest related to Sniper Shootings."

I must have been feeling pretty tense. I saw the draft of our flyer and had concerns. We needed to be exact. I asked Assistant Chief Walker a series of questions about the flyer. The draft had been written by Assistant Chief O'Toole, but he was still at the JOC and Assistant Chief Walker was the assistant chief in the room, so she's the one that served as the sounding board.

She had the language on the flyers changed. They went out saying only, "Wanted for Questioning Reference 0-100s." A "0-100" was Montgomery County cop code for "murder."

It looked, that Wednesday night, like we'd done all we could do. I called Sandy and told her I'd be home relatively early. I told her we might even have an early dinner—that I'd be in by eight o'clock or something like that. But little things kept coming up. There kept being one more thing to look at, one more detail to check out. Pretty soon it was eight o'clock, and then it was nine o'clock. Sandy called and said she was going to the store to get something to make dinner with.

She was calling a lot around then. Sometimes she'd have an urgent need to tell me something. She'd page me and then enter her secret code for "emergency," the numbers 1-2-3-4. In Portland, that was the police code for an emergency involving a mentally ill person. It was her humorous way of saying, "I really need to talk to you *now*." One time she called with that code, and when I called back she said she had seen a white van, parked backward in a parking space, with its back door pointed directly at a Michael's craft store. I told her, "Why don't you call Sergeant Emanuel? I'm busy right this minute." She didn't like that.

The warrant for Muhammad took much longer than we'd hoped. When it finally came through, from the South Precinct of the Seattle Police Department, it was time-stamped 7:54 P.M.—Seattle time. So it was nearly 11 P.M. before we had it in our hands in Maryland.

Late Wednesday night the task force held a press briefing that officially identified Muhammad and Malvo as being materially connected to the investigation. We noted that Malvo, as a juvenile, could not be identified fully. Bouchard said that a warrant, being executed in the state of Washington, might lead to an arrest.

We had hoped to get this information out there to the public via the evening news. By now, it was much too late for that. It was even too late for the 11:00 news. We'd have to settle for reports going out the next morning.

That last press conference was held at 12:05 A.M. I had a prepared statement, a *carefully* prepared statement, to read. Every word in it was designed to give the snipers reassurance, to make it appear we were far away from them, to draw them closer to us, to prevent them from running away from us, and to convince them that we were getting ready to give in to their demand for the $10 million.

We had worked on the statement for hours. Captain Nancy Demme had written it and rewritten it five or six times. Each time, mindful that we were trying to speak directly to the snipers, we had the FBI and ATF profilers and negotiators review the communiqué and offer us their comments. They had plenty of comments, and they were always different. That's because they had different jobs. The negotiators wanted to draw the suspects out into the open. The profilers wanted to figure out what the suspects' next move would be. They were both kind of like the weather forecasters—they were not responsible for the outcome.

We wanted the suspects to know we were talking to them. We wanted them to know we wanted to talk to them. We also wanted them to see that we were in control. We didn't want to say anything that might serve as a catalyst for them to start shooting again. We went through several more drafts before we had the language right.

After describing the suspect, for the media and the public at large, as "armed and dangerous," I said to the microphones and TV cameras:

"We understand that you communicated with us by calling several different locations. Our inability to talk has been a concern for us, as it has been for you. You have indicated that you want us to do and say certain things. You have asked us to say, 'We have caught the sniper like a duck in a noose.' We understand that hearing us say this is important to you. However we want you to know how difficult it has been to understand what you want, because you have chosen to use only notes, indirect messages and calls to other jurisdictions. The solution remains to call us and get a private toll-free number established just for you. We still ask you to call or write us at P.O. Box 7875, Gaithersburg, Maryland, 20898-7875. If you are reluctant to contact us, be assured that we remain ready to talk directly with you."

Since the sniper had used certain code words and phrases, I decided to do the same. I said, "Our word is our bond. If we can establish communications with you, we can offer other means of addressing what you have asked for. Let's talk directly. We have an answer for you about your option. We are waiting for you to contact us."

I left the station almost immediately after delivering this message. I drove home. I was running so much later than I'd planned. Going out to eat was no longer possible—it's not New York City where we live, and your dining options start to disappear pretty fast after nine o'clock or so. By midnight, they're gone.

I don't think I had any appetite anyway. I was tired. I was keyed up, too. We knew we were closing in. We had lots of information on Muhammad, and some details on Malvo. We had the information on the car they were driving, or had been driving. I knew that whatever was going to happen next was going to happen pretty soon.

When I got home, I told Sandy, "I think we may be getting close." I sat down in the rocking chair in the living room. I said, "I really hope this turns out to be it." I said, "I really hope tonight turns out to be the night."

I didn't tell Sandy what I meant. She didn't ask. We

just sat and talked. I worried, as much as anything else. I knew there was nothing I could do but wait. Tomorrow was going to be a complicated day. So was the day after that, and the day after that. Despite the developments, there was no end in sight.

Sometime early Thursday morning, I went to bed. I slept for a while, fitfully. Sandy told me later that I tossed and turned like someone having a bad dream. That makes sense. Being awake was like *living* a bad dream.

I had been reluctant to give out too much information. As always, my fear was that Muhammad would find out what we had found out, and understand how close we were, and make his escape. I didn't want the description of his car, or the car license plate number, released to the media. I know some people have criticized this decision, thinking that somehow I was planning to make a more spectacular arrest without the help of the media or the public.

That's wrong. I was just afraid the suspect would run. If you were Muhammad, at that moment, and you heard the police were looking for you in a blue 1990 Chevy Caprice with New Jersey license plates NDA-21Z, in connection with the serial sniper shootings in Maryland, Virginia and the District of Columbia, what would you do?

If it were me, I'd get rid of the gun, and I'd get rid of the car, and I'd get another car, and I'd get the hell out of the area.

Mike Bouchard, Gary Bald and I had disagreed about what information to release. We wanted the police officers in the area to be aware of what was going on. We also wanted to contain the information as much as possible. Gary Bald wanted to release the names of the suspects and identify them as suspects. He wanted all the information we had out there, available to all our people. Mike Bouchard disagreed. He said, "What if these are not the guys? What if they just know something about this case, and it's something we need to know?"

We knew the two suspects were connected to the car, and we knew the car was connected to the killings, but we didn't know for sure that these were the killers. Mike Bouchard was concerned that an officer, thinking these were the prime suspects, might try to apprehend them, and get into a fight, and kill them. They might know something useful that we'd never find out, in that case. If the killings continued, we would have eliminated our principal source of information.

In the end, we decided to put out most of the details, but to leave some of the information between the lines. The media, fed by leaks from within the task force, or by police agencies working with the task force, did the rest.

Just after 10 P.M., Wednesday night, CNN reported that we were looking for a 1990 Caprice, with New Jersey license plates. They said the task force was considering releasing the names of two men, but added that the police had asked the media not to refer to them as suspects.

Just before 11 P.M., Fox reported that police were looking for John Allen Williams, who was also known as John Muhammad, and Lee Boyd Malvo. They also reported the license plate number for the Caprice.

Three minutes later, CNN reported the names of the suspects, too.

It was after midnight before we officially said anything. We put out the information that we were looking for two men in connection to the case. We put out the information about the material witness warrant and the warrant on federal gun charges. We released a photo of Muhammad and a detailed description of the car.

While I was home resting, the task force was working through the night. Little pieces continued to come together. With identification now of Muhammad and Malvo, and a fingerprint on Malvo, more pieces were available. At eleven o'clock or so that night, investigators had learned that Malvo had been detained briefly by Montgomery County Police and that the officer making the stop had run a "10-29" on him, on October

2. A 10-29 is a request, usually made by an officer in the field, for more information. He or she might want to know whether there are outstanding warrants on an individual, or whether a certain vehicle has been reported stolen. But Malvo's car had been purchased legally and was legally registered. The driver evidently had a legal driver's license. We would see later that the suspects knew how to keep a low profile, and knew how to behave around the police. They didn't drink or take drugs, to our knowledge. They just said "yes, sir" and "no, sir" to the officers, showed the proper paperwork and kept their mouths shut. Montgomery County Police had stopped Malvo and released him on that date, having no reason to hold him.

This, for the first time, put the suspects in the area during the time of the shootings.

Sometime after 12:45 A.M. an out-of-work refrigerator repairman pulled into the rest stop off Interstate 70, at exit 42, just past the line where Montgomery County becomes Frederick County. He had been listening to the radio and had heard a report about the police looking for a Caprice with New Jersey plates. Pulling his white van into a parking spot in the rest stop, the repairman noticed the Caprice parked there. He called 911 on his cell phone. The police dispatcher told him to sit in his car, with the windows rolled up and the doors locked, and wait.

A few minutes later, a rest stop employee named Larry Blank walked out to the parking lot. He had been listening to the police scanner and heard a report about on-ramps and off-ramps being closed up and down Interstate 70, all around his rest stop. Blank, thinking it might have something to do with the sniper, went outside to see what was going on. He recognized the driver of the white van, who was a regular visitor at the rest stop. The driver had also been listening to the radio. He asked Blank to come sit in the car with him. Together they sat with the doors locked, staring at the Chevy Caprice. Blank had parked right next to it when he arrived for work, but hadn't noticed the year or the color, and hadn't thought anything about it.

Within ten minutes of the first 911 call, police received another, from a trucker named Ron Lantz. He had also spotted the blue Caprice and reported in to the authorities like a good citizen. The police told Lantz to try and use his big rig, a bright purple Kenworth eighteen-wheeler, to block the exit from the rest stop. They asked him to try and get a buddy to block the entrance. Lantz did as he was told.

Bill O'Toole had been making it a habit to stay until one o'clock in the morning during the investigation. He was supposed to be on the night shift, while Dee Walker did the day shift. That meant she came in around three in the morning, and stayed until three in the afternoon. O'Toole was working very long days, and that day had come in especially early, around six or seven in the morning.

We had started ordering officers to take a day off—not requesting, or suggesting, but actually ordering—because we were afraid of burning everyone out. It had been three weeks of fourteen- to sixteen- to eighteen-hour shifts, with no days off. Everyone wanted to stay. No one wanted to miss anything. O'Toole said, as others had already said, that every officer on the force had this idea that he or she was personally going to be in on the arrest, or was going to turn up the lead that led to the arrest, and no one wanted to miss the opportunity.

O'Toole was getting ready to leave that night. Having seen the announcements go out on Muhammad and Malvo, though, he had a second thought. He went down to speak with John Fitzgerald, commander of the tactical division, and told him, "Since we've got this manhunt going, I'd like you to hold over the SWAT people until five o'clock in the morning. We may need them."

Fitzgerald told him, "It's already done."

Having taken the extra time to do that, O'Toole was still in the building when the first calls started coming in from the rest stop.

O'Toole called Drew Tracy, waking him at home. Tracy immediately decided he ought to be on the scene, directing the tactical units and uniformed officers. He left at once to drive to the rest stop.

O'Toole passed the word to other officers at the JOC. Within fifteen minutes, fifty police officers had made it to the rest stop. The report of the Caprice being located had gone out. There was no information on who was in the car, or whether anyone was in it at all. They weren't going to wait to find out. Units started being dispatched at once.

Seven miles of I-70—between the interchanges to Maryland Route 17 and Route 66—were closed. Police cars were placed at entrances and exits to guide motorists away from the area and prevent them from getting too close to the rest stop.

The parking lot of a McDonald's restaurant in nearby Myersville served as a temporary base of operations. Task force officials staged planning meetings there as they prepared to make an assault on the Caprice.

They planned carefully. At this point, no one had gotten close enough to the car to know who was in it. They didn't know whether anyone was in the car, whether they were armed, or what kind of resistance they were going to present. The task force might have been making an assault on an empty vehicle. They might also be walking into a trap. What if the snipers had heard them coming and taken up positions in the trees, and were planning to fire on the officers when they approached the vehicle? The task force planners wanted to do it right.

Right around one o'clock, sure that this was a confirmed sighting of the car we were looking for, O'Toole got on the phone and called me. I was sleeping, though fitfully, when the phone started ringing. I woke up fast.

O'Toole told me the little that he knew—they had spotted the car, secured the rest stop, blocked the interstate and dispatched the tactical units to the scene. He promised to call me as soon as there were any developments.

By then, the entire task force was scrambling. Maryland State Troopers were on the scene within fifteen minutes. They had the car under surveillance and were getting the area secured. Within the next short while, SWAT teams would be dispatched—all but two of the teams we had at our disposal. O'Toole made the decision to hold two back, in the event that some other kind of trouble started at some other location. Officers armed with high-powered rifles and fitted with night-vision goggles would begin to surround the rest stop. An airplane fitted with heat-sensing surveillance equipment would be in the air above the rest stop.

O'Toole remembered that we had use of a Maryland State Police helicopter. He scrambled that, too, and used it to fly three counter-sniper marksmen to the rest stop, just in case. The helicopter was on the ground at at Richard Montgomery High School, off Route 355, at 1 A.M., picking up the sharpshooters. Then the helicopter headed for the rest stop.

I was at home, waiting. I told Sandy, "It's getting ready to happen. It's going to happen now."

I could have been there in twenty minutes. I didn't move.

Sandy asked me why I wasn't getting up and leaving. I told her I didn't think it was my job to go. I'm not that kind of police chief. I don't go to every crime scene, or try to make every arrest. That would be the opposite of how I run the department. I thought it would be insulting for my officers to have me there. The people who should be there were the people who were experts in doing what had to be done—and I was not an expert in this kind of work. If I'd wanted to be a SWAT team expert, I would have spent my time learning how to be that. I hadn't done that. And the people who were going to handle this arrest had to be experts.

Sandy said, "But don't you want to be there? I would!"

I stayed in bed. If this was just another empty lead, there would still be tomorrow's work to do. I knew I needed the rest.

I thought about how ironic the location was. John King had a child who played soccer, and he was a coach on the soccer team. All of the games had been cancelled during the sniper shootings, as had so many events that involved large groups of people sitting or standing outside, exposed, where they'd make inviting targets. A week earlier, one of the people from the soccer league had proposed holding a match up in Frederick County, far from where the shootings had taken place, thinking that would be safe. King had told him, "In my personal opinion as a dad, the answer is no. In my professional opinion as a police officer, the answer is also no. It's not far enough away to be safe." The soccer field they were considering using was right there, where this rest stop was. King had been right to think it wasn't far enough away to be safe, because there they were.

It was a long, long night. By 2:00, we had not received another call. I tried to go back to sleep.

There was so much to worry about. I was worried that we'd found the car, but not the suspects. I was specifically worried that the suspects had heard the same media reports I had heard, and had taken off. Maybe they had dumped the car. Maybe the rest stop was a great place to steal another car. Maybe they had stolen the car and had a hostage. Maybe they hitched a ride, and had a hostage. Maybe one of them was in the car and the other was in the woods, keeping lookout, rifle ready, waiting for some kind of attack.

After all the terrible violence of the shootings, I expected there would be some kind of a fight, if these were the right guys. They were obviously not afraid to kill. I was worried that my officers would be injured or killed trying to bring these suspects in.

Finally, at 2:15 A.M., when I couldn't think of anything else to worry about, I went back to sleep. I knew that, whatever happened tonight, tomorrow was coming fast. And, no matter what happened tonight, tomorrow was going to be an extremely demanding day.

By 2:30 A.M. the SWAT units were in position at the

rest stop. More than one hundred officers were on point, surrounding the car. More were in the woods, ready to prevent the suspects from running, should they escape the vehicle.

Captain Barney Forsythe got the call right around then. He was at home, sleeping, when the phone rang. Sergeant Roger Thomson told him the Caprice had been located, in this rest stop, at exit 42 off of the I-70. Forsythe lives a very short distance from there. He decided to go to the scene at once. He jumped up and got dressed and called his assistant, Lieutenant Phil Raum. There were at the scene within a half hour.

Forsythe remembers the night as cool to cold. As he and Raum pulled up toward exit 42, they found the interstate shut down. They stopped and identified themselves to the control cars and were let through, and made their way closer to the Caprice. They got as far as the exit to the rest stop. Forsythe conferred with officers from the Maryland State Police.

The exit to the rest stop had already been blocked by a convoy of four or five eighteen-wheeler big rigs. As Forsythe and Raum waited, they could hear the low rumble of the big trucks—the only noise on this otherwise quiet night.

Sometime around 3:10 or 3:15 there was a call for radio silence. All the officers on the scene turned their radios off. Forsythe, though he was not at the front line of the assault, knew this meant the SWAT teams were making their move. For a very tense five or six minutes, he and Raum waited.

At 3:19 the takedown began. SWAT teams stormed the Chevy Caprice. Officers smashed out the car's side windows with sledgehammers and tossed "flash-bang" grenades into the car, blasting the inside of the Caprice with blinding light and a deafening roar. Overhead a police helicopter flooded the area with a million watts of midnight sun. Officers screamed at the occupants to get out of the car, and began dragging two stunned-looking men out of the Caprice—Malvo from the front seat,

Muhammad from the back. The men were pushed to the ground and handcuffed.

It was over in less than thirty seconds. Muhammad and Malvo were in custody.

Malvo would later tell investigators that he and Muhammad had a 99.9 percent "success rate," and that they were "unstoppable." The capture was the result of Malvo's own "0.1 percent failure": He had fallen asleep, at his lookout post, and failed to warn Muhammad that the police were there.

Forsythe and several others walked quickly down the hundred yards or so that separated them from the rest stop. Forsythe found the crime scene well under control. Under the bright lights of the well-lit parking lot, he saw the Caprice parked, nose in, its doors flung open. The two suspects were seated on the ground, on opposite sides of the car. They were both handcuffed. Forsythe thought they looked disheveled, as if they had just been awakened. He also thought they looked "resigned." That was his word. They looked "resigned" to what had happened. Slump-shouldered. Heads down. Tired. Showing no resistance at all. Just sort of . . . done.

Free now to walk into the crime scene, and with the radio silence lifted, Forsythe was able to confer with his counterparts. Gary Bald of the FBI was there. The ATF had a mobile crime lab vehicle on the scene. The people attached to that unit, along with the Maryland State Police, were responsible for securing and searching the overall location for evidence. They went to work right away. Forsythe, because he didn't want to spend all night standing around at the rest stop, called down to the JOC. He wanted to get some executive-level people from the task force to come relieve him, so he could drive down to Montgomery County when the suspects were taken there. He got one ATF agent and one FBI agent to come up to the rest stop to relieve him.

The suspects were placed into separate police cars and driven down I-70, back into Montgomery County. They were to be driven to a juvenile assessment facility, part of the family services branch of the Montgomery Police Department, in Rockville. This was not the usual facility for suspects of this nature, but we had chosen it because it was relatively unknown, relatively quiet, and was outfitted with equipment that would allow us to easily videotape and audiotape the suspects as we interviewed them.

The location was also not very well known to the media. We thought we could get the suspects there and conduct our business without the press making a circus out of it. I don't think anyone was expecting there to be a lynching or anything like that, but we wanted the location as secure as possible, and less media coverage would make that easier to guarantee.

The location was also not very well known to members of the various law enforcement agencies. We had to place an escort vehicle near a certain off-ramp, so the cars bringing the suspects down to Montgomery County could be led to the facility. It's only a couple of miles from the main Rockville police station, but it was not familiar to the people driving the suspects.

Back at the rest stop, the Caprice was secured. Forsythe said it was obvious from the look of the car that the suspects had been living in it, as well as driving it, for quite a while. There were clothes and containers of food and other evidence that the car was being used for more than commuting.

A decision was made almost immediately that night not to search the car until a search warrant could be obtained and the car could be moved to a secure location. In the morning, it would be loaded onto a trailer and hauled to a place where it could be thoroughly inspected.

Gary Bald called me about then. He said, "We've got them." He told me no one had been hurt.

Drew Tracy called John King, at the FBI academy down in Quantico, a little after that. He said, "We got 'em."

King had already heard some of the news. He had

also already seen a lot of great-looking suspects go up on the board and then come down off the board. He said, "I know we got the guys we were looking for. Do we know they're the guys we really want?"

"These are the guys," Tracy told him. "They cut a shooting port out of the trunk of the car. That's how they were doing it."

That's when King knew: These were the snipers.

Back at the JOC, O'Toole attended the 5 A.M. daily briefing, held for the officers who were just coming in for the day shift. There were eighty to a hundred officers in attendance. Some of them had heard bits and pieces of the news on the radio as they drove into work. No official announcement had been made, but reporters listening in on police band radio had obviously figured out that some kind of arrest had been made. The room was electric with energy.

Drew Tracy had led all the morning briefings for the duration of the sniper case. Today, he brought with him one of the SWAT officers who participated in the takedown. The SWAT officer gave the troops a firsthand account of the event.

O'Toole told me later the scene of relief in the room was overwhelming. There was no applause. There was no shouting. There were no high-fives around the room. Just a sense of great relief. For the average officer, it was all over.

One thing worth remembering: Many of these officers were residents of the target area. They all had cars they had to fill with gas, and parking lots in front of malls where they had to leave their cars to do their shopping. Some of them had wives or husbands and children and parents who lived in the area, too. Every time there was a shooting, each of them had to be thinking the same thing: Is it one of my people? The officers on duty had responded to all kinds of calls, all day long, for three weeks—sightings of the white van, reports of suspicious behavior, reports of shots fired. They were exhausted. Each day, going about their business, being in uniform, each of them had to have been wondering whether he or she was going to become a target, too.

Even senior officers, like O'Toole, had been working very long days. He had made it a habit for most of the last three weeks to put on his uniform at home, drive his child to school, stand outside his child's school in uniform for an hour while the kids all made their way onto the campus and into the classrooms, and then come to work. He did this five days a week, for the duration of the three weeks, before he got to work every day.

So the relief was much greater than the one that normally comes at the end of a big case. The job was done, plus all these people knew now that they and their loved ones were no longer in danger.

For Barney Forsythe, the moment of relief was slower in coming. He told me later that after he got the suspects over to the juvenile assessment center he went back down to the JOC. He worked through the rest of the night there. At about seven o'clock the next morning the search of the suspects' vehicle was complete. Captain Forsythe got a call from one of his sergeants telling him that the search had turned up a high-powered weapon, a Bushmaster that fired a .223 round, hidden under the backseat.

Captain Forsythe made the announcement to all the officers and investigators working in the JOC. There was cheering and applause. Then Barney told Dee Walker he was going home for a few hours, to get some sleep, and that he'd be back later in the morning.

Even then, he didn't go straight home. Captain Forsythe drove to the school where his wife teaches. He took her aside and said, "You can't tell anyone this, but we got them. We got the guys. Only you can't tell *anyone*." Then, when he got home, he called his parents. They were elderly, and the week the sniper shooting started they had just moved back to the Montgomery County area. He called them and said, "We got them. You can't tell anyone, not *anyone*, but we got them." Then he went to bed.

I would like to say that I woke my wife up and opened a bottle of champagne. But it was not time for drinking champagne. We had the suspects in custody. More important, we had taken them without any shooting. I was very relieved about that. We had made the arrest. We had arrested the right people. The killings were over.

We still did not have a complete case. It was still in my mind that no one had seen these suspects do anything. We needed to confirm all the existing evidence, and to find a weapon. Even if we found a weapon in their car, what if it was a different weapon? So far the ballistics tests had shown that the same rifle had been used in almost all of the shootings. What if, knowing we were closing in, they had switched rifles, or destroyed the one they'd used in all the shootings?

I didn't ask any of those questions out loud. And Gary Bald didn't tell me, because he didn't know then, whether the gun was in the car. No one was going to touch the car until it was light out, and until everything could be done in a very professional way. If this was the right car, there was going to be a lot of work left to do. If it was not the right car, I didn't even want to think about that possibility. But either way, the investigation was far, far from over.

Despite that, I said to Sandy, as we lay in bed, "It's over. I think it's over."

It was about 4 A.M. by then. I made a conscious decision to try and get some more rest, even though it was almost morning, and I would have to get up in a couple of hours. I went back to bed, and stayed there for an hour. I knew that, if these were the right guys, we were at step one of the end of the case. Or I knew that if they were the right guys, and it was the right car, and there was any evidence in the car, we were at step two. If the gun was in the car, we were at step three.

The first piece of the final investigation had already begun by then. The suspects were already being interviewed. We had two Montgomery County Police officers on that. Detective Jim Drewry, of our major crimes unit, was on one team, paired up with either an FBI or an ATF agent. Detective Terry Ryan—the plainclothes detective I'd bumped into at the Mobil station the very first day of the shooting spree—was on the other team, also paired up with a counterpart from FBI or ATF. Both these guys were very experienced investigators and very experienced interviewers. They would go through the night, starting before dawn, beginning to ask the questions we had all been wanting to ask since the evening of October 3.

But there were still a lot of steps to go.

10. A Question of Color

As the manhunt for the sniper suspects drew to a close, starting with information we received on Tuesday, October 22, a startling fact began to be apparent: Our two principal suspects were both African-American.

This was an unusual development. In American criminal history, serial killers are rarely black. The profilers had missed this entirely. No one expected the sniper suspects not to be white men. As a black police chief, I could be expected to have complicated feelings about the suspects being black. I did. I have complicated feelings about everything involving race.

The issue of black and white is still, for me, a defining characteristic of life in America. It is still a very central issue—maybe *the* central issue—of life in America.

I see it everywhere. I've seen it everywhere for as long as I can remember.

When I was a kid in Lexington, North Carolina, blacks were a distinct minority. There were two or three neighborhoods where blacks lived, spread around the town, but I probably knew all the black kids of elementary to high school age. Even though the difference between white and black was completely polarized, and perfectly visible, there were differences within the black community, too.

We were from Smith Avenue. That was the high end of things. If you told someone you lived on Smith Avenue, that said quite a bit about how you were doing. At the far end of Smith, in fact, at the very top of that rise, there were houses that belonged to white families. Smith was as close as Lexington got to being a mixed neighborhood.

If you told someone you lived in Parkertown, though, the opposite was true. That was at the other end of the things. That stretch was lined with rough little tar-paper-lined shacks, little wooden-frame one-room shacks that looked like a strong wind would knock them down. If you said you lived there, you were saying a lot about your status.

Same thing if you lived in the projects. These were red-brick duplexes and triplexes, built in a large circle, decorated with little shrubs and fronted by tired lawns. There was a stigma to living in public housing, but these were a step up from Parkertown, to be sure. They were insulated. They had roofs that didn't leak. But they were still the projects.

If you lived on Pine Street, where we had a house when my father first came down to Lexington, you were a step up from that. This is another few blocks of little wooden frame houses. But these had brick foundations and brick fireplaces with chimneys and coats of paint on the wood.

It wasn't just where you lived. There were other ways of guessing someone's status. The most obvious one was the car. If a man drove a fancy car, or an expensive car, that told you a lot about his financial station. It didn't always tell the truth, but it said something.

For example, after my mother died, I inherited her Plymouth Valiant. I drove that car to school and to the jobs I had during the summer vacations. If you hadn't known better, you might have guessed that my folks had bought me my own car to drive around, which would have suggested we were a family with a certain amount of disposable income. Even though we weren't.

One summer that bad guess was even easier to make. My father had just bought a brand-new 1971 Grand Prix. I had just graduated from high school. I knew I was going off to Chapel Hill in September. But that summer I had a job at a construction site. For some reason my dad gave me that Grand Prix to drive. I drove it to work. I drove it after work. I styled around in it at night. Everyone thought my dad had given me a brand-new Pontiac as a graduation present. I let them think that.

I wasn't even aware of there being poor white people at that time. I'm sure there were. But I didn't know anything about that. The idea that there were white people worse off than me would have seemed strange, I think. I thought white people had it all.

Among the various economic levels of blacks, there were still more distinctions—more subtle, more insidious distinctions. One of them had to do with color.

As a boy, I ran around with the neighborhood kids. We all used to cut up and goof off and get into little bits of trouble. Nothing big or bad, because we weren't real bad kids. There was the time we spent the whole afternoon shooting out the glass in that guy's tractor with our slingshots. Another time, a bunch of us found the door to the Dunbar High School gymnasium unlocked. We snuck in and spent the afternoon playing basketball on that beautiful wooden floor. We got caught—by Charlie England, who was the football coach there. He could have called the cops. He could have got us in a world of trouble. As it was, he gave us a lecture and told our parents, and made sure we got punished. But he did it without the law. I sometimes wonder how my life would have been different if he had called the police and filed a report and gotten the juvenile justice authorities involved. I'm grateful he didn't. Later on, after integration, they renamed Dunbar School after him. Even today the school is called Charles England Middle School.

That was little-kid trouble. I knew kids who got into more grown-up kinds of trouble. Later on, in high school, I knew kids who were fooling around with drugs. There was marijuana around, and some of the high school kids were smoking it. That led them into all kinds of trouble, too.

There were two boys we used to play with. They were brothers, and they were the lightest-skinned black kids I knew. With these boys, because they were so light-skinned, it was like they had to prove they were even tougher, even crazier, than the other kids. They had to prove how "black" they were. They did that by getting into trouble.

It wasn't until I was in high school that I started to really feel the inequity of black and white. I had lived in it my whole life. I had seen evidence of it. But I didn't really have a strong consciousness of it until I was a little older.

I was on the football team. I was kind of a star, in fact, on the football team. I was a running back, and in my senior year I was named "best blocker."

Off the field, though, I was a second-class citizen.

When I was a college student and working as a book salesman in Mobile, Alabama, I'd started in a certain neighborhood and then fanned out. I guess I fanned out a little too far. I worked my way out of the black side of town and into the white side. Eventually I got stopped and questioned by a couple of white cops. They weren't mean to me. They didn't handcuff me or beat me or shoot me. But they made it absolutely clear to me that I was in the wrong place and that I'd better get out now if I didn't want trouble.

I understood, without putting up any kind of fight, that it was time to move on. I didn't want an ass-whipping. I didn't want to be in the wrong part of town. And, truth to tell, I wasn't going to be able to sell as many dictionaries in the white part of town as I could in the black part. It probably didn't even occur to me to think about any of this as unfair. It was just the reality of the time.

No matter what has changed in this country since then, there is still that same kind of reality in most cities in America. Right or wrong, there is still the white section of town and the black section of town, in most places. And a black man is not going to feel as safe and comfortable in the white section as he will in the black.

If I'm traveling around America, and I'm in a new city that I don't know, and I want to find someplace to get a haircut, or to get a certain kind of food, or find people hanging out who look like me, I have to find the black part of town. Nowadays, that's gotten pretty easy. All you have to do is ask, "Where is Martin Luther King Jr. Boulevard?" Most cities have one of those now, and the cab driver always knows where it is. Find that, and you'll find the black part of town. You'll find the people that look like you. Martin Luther King Jr. Boulevard is never, never in the white part of town.

It's never in the "nice" part of town, either. It probably doesn't occur to most people to think about whether that's unfair, either. It is just the reality.

And the reality does not change. Something that may be hard for the average white person in America to understand is that a black person in America never, ever stops being a black person. Everywhere you go, it's the thing that people see first—not that you're successful or not, not that you're wealthy or not, or handsome or not, or intelligent or not, or friendly or not. First, you're black.

I wish I could say I haven't experienced much of that personally. In fact, I've experienced a lot of that. It's one of the reasons I think I was reluctant to engage in any aggressive "profiling" on the sniper case. I've seen how confining it can be, how blinding. If you tell people what to look for, that's what they see. If you don't tell people what to look for, they have a better chance of seeing everything.

I have been on the receiving end of profiling, more times than I care to think. A lot of it happened when I was young, in North Carolina. But a lot of it has happened recently, too.

My wife and I were stopped and detained by the Washington, D.C., transit police quite recently. We had taken the train into the District from our home in Gaithersburg, to meet my son. He was a new student at Howard University. I wanted to help him figure out the subway system. Sandy and I rode into the District on the train alone, and we were going to ride back home with my son, so he could get a feel for it.

These transit police stopped us and demanded to see some identification. They took my Montgomery County police I.D. and went into their little office to run it down. When they came back, they challenged me on it. One officer, a white woman, said, "This tells me nothing about who you are and what you're doing here."

So, I told her who I was and what I was doing there.

She didn't believe me. She said to her partner, "He's just trying to impress this white lady."

Sandy was furious. She said, "You've insulted a police chief, and his wife. And his wife is an attorney!" She wanted to file a lawsuit. I wanted to forget it. In the end, that's what we did.

For me and my wife, the "profiling" also extends to what people see when they see a black man and a white woman together. Unfortunately, some people come to some ugly conclusions. On several occasions we have been stopped and questioned in hotel lobbies, or walking down the hallway with our room key in our hands.

It is difficult to calculate the price that Sandy and I have paid for being a black-and-white mixed couple. It doesn't matter, either, because I wouldn't have it any other way. But it's something I think about—what chances I might have had, what opportunities I lost, because of this.

For example, I know I lost a police chief job once for exactly this reason.

I was a candidate for police chief in Jackson, Mississippi, in 1990. I had applied for the job. I had been interviewed for the job. Members of the Jackson mayor's hiring committee had been to Portland to meet with me several times. I thought it looked like a great opportunity. I told Sandy, "We can do this."

By December, I was told the committee was down to three candidates—all three African-Americans—and the members were getting close to making up their minds. The other candidates were the acting chief of Jackson, and deputy police chief from Dallas. I was reported to have the support of the powerful Jackson Police Officers Association, the mainly white police officers' union.

Then the mayor's office called and said, "We'd like you to come down to Jackson and stay a few days. Bring your wife."

They put us up in a hotel where they were actually flying the Confederate flag. It was Christmastime, and there was a Christmas party that night. We met the other candidates. They were both black. They both had black spouses. Everyone was cordial, but there was something wrong. I could feel it.

No one said anything. We went back to Portland. I was later told that I had not been chosen for the job.

A newspaper article some days later told me why. Following the Christmas party, I had fallen from favor. The *Jackson Advocate*, reporting on the police chief selection process, quoted a member of the mayor's hiring committee, "Moose walked in with a blonde-haired, blue-eyed white wife and that killed any chances he had of becoming police chief here." The committee member said that he personally had no problem with a black police chief having a white wife, but said the citizens of his city might. "This is still Jackson, Mississippi."

The article went on to report that I had a poor reputation with African-Americans in Portland, quoting one community activist as saying, "He ain't going to do nothing to help Black folks. He wouldn't give a Black man a break if his life depended on it." The reporter even went so far as to contact my ex-wife and quote her: "I remember when he was promoted to Sergeant, other Black officers asked him for help and he ignored them. I had the impression he didn't care about them."

I was screwed both ways. I had a white wife, which

was bad news for white people, and I didn't like or support African-Americans, which was bad for everybody else. I wondered how in the hell I had become a candidate in the first place.

Then I got a call from the mayor of Jackson. He told me how sorry he was that it hadn't worked out. He told me I had been the front runner. Then he said, "This town is just not ready for a police chief with an interracial marriage."

That was a brave thing to do. He was going out on a limb telling me that. I appreciated his honesty, even if it was painful to hear.

For a while, I thought about suing the city of Jackson for discrimination. I contacted Morris Dees of the Southern Poverty Law Center and asked him to look into it. He and I had become friends. I wanted his advice. He looked into the matter for me and then said, "I can file a lawsuit, and I can get you the job. But maybe that's not a job you really want."

I had to think about what it would be like to have that job. What it would be like to be the police chief in a city like that. What it would be like for Sandy to be the police chief's wife. So I let it go. In January, I learned that the city of Jackson had not hired any of the front runners for the job, giving it instead to a former lieutenant with the Houston Police Department. He was a Mississippi native. He was black, too.

Four years later, the Jackson Police Department invited me to come down and teach their police force a few things about community policing.

I see the question of race in other, less lethal places, too. The door can swing both ways. I recently had to handle a grievance in my police department. There were some people up for promotion. A couple of the candidates were white. One of the candidates was black. I promoted two officers—one black and one white.

One of the white men who was not promoted filed a grievance about how the department passed him over in order to promote a black guy. The grievance was all about how he was more qualified than the black guy, had more experience than the black guy, did better on the tests than the black guy, was more deserving of the promotion than the black guy.

He *never even mentioned* the white candidate who got promoted. He never claimed that he was better than that person, or did better on test scores, or had more experience. All he could see was that the black guy got the job and he didn't. And that's all he claimed in his grievance.

I think it's possible that growing up black prepared me for being a police officer. It heightened my sense of right and wrong. It made me more aware of people being victimized or taken advantage of. I had a lot of feelings about the world not being fair. I saw how people treated my father. I saw how people treated Martin Luther King Jr. and the other people who were working in civil rights.

Unfortunately, I saw that the police in the South were a big part of the problem. From my perspective, they weren't protecting the people who were being victimized. They were doing the victimizing. They were taking sides, and it was sometimes taking sides against the people who were trying to make the world a better, fairer place.

That certainly didn't make me want to be a police officer. But it might have prepared me for being a police officer. Because when I was first exposed to police work, and realized that I actually had the power to help the people who were getting hurt the worst, I responded very positively to that.

Albina, the area in the Northeast section of Portland where I was first assigned to work, was mostly black and mostly poor. The other end of the spectrum would have been Lake Oswego, a suburb that was mostly white and mostly wealthy. When I started working undercover in Albina, I saw that all the stuff that was being stolen and brought to me was stuff that had been stolen from Albina. The stolen goods, and the victims, and the criminals were all from Albina. The crooks were stealing from poor people. I used to say, "What's wrong with these guys? How come they stay here, where there's nothing worth stealing? Why don't they steal stuff from people in Lake Oswego?"

The bad guys weren't raping people in Lake Oswego. They weren't selling drugs to people in Lake Oswego. They were raping the wives and daughters of Albina, and selling drugs to the young people of Albina. They were ruining the lives of the people they lived with—their own people.

The police weren't doing as much as they could have to stop this, but the police were not the bad guys. And, what's more, the white people were not the bad guys. This was black on black crime, pure and simple. It was poor people victimizing poor people.

Being a black police officer gave me a special opportunity. It may have made it easier for me to think about ideas like community policing and a holistic approach to protecting citizens from crime. I had a way of relating to the victims and the criminals that maybe the white police officers around me didn't have.

But being a black police officer, I think, represents all kinds of challenges. I don't think a white guy, for example, has to spend a lot of time apologizing, or thinking he ought to apologize, for being a cop.

There's a perception in the black community that if you are a police officer you are automatically an Uncle Tom, or some kind of traitor to your people. Everyone can recite chapter and verse on how abusive the police have been to black people in America. Whether they think Rodney King was innocent, or O.J. Simpson was framed, or whatever, most African-Americans see the police as part of their problem, and not part of their solution.

I first got a taste of this when I was a young police officer and was trying to date, and I met women who just wouldn't have anything to do with a police officer.

Later, I got it from family. I got it from my father. He wasn't exactly thrilled that I'd become a police officer.

A lot of white people were surprised I was a cop, too. I mostly worked in the North and Northwest sections of the city. But every once in a while I'd have to make a police call out to the West Hills area. That was the "nice" area, where the people with money lived, and the people with money were white. A lot of the time, when you'd make the calls out there, you'd be told to come around to the back of the house. You'd be told to take your shoes off before you came inside. If you took offense at that, or if you refused to be treated like a second-class citizen, you'd be hearing from your captain, or from the mayor. You'd go on report for not being respectful, for causing trouble, for being difficult.

You knew that wasn't going to happen on calls you made in Northwest. If someone called to complain about your behavior from a house in that area, they'd probably just be laughed at. Their attitude was more along the lines of "How can a black man become a cop? Don't you know what the cops do?" I'd get people I was trying to arrest saying to me, "Come on, man. Give a brother a break. You ain't gonna arrest a brother, are you?"

I don't think white cops get that too much from white suspects. "Come on, man. You aren't going to arrest *me*. I'm white like you!" I don't think that comes up for white police officers. But it came up a lot for me. Lots of black people, including the criminals, thought that it was a question of choosing sides—and that I would choose being black above being a cop if I was given that choice.

I wasn't given that choice, so I never had to make that choice. But I think I developed a kind of split personality about the whole question. On the one hand, I was a police officer, and I had dedicated myself to being a police officer, and I was working with the system of the police department. I was going to uphold the law and follow the rules.

On the other hand, I was going to challenge the sys-

tem wherever I saw the system wasn't fair. I was a police officer, and I was ambitious to get ahead, so I was
trying for promotions. I wasn't going to cheat or lie to
get a promotion, but I saw that the promotion process
wasn't fair. So I challenged that. Some people thought
that was wrong. They thought I should accept the system for what it was. I didn't agree. I thought it was my
job to challenge the system, from inside the system, to
do what I could to make sure the system was more fair
when I left there than when I got there.

Surely that was the lesson of Martin Luther King Jr.
and Medgar Evers and Rosa Parks. You couldn't change
the system without challenging the system, and you
couldn't challenge the system if you were a criminal. So
instead of breaking the law, you pushed the limits of the
law. Or insisted, in some cases, in the letter of the law
being applied fairly to you, just like it was to everybody
else.

Part of the problem of being a police officer who
wants to instigate change is that it is usually the police
officer's job to *defend* the status quo—not to challenge
it. Things change slowly in our society. When things do
change, it doesn't usually start with the police department. It usually *ends* with the police department, because that is one of the last places to embrace change.

Like the issue of arresting homosexual men for what
they do together in private. There are still lots of states
in America that have sodomy on the books as a crime.
Technically, you could fill up your jail every day with
nothing but sodomy cases, if you wanted to arrest people for that.

In Portland, the traditional approach to this situation
was to put male officers undercover in places where
there was a lot of activity, and just start arresting anyone
who approached or propositioned the officers. That was
counterproductive.

The alternative I favored was to go to the same area
with uniformed officers and with members of the gay
and lesbian community and say, "This park may have

been the place where this kind of activity was the status quo, but things have changed. There are other people using this park now, and that kind of behavior, in public, is no longer acceptable." We had the choice of just arresting people, or of using the gay community to help change the culture of the park. I found we had more success using the second strategy—even if the letter of the law suggested we should just be arresting everyone and letting the courts prosecute them.

I think that's a daily challenge for police departments everywhere. Is it going to be your job to wait until a crime is committed and then come in and arrest the people doing the crime? Or is it going to be your job to look at the place in your community where crime is going to be committed and ask yourself what you can change to prevent the crime?

I see it everywhere we go. My wife and I were recently in Philadelphia. I really like Philadelphia. But whenever we stay there, we'll be going out to do something and it's two in the afternoon, and there's these little groups of black men standing around on the street corners. You can see there's nothing going on around these street corners. You can tell from looking at the men that they didn't just get off the night shift. You have to wonder, "Why isn't there someplace for these men to be? Why isn't there someplace for these men to go— and something useful for them to be doing?" I'm not saying these guys are breaking the law, or that they're planning to. But there's nothing good about groups of men hanging out on street corners at two in the afternoon with nothing to do. That's a place where trouble is going to start.

For some people in the black community there might have been a dilemma in the resolution of the sniper case. Some people might think it's bad for the black community that the accused men were black. We have not, as a race, been serial killers. We haven't been mass murderers. We've had more than our share of crime. But that kind of insane mass violence has not been associated with black people.

When the two black men were arrested in the sniper shootings, the black radio talk show host Tom Joyner remarked that he was disappointed. He was sarcastic about it. He said, "First they let us into baseball. Then they let us into golf. Now we've made it into serial killing!"

I felt the same way: African-Americans were already associated with so many bad things in America. Now this.

For many black Americans, there wasn't a lot of cheering that the suspects might face the death penalty. Blacks have been the victims of the death penalty, in disproportionate numbers, for a long time. Most black Americans have someone in their family, or close to their family, who can tell a story about a lynching, about a family member that got lynched. So the idea of that kind of justice is frightening to them. I don't think there was a lot of cheering in the black community that these guys were going to go on trial in a death penalty state. It isn't that anyone decided they were guilty or not guilty. There just isn't the enthusiasm for the death penalty that you might find in the white community.

Don't get me wrong. I'm not saying I'm against the death penalty. But I have mixed feelings about it. In most cases, I think that life without possibility for parole, for the worst of the criminals, is fine. But I understand the call for the death penalty, too. If someone did something awful to my wife, or my child, I'd probably be demanding the death penalty. I might demand the person be killed. I find it tough to say I don't believe in the death penalty.

And I recognize it has a certain power of deterrence. I've always known that when I am in Texas, for example, I'd better behave. The snipers should have known that they were in Virginia, and they'd better behave.

Early in 2003 I participated in an event held on a cold, snowy Saturday morning at the Ebenezer African-

American Episcopal Church over in Prince George's County, Maryland. The event was chaired by Tavis Smiley, the syndicated talk show host. He and I and a half dozen other men and women from the area spoke to a group of about three hundred African-American young people and their families.

The questions facing us were the questions that face all African-Americans today: How will we be part of the solution? How will we be part of the system? How will we be part of the society? What is our role? What is our responsibility? And what do we have for our young people?

The choir sang. The minister, a rap star–handsome young man in braids and a beautiful suit, shouted at the young people to join him in some "holy hip-hop." Then the band struck up a hip-hop beat, and a young singer started rapping about God. When he was done, the minister pointed down at me and said, "When the chief of police is getting his roof on for holy hip-hop, you *know* God is in the house!" Then he asked the congregation to join him in "Lift Every Voice and Sing," which some folks refer to as the "Negro national anthem."

Tavis Smiley talked about his Youth To Leaders program. He quoted the great African-American thinker W.E.B. DuBois's idea, from his 1902 book *The Souls of Black Folk*, about the "talented tenth," the 10 percent of the black population that DuBois said would be the great leaders. Tavis talked about harnessing that "talented tenth" and finding the young men and women in America today who are going to be the leaders of America tomorrow, and making sure they know, today, that they can make a difference.

There was a lot to talk about that morning. America was preparing for war. America was preparing for more terrorist attacks. There were tanks and rocket launchers posted outside the airports and monuments of Washington, D.C.

When it was my turn at the podium, I said, "We as adults are not doing our jobs as role models. We want our children to find resolutions to their conflicts in non-violent ways. But we as a nation are about to solve our conflict with bombs and the might of the greatest military power in the history of the world. As a nation, we are a poor role model.

"There's a recklessness in our society with violence and guns. There's a recklessness with sex. There's a recklessness with drugs. Young people who do not know their bright history may not think they have a bright future. It is our responsibility to teach our young people their history, and to serve as responsible role models at the same time."

Later, when there were questions from the audience, someone asked me what was the role of a black police officer in this world I was talking about.

"It's a confusing issue," I said. "You talk about DuBois. You talk about being black in America. I have that problem every day. I am treated differently by the system because I am black, but I am part of the system, too. But that doesn't mean I can't do anything about it.

"We can all be social engineers. We have to be. We have to get angry when we see injustice being done to another human being, just as we get angry when an injustice is done to us. We have to take responsibility, as human beings, for that.

"I've decided to do that as a police officer—to ensure that there will be no injustice done where *I* am. And we can all do that, in our lives. We can't assume that somewhere among us is a Martin Luther King Jr. who's going to march for us, or a Johnnie Cochran who's going to speak out for us. We all have to be the person who marches and speaks out. If you see someone committing an injustice against another person, it is your job to speak out against that."

There was another question, from a young person, about personal responsibility and the powerlessness of the average citizen to change society. I disagreed. I said, "You *can* do something, right now. Even if it's as simple and small as name calling. We're all part of that. We're all part of a group that laughs at something someone says about someone from another group. If you laugh along with that, you're part of the problem. And you can change that, right away, if you stop joining in."

I really believe that. I really believe that each of us has that job.

Ultimately it's a question of personal responsibility. It's not a question of law or law enforcement. The law isn't always going to be there. It comes down to each person being responsible for his or her own action.

Even at the level of something as basic as name calling, it's a personal choice. If you are around people who tease, or engage in name calling, you're participating. We're all part of a group—at work, at school, whatever—where people do that. And if we laugh along with them, we're part of the problem. The problem won't stop unless *we* stop.

If you get a police officer that shoots an African-American kid, for example, and then a police officer from the same police department shoots another African-American kid, people will start protesting. They might hold a march in front of the police station to register their outrage. But if Mrs. Johnson's kid shoots Mrs. Jenkins's kid, you don't see anybody marching on Mrs. Johnson's house. Why not? It's the same thing. It's another act of violence against a young African-American male. It's another death. Maybe we'd get a handle on violence in America if more people started marching on things like that—started saying, "We're not going to put up with any more violence."

I think I got my sense of personal responsibility from my dad. I got a lot from coaches I had in school. I got a lot from Bob Lamb, too.

He was a retired captain, off the Atlantic City Police Department. Later he became a longtime employee of the federal Community Relations Service. His territory was the Pacific Northwest, during the time I was in Portland, Oregon.

He called me a lot. He'd talk about what he was reading, what he was hearing, what he was thinking about. He was one of the founders of NOBLE—the National Organization of Black Law Enforcement Executives. Bob would call, and he'd force me to talk. He'd call at nine o'clock or even ten o'clock on a Friday night. He wouldn't wait for me to call him with a problem. He'd call me and find out what the problem was, if I was having one. He was just checking on me. He had a way of telling a story, or remembering something that had happened to him, that made me comfortable. He'd get me talking about what was going on.

I'd like to be better at that. I'd like to do more of that. I don't know if you get permission to give advice just because you get old. Or if you get permission to stop taking advice just because you get old. I don't really have anybody I call these days, or who calls me, for that kind of conversation. I don't really have anybody I can call now and ask for help. I don't really have a mentor. I think it's more important for me to *be* a mentor, to younger officers, or younger people, who are just coming up.

I'd like to be Bob Lamb to someone. I'd like to be Lee Brown.

Lee Brown was a great role model for me. He isn't a personal friend. I wouldn't presume to call him a mentor, exactly. But he's someone that I admire, and someone who represents for me some of the opportunities available to a person like me.

Lee Brown was a police officer in a medium-sized town in California before I met him. Then he became one of the first African-Americans to get a Ph.D. in criminology and was hired by Portland State University to run their criminal justice program. He eventually became sheriff of Multnomah County, Portland's county, at a time when the county police department was much stronger than it is today. He made his sheriff's department one of the first police agencies in America to require a four-year college degree for its incoming deputies. He made other changes, many of which were later adopted by other agencies.

He left Portland and became the police chief for Atlanta, Georgia. He was there during that terrible serial killing of children. He solved that. Then he became police chief of Houston, Texas. Then he became the police commissioner for the New York Police Department. Then he became Bill Clinton's "drug czar." Then he became a professor at Rice University, where he became part of the Baker Institute. Then he ran for mayor of Houston—and now he's finishing his fourth term.

I really got to know Lee Brown in the late 1980s, when he was police chief in Houston and was hosting an event there on community policing, with an emphasis on the black community and black police officers. I remember, to this day, a man at that event complaining about black police executives specifically. He said, "The problem is black police officers get promoted in their departments and become lieutenants and assistant chiefs and deputy chiefs and even police chiefs, and you have the same policies that the white guys did. The people in the streets, doing all that protesting, making it possible for you to get promoted in the first place, we did all that work for nothing. If you're not going to change the policies, why did we struggle so hard to get you guys in charge?"

I never forgot that. I realized, when I was promoted to chief, that I could just take the job and be a caretaker. That would be safe. That would be popular. Or I could try to change the way things were done in my city. I realized that being chief, and being well liked, was not going to go along with that. And I decided I would risk being an unpopular, not-well-liked police chief, if that was the price for making change.

Since then, I see Lee Brown at police conferences. Sometimes I overhear people laughing at him, or about him, and the way he's managed his career. They say he's going to have to keep working forever, because he's never stayed at one job long enough to qualify for a pension. For me, he's the consummate role model—in terms of working hard, getting the education, being willing to risk making the changes, being willing to take on new jobs and new challenges.

When he was police commissioner in New York, he and then-mayor David Dinkins set about instituting a new kind of community policing. They increased the size of the police department, and they changed the way police officers worked in the community. And they cleaned the city up. Then, Dinkins was out, and a new police chief came in. The new chief, Bill Bratton, inherited this community policing model, and he inherited the benefits of that. He gets all the credit for changing New York, when it was really Lee Brown that did a lot of the hard work.

During the sniper investigation, I got a couple of notes from Lee Brown. That meant a lot to me. I hope I can be that kind of mentor, or role model, for someone else someday.

During the sniper siege I found myself having, again, a dream that has been a recurring dream for me since I was a child. In the dream, I am being crushed by falling rocks. It's a whole mountain of falling rocks. I struggle to get free, but I can't. I'm crushed. I die in the dream, crushed under this mountain of falling rocks.

I don't know what the rocks mean. I don't know why I have this dream. I suspect it has something to do with growing up the way I did, in the time I did, in the place I did—and I suspect it has a lot to do with being an African-American. Every time I start thinking that the race issue in America has been solved, or that my problems as a black man in America are no long serious problems, something happens to remind me how little has changed.

After the sniper suspects were caught, I got a fax in my office from something called the National Alliance, in Baltimore. Featuring pictures of the sniper suspects and titled "Do You Feel Safe Yet?" this document attacked the sniper task force generally, and me specifically, for intentionally screwing up the sniper investigation.

Why? Because I'm black and the suspects were black, and I didn't want to arrest a black person for this heinous crime.

"Charles Moose had access to the telephone messages from the snipers, and surely must have known that the caller was Black," the paper says. "Yet Moose, Black himself and a vocal opponent of 'racial profiling' (when it affects Blacks) did not reveal that fact to the public until it became inescapable.

"What frightens you more: The two killers, or the fact that a man like Moose, who put his race above our safety, is the head of the task force meant to capture them? Is that the type of person that you want to have safeguard your children?

"Do you feel safe yet? Don't let your guard down, because every formerly White nation on this planet is crawling with dangerous non-White criminals, parasitic non-White immigrants, and incompetent non-White or anti-White public officials. It's being done purposely. It's time to take our country back."

I read that, and I stop wondering if I'm being a little paranoid about my position as a black man in America. Anyone that thinks it's not tough isn't living in America. Or isn't black.

11. Caught Like a Duck in a Noose

The next day was Thursday, October 24. It was in some ways the longest day of the entire ordeal. We had the snipers, but we couldn't say we had the snipers, because we didn't know, for sure, that they *were* the snipers.

With every hour that passed, though, we were more sure. It was clear in the middle of the night that we had the right car, with the right plates. It was clear by 3:30 A.M. that the two people in custody were, in fact, John Allen Muhammad and Lee Boyd Malvo.

As the day progressed, we got a look inside the Chevy Caprice. The snipers had modified this nondescript car—which we later learned had been purchased at a New Jersey used car dealership, with the ironic name of Sure Shot Auto Sales, and had previously been used as an undercover police vehicle—and customized it for long-distance killing. They had drilled a porthole in the trunk lid to accommodate the muzzle of the rifle and the scope. They had removed part of the backseat, so that the shooter could lie flat in the car, his feet resting against the back of the front seat, stretched out comfortably to shoot. They had even built a small platform in the trunk so the rifle's tripod was raised to exactly the same height as the hole in the trunk lid. Shooting with the trunk down kept the sound of the gun and the muzzle flash to an absolute minimum. The snipers had a pair of blue socks—exactly the same dark blue as the blue of the car—to shove into the holes in the trunk lid so they wouldn't be too conspicuous.

Also in the car were the snipers' clothes, in duffel bags, plus a silencer for the rifle, plus the scope and the tripod they'd used to target the victims. There was also a laptop computer, and in the computer were files relating to the shooting—a log of the whole killing spree. The pair had used walkie-talkies, too, so the spotter could help the shooter choose a location, pick a victim, time his shots and make his getaway.

In the world of the true crime novel, this whole setup would be considered hokey and crude. In the real world of October 2002, it proved to be extremely effective.

Through the day, we began to piece together everything we knew about Muhammad and Malvo, too.

Muhammad had been a soldier. He'd fought in the 1991 Gulf War, and been awarded something called the Kuwait Liberation Medal for his work as a combat engineer. He earned an honorable discharge in 1994.

Muhammad had been married twice. He had four children. He was estranged from the mother of the last three, Mildred Green, and during the separation and divorce lost custody of the children. He was also hit with a restraining order, preventing him from being anywhere near his ex-wife.

That didn't stop him from seeing his children. He took them to Antigua, in March of 2000, in what his ex-wife Green called a kidnapping. In Antigua, he may have met Malvo and his mother.

Sometime after that, according to INS documents, Malvo and his mother, Una James, were smuggled from Jamaica to Haiti to Miami, in a cargo ship. They found work in a Red Lobster in Ft. Myers, Florida. They later traveled to the Tacoma, Washington, area—perhaps to be with Muhammad.

By December 2001, they were all reunited—though

not very happily. Police in Bellingham, Washington, responded to a domestic disturbance call there and found Muhammad and James doing battle.

Muhammad and Malvo both wound up living in a homeless shelter, and later a YMCA, in Bellingham. Malvo attended area schools. He and Muhammad played basketball and worked out at the Y. They lived at the Lighthouse Mission, in Bellingham, from at least October 20, 2001, to January 19, 2002.

By then, Muhammad was introducing Malvo as his stepson.

And Muhammad was beginning to show off his fascination with guns. Sometime during this period he visited a friend in the Seattle area, and brought with him an AR-15 assault rifle fitted with a long distance scope. He took some target practice and talked about how effective the weapon would be for sniper work, with a silencer attached.

All of this was fascinating. But it didn't mean a thing. Nothing in what we were learning made for solid evidence.

But through the day the information continued to come together. Sometime later in the day we began to have a clearer sense of the snipers' movements.

We were able to place them in the Montgomery County area as early as September 15. We figured them as suspects in a shooting on that date, in which a pizzeria owner in Clinton, Maryland, was shot six times with a .22-caliber handgun and robbed of $3,000 and a laptop computer—the same one that was found in the back of the Caprice on October 24.

We were able to place them at the scene of another shooting on September 14, in Silver Spring, Maryland, where evidence connected them to an attempted murder outside a liquor store.

The following day, in Prince George's County, the same .22-caliber handgun that killed the pizzeria owner on September 15 was used to shoot a liquor store employee as he was closing up shop. The employee was robbed of his wallet.

By then, the suspects had already obtained the Caprice. Records show the car was purchased in Trenton, New Jersey, on September 10, for $250. Muhammad told the dealer at Sure Shot Auto Sales that he intended to use the Caprice as a taxi. (Two days before, he had said he wanted to buy a car for his son. He had originally visited the dealership in the company of another man. This was probably Nathaniel O. Osbourne, a New Jersey resident who was listed as co-owner of the vehicle. Osbourne was later sought, apprehended, questioned and determined to have had nothing to do with the shootings.) The car had 146,975 miles on the odometer.

Then, for reasons we had yet to establish, Muhammad and Malvo left the area. On September 21, they were in Montgomery, Alabama. On that date, they shot two women outside another liquor store. One was shot with a .223-caliber assault rifle, the other with a .22-caliber handgun. The woman shot with the assault rifle died.

Two days later, a woman was shot once in the head with a .223-caliber assault rifle as she walked from the beauty parlor where she worked in Baton Rouge, Louisiana. Witnesses put Malvo at the scene. Plus, this murder may have been the one the snipers referred to in one of their phone communications with the task force hot line operators. At one point they had made claims about a killing outside a casino in Louisiana. At the time, we had not been able to determine if there had been any killings outside any casinos in Louisiana. We had been looking in the Gulf Port area, where the riverfront casinos are. This killing in Baton Rouge may have been the one the snipers meant us to find out about.

The task force would later be asked to conduct ballistics tests on a bullet fragment connected to a shooting in Georgia. On September 20 a forty-one-year-old Ethiopian immigrant was shot and killed outside a liquor store in southwest Atlanta. We had reason to believe the two suspects had been in Montgomery County on September 14 and had shot a man outside a Silver Spring liquor store. We had evidence to suggest these two men had been in Montgomery, Alabama, on September 21. Had they passed through Atlanta on their journey south? The ballistics tests linked the bullet fragments to the other shootings.

We had one more weird puzzle piece: Muhammad's ex-wife lived in the snipers' target area, in Clinton, Maryland, in Prince George's County. She worked, or had once worked, in a Michael's craft store.

And Muhammad's other ex-wife lived in Baton Rouge, Louisiana.

There was some theorizing that day about a possible motive. Was Muhammad originally trying to kill his ex-wife? Was he trying to raise money to get her back? To get his family back? To get his family back and have the money to run away with them forever? Was he going to kill all these people, and then kill his wife, using the other murders to camouflage his true motive—getting even with the wife? Was he just a good squared-away family man trying to settle down and raise his kids—with the $10 million he'd need to do it right?

We talked about what made the snipers suddenly freak out, that day, in that place. They had done several killings already, it looked like, but those were killings where robbery was also a motive, or maybe the only motive. In Montgomery County, starting on October 2, they didn't attempt to rob anyone.

Maybe that way was the best way to get our attention. The killers never tried to change guns, never tried to change the ballistics on the gun. They wanted us to know it was one person doing this, and that he was a real badass, so we would give them the money. We talked about the amount, too. Why $10 million? It's not very much money, on one hand. But it's probably in the range that they assumed we would pay. If they'd asked for $800 million, no negotiations could have taken place. With $10 million . . . Maybe this was nothing but a financial arrangement from the beginning.

The investigation continued to show that anything was possible.

All day long, as this information began to collect around us, we were waiting for the one piece that really mattered. The ATF ballistics experts were conducting their tests on the rifle we'd taken out of the Chevy Caprice. We knew it was a Bushmaster XM-15 E2S. We knew it fired .223-caliber bullets.

We would learn later that the weapon was shipped by the Bushmaster Firearms Company to a distributor in the Washington State area, probably Tacoma, in June 2002.

But we didn't know whether the results of the forensics tests in the Rockville lab would come back positive, negative or inconclusive. We knew it could be any one of those three.

And we didn't know it was going to take so long.

We got the gun out of the Caprice at something like 6 A.M. on the morning of October 24. There was some disagreement, right away, about where it should go first. It was decided it would go to the FBI lab first, where it could be swabbed for DNA and any other evidence. Then it would go to the ATF lab for ballistics.

The gun stayed with the FBI for far longer than we'd expected. It didn't get back over to the ATF lab until about two in the afternoon. The ATF ballistics team consisted of seven examiners, led by a dapper-looking African-American firearms and tool mark examiner named Walter A. Dandridge Jr. They went to work right away. I guess I figured they'd be out pretty soon. But it took six hours. Six hours! It was a long time to wait.

The ATF guys were slow and methodical, and tested each bullet and bullet fragment we had, one at a time. When they were done testing them all, and had all their results, the man conducting the forensics experiments stepped aside, another ATF expert came in, and the tests were done all over again from the beginning. They didn't want there to be any possibility of a mistake, or any possibility of doubt, when they were done.

The ATF people had decided to go all the way through and finish before they said anything. They didn't want, and I agreed with them, to come back with partial results. We didn't want to go out early and tell the media that we had positive results on two of the killings—because the media would want to know which ones. Then we'd have to say. Then we'd have to deal with the feelings of the families of the victims where there was no result. We wanted as much closure as possible, and to not leave anyone hanging. So we had agreed from the beginning to be very thorough.

The media was already reporting, or trying to report, that we had apprehended the right suspects—but they were premature, and basing their conclusion on erroneous assumptions. I had arrived for work that morning as usual. I pulled around the back of the building, to the parking lot, and then walked across the parking lot and into the building. I was wearing jeans and running shoes, the way I do every day except for the days I teach in the evenings. I got out of my car, walked to the back of the building and bumped into Lieutenant Raum. He had been up all night, interviewing the suspects at the holding facility. I asked him how he was doing, whether there had been any developments, whether he'd been able to spend any time with his family lately and so on.

Lieutenant Raum told me they weren't finished interviewing the suspects yet, that the car hadn't been properly searched yet, so there was still a lot to learn. He told me, "It looks good, though. It's all coming together." I thanked him for all his hard work, and then I went inside.

What I didn't know was that a cameraman had snuck around the back of the building and gotten all this on tape. So now the reporters at his TV station were coming to all these conclusions. I was arriving for work out of uniform, very casual. That must mean the case was closed. I was coming in the back door, and chatting with a plainclothes officer, very casual. That must mean the end was here.

They were wrong about everything. But they had not been able to get a camera on the back of the building since the case began. They had never seen me arrive for work in jeans and a sweater. They had never seen me park my car and then stop to chat with a member of the task force. I did all this stuff every day, but to the untrained eye it looked like a fascinating new development, and the end of the big sniper drama.

I learned later that Dandridge was just as affected by this crime spree as the rest of us. He lived in Fairfax County, Virginia. He had three children, all in area grade schools. He said he and the other members of his team were very conscious of the time passing, of the world waiting and of the pressure being put on them by the media. So they paid no attention to that, but went slowly and methodically about their business.

Meanwhile, we waited, and the task force team continued to assemble. Chief Ramsey, of the Washington, D.C., Metropolitan Police Department, arrived. So did Chief Manger, of the Fairfax County Police Department. My corner office didn't have enough seats at the eight-sided table. Soon it didn't have enough room, almost, for me. It's not some big executive suite to start with. And it was filling up with all kinds of people. There were my assistant chiefs. There were Gary Bald and Mike Bouchard. There were representatives from all the other police jurisdictions. There was Superintendent David Mitchell from the Maryland State Police. There were people from the Virginia State Police and the sheriff's office in Spotsylvania County and from Prince George's County police. There was Charlie Dean, the Prince William County police chief, which was great. I'd met Charlie in 1993 at the FBI National Executive Institute when I was still in Portland, and always found him to be a very experienced and thoughtful man. He dealt with the sniper situation well, reaching out to the task force for help and remaining an active player in the investigation, contributing a number of important ideas and suggestions during the three-week manhunt. It was good to have him there at the end.

We also had the Montgomery County executive,

Doug Duncan—the only political leader to be part of this final briefing.

It was pretty tense. I don't like a lot of people around me in the best of times. My staff assistant, Sergeant Emanuel, works hard to control the flow of traffic in and out of my office. He knows I want to see everybody who wants to see me. He knows I also have to get my work done. Sometimes I tell Sergeant Emanuel, "I need twenty minutes undisturbed."

Sometimes that's because I have paperwork that requires all my concentration. Sometimes I need to make a phone call that requires all my concentration. Sometimes I need to speak with my wife. Sometimes I just need a few minutes of quiet.

Other times, I want everyone to have access to me. When I took the job in Montgomery County, I told the assistant chiefs that there was no such thing as bothering me too much, that there was no such thing as a bad time to call. If my door was shut, they had the authority to open it.

I made the open door policy known to the rest of my employees, too. I explained that the policy meant that anyone could call my scheduler, Nancy Marsden, and tell her they wanted to meet with me, and that it was personal. They didn't have to supply any other information. The meeting would be scheduled, and as an added protection of their privacy, their appointment with me would not appear on my daily schedule. I have that sent out department-wide, every day, so that all my people know how I'm spending my time. But the personal appointments with people on my staff were never made public. I thought the employees deserved that protection.

When I hired Sergeant Emanuel to be my aide, he asked me how he was supposed to do the job. I said, "You've been in the military," because I knew he had been a Marine. "Do it just like a general's aide does it." He understood that.

So when I'd say, "I'm closing my door for twenty minutes," he'd post himself on the door and no one would get in. Sergeant Emanuel would tell them, "Unless an officer has been shot or you have caught the sniper, you are not getting past me."

The department had never been under this kind of pressure before. I had never been under this kind of pressure, either—especially not for three weeks running. There was a lot to do, every single minute of every single day. In addition to the largest American manhunt in history, there was also the department to run. There were promotions to attend to and job vacancies and discipline issues and investigations of grievances. There were all kinds of budget worries. In addition to the regular police work and in addition to the sniper work, there were also all these meetings with the press, and meetings with the county executive. Every day was a very full day.

I don't know how much I was showing the strain of that. I notice from the TV clips how long my hair was getting. I was afraid to take any time off to get a haircut. I didn't think that would look too good: The chief is off at a beauty parlor while a cold-blooded killer stalks his county. Luckily I had been in for a cut not long before this all started. But three weeks in, I was starting to look like I was going for a full-on Afro.

I know my clothes were still looking okay, because I'm fastidious about that. And in Montgomery County this was a little easier than it was in Portland.

Before I took the Maryland job, I made several visits to the police department. I remember telling Sergeant Darrin McGee, the chief's aide during that time, how impressed I was that the officers I met always looked so sharp. They didn't know I was coming, didn't know who I was, and yet they always looked very well turned out. McGee explained to me that the Montgomery County Police Department paid for all its officers to dry clean their uniforms. In Portland, the officers had to pay for their own dry cleaning. Years ago, the department had made the switch from wool uniforms to wash-and-wear uniforms, so the officers laundered them at home. But the ones who could afford it still had them professionally cleaned and pressed, so you had some officers looking sharp and some looking not so sharp. And even the sharp-looking officers were not getting their uniforms cleaned as often as the Montgomery County officers.

It's a big budget item. But if you want the officers to look really sharp, you pay for them to get their uniforms done. And you set the example.

I try to do that, personally. When I've got a little extra time before going to work—my wife kids me about this—I even take my military uniform out of the dry cleaner bag and go over it one more time with a hot iron. I like to make sure the creases are straight and sharp, and sometimes they don't come back from the dry cleaner that way.

This comes from years of experience with the Air National Guard. They take their uniforms very seriously. The whole spit-and-polish image is important to them. So it's become important to me, too. I order my uniforms over the Internet from an outfit down in San Antonio. They'll customize the uniform for you, to help keep it looking perfect for a long time. The buttons on the pockets, for example, are all covered with a flap of fabric, so you don't see them. But every time you press the uniform, the press makes a little indentation in the fabric when it passes over the button. So this company will remove the buttons and sew the pockets shut—and then the pockets also won't bulge from having stuff in them. They'll even Velcro the pockets for you, if you want. All of this costs a little extra, but it's worth it if you want that extra spit-and-polish look.

My uniform was looking good, but I know from some of my behavior that I was getting worn down. One morning, for example, I was sitting for an interview with a reporter from one of the TV stations. I had been going around since about 6 A.M., as I did every morning, taking time for each of the news outlets, trying to stay friendly. Then I sat down with the county executive, Doug Duncan, for an interview with a reporter from one of the network stations. The reporter was a New York anchor, interviewing me by remote from her New York office, working with her Washington, D.C., affiliate's crew. She started to ask me a question, and when I answered she cut me off. Then she did that again. Then she did it again, and I said, "You asked me a question. Let me answer it." But she cut me off again.

I unclipped the microphone from my shirt, pulled the earpiece out and got up and walked away. Doug Duncan said, "I guess this interview is over." It was. I didn't have time to be abused, or the patience.

As I walked off, the reporter's crew started cheering and applauding. That was a little weird, taking my side against their own colleague. I guess they'd never seen anyone refuse to cooperate with an anchorperson before. I'm always surprised at what people will do in order to be on television. I wasn't doing this.

Another time, I came down to do the morning briefing, in the company of Doug Duncan, Gary Bald and Mike Bouchard. We had a system for how we did these briefings. We'd thought it all out. We had it all set up. We wanted to speak to the citizens, and for that matter to the sniper, and we wanted it done in the same orderly way each time. We wanted to make sure, too, that no one was the star of the show. The people in the FBI and the ATF needed to know that their leaders were just as much in the spotlight as the chief of police—that this task force was still a team.

This particular morning the chairs had all been moved around. Some producer had come up with a new arrangement. I said to the producer, "You may not have gotten the memo on this, but we have to rearrange the chairs so it's in this order."

She got huffy and said, "We don't have time to rearrange the chairs. We did it this way. It has to stay this way. Please take your seats."

I told her again that the seats needed to be moved.

She said, "We don't have time. We go live in a minute and a half."

I said, "I have things that need doing in my office," and I walked off.

The chairs went back to the original configuration. We did the interview in the usual way.

I don't know if I would do it that way again. At the time, though, I knew that this was the most important case of my life. I needed to do it right. I needed to insist on us being a team, right to the very end, even after the very end.

After the incident with the anchor from New York, Sergeant Emanuel said, "I guess we won't be doing any more work with that news organization."

I said, "Sure we will. I just needed to make a point."

Sure enough, the next day this enormous fruit basket arrived with a nice note from those folks, apologizing for the interview.

I said to Sergeant Emanuel, "Wow. It looks like the police are back in charge of the media." I could only wish!

This afternoon and evening there wasn't going to be any chance for a twenty-minute break. There were too many people around. My office was standing room only.

The tension of having all these people around increased because it took such a long time for us to get the reports back from ballistics. We had thought we were going to be able to get out and make a statement as early as six o'clock. In fact, it was hours later than that.

I was gradually feeling a sense of relief. We had the suspects. We had the car. Then we had the gun. Then other pieces started coming together. Every hour that passed with no new shooting, and no one new getting killed, helped, too. I guess my nightmare scenario at that point would have been, we've got the guys and the car and the gun, and guess what? Someone else has just been killed. I can't imagine how that would have felt.

At some point in the late morning I told Ellen Alexander, our victims' liaison person, to start contacting the families of the snipers' victims. I decided earlier that day that I wanted them to hear, from me, personally, that we had captured these men and that we were certain they were the men responsible for the deaths of their loved ones. •We decided to hold a meeting in a classroom at the police academy. No media. No other law enforcement representatives. Just the core group of task force people—County Executive Doug Duncan, Gary Bald, assistant chiefs Dee Walker and Bill O'Toole and me—but not Mike Bouchard, who was still back in the ATF lab ramrodding the ballistics stuff—and the families and loved ones of the Montgomery County victims.

I wanted the families to have the respect of hearing everything we knew, from us directly, delivered in the kindest, softest way. I did not want them to be having dinner and watching TV that night and find out it was just over, without us having the courtesy to tell them ourselves.

Once they were assembled, after a lot of hugging and crying, we made sure everyone had a chance to meet everyone else—bearing in mind that the more recent victims' families were newer at this than some of the others. There were fifty or sixty people in the room— wives, husbands, children, parents and others. None of these people had known each other before this started. Now a lot of them had become close. I had not met most of them either. Doug Duncan had been to every funeral and had met the victims' families. I had not been to any of them. These were new faces for me, too.

I got up and spoke. I started with an apology. I said I was sorry that this ever happened, sorry that I didn't know why it ever happened and sorry that we were not able to solve it, and stop it, sooner. I told them that even this afternoon, we didn't really understand why it had happened here, and now, and why their loved ones were the victims. I explained to them that nothing we had learned suggested that the victims had done anything to become targets. None of them was doing anything they shouldn't have been doing. None of them were anyplace they shouldn't have been. There was nothing going on that was going to show up in the newspapers and embarrass the families.

I wanted them to understand the truly random nature of the killings. I wanted them to understand there was no connection between the victims, and no connection between the victims and the killers. I didn't want there to be any doubt lingering in their minds that their loved ones were doing something wrong that got them picked to die.

I commended them for their courage. I said I knew that no one really understood how they felt. I told them that I couldn't imagine what it would be like to suffer a loss like that, and to suffer it in such a terribly public way.

Then I told them what we knew so far. We had these two suspects. We had their gun. We had enough information to keep the two men and the gun off the street. We weren't going to announce indictments yet. They weren't going to hear about specific charges yet. But I told them not to be concerned about that. These two men, I promised them, were not going to be released. They were not a danger to anyone anymore.

I tried to give them some kind of sense of what would happen next. The trials would be a long time in coming. The victims' families would not have to attend, or participate, unless they wanted to.

But the media part of the story was going to continue. I told them to accept the fact that this was going to be in the news for a long time. I understood that they needed closure, that their lives had been changed forever, that their heartache was going to continue. Unfortunately, the news story was going to continue, too. They were going to have to read about these killings, and the people responsible for them, for months and months.

I suggested various ways they might protect themselves from the media. One family had made the mistake of allowing some reporters to come to a funeral service. The media people had agreed not to take any pictures inside the church. The family was very surprised, and very upset, to see a picture in the paper the next day—of the victim, inside the casket. I suggested that maybe each family could designate a person to answer the phones, to stand at the door, to be a shield against the requests for interviews, photographs, whatever.

Conrad Johnson's family had not held their funeral yet. Many of the families of the victims who were already buried reached out to Conrad Johnson's family. They had some advice, and they offered to help. There was some more hugging and crying.

It was very emotional for me, maybe the most emotional moment since I had to go out and talk about the shooting of thirteen-year-old Iran Brown. It was very real for me, seeing the pain these families felt, feeling the loss they had experienced. It made the case all the more human and horrible.

It also made it impossible, somehow, for me to feel any jubilation about solving the crime. This was not a happy day. It was a good thing it was coming to an end, but the reality, for me, was how much I wished I had gotten it done sooner. How much I wished I could have ended it before all those victims had to die.

It was almost 8 P.M. that night before, finally, we were told that the ATF was finished with the ballistics on the rifle.

The ATF laboratory man Dandridge came in person. He explained how the lab technicians had gone through each shooting, individually, painstakingly, until he had compared every bullet fragment with bullets from the gun we'd taken from the Caprice. Then, when he was all finished, he'd had another guy go through and do it all over again—without knowing the results of the first set of tests.

We had waited six hours for this. Now it was clear. The ballistics tests positively connected the snipers' gun to the shooting deaths of Premkumar Walekar, Sarah Ramos, Lori Ann Lewis-Rivera, Pascal Charlot, Dean Harold Meyers, Kenneth Bridges, Linda Franklin and

Conrad Johnson, as well as to the nonfatal shootings of the woman in Spotsylvania County, the boy at Benjamin Tasker Middle School and the man outside the Ponderosa restaurant. There was no doubt whatsoever in the minds of the ATF experts that this was the murder weapon. Later, they would connect the weapon to all the victims.

I don't remember feeling anything but relief. I don't remember smiling or laughing or yelling or anything. But other people were doing all that. There were high-fives and people cheering and shouts of congratulations. There were outbursts of applause. Someone called the people over at the JOC, and there were spontaneous outbursts of applause over there, too.

Once we knew, for sure, we gathered up the rest of the task force team. There were still a couple of people missing, people who had a two-hour drive to get there. We had discussed sending a helicopter to pick up some of them. We tried to get all the Virginia people to join us, and some of them did. We wanted to make an announcement, and we wanted to show a completely united front.

When the team was assembled, I went out to face the media, with the other members of the task force leadership team at my side. As usual, I stood with Gary Bald, Mike Bouchard and Doug Duncan.

I began by asking for a moment of silence for a fallen colleague. A Virginia state trooper named Mark Cosslett had died that day, in a motorcycle accident, while rushing to the scene of a 911 "shots fired" call. If you look closely at the pictures of the officers at that press conference, you can see most of them wearing a little black band across their badges—again, in honor of the fallen officer.

Then I read the following statement:

"At approximately one A.M. a motorist called 911 to report seeing a 1990 Chevrolet Caprice, bearing the New Jersey license plate NDA-21Z, associated with John Allen Muhammad, parked in the parking lot of the rest stop. The rest stop is located at I-70 and marker 42, approximately four miles from the Washington County line, eleven miles west of Frederick City. Maryland State Police responded, verified the tag number and kept the vehicle under surveillance while task force members responded to the location. Members of the task force approached the vehicle and found two males sleeping inside. They took both men into custody without incident, and they were taken to an undisclosed location in Montgomery County. The vehicle was secured and transported to a Montgomery County facility. A search warrant was secured and executed on the vehicle. One of the individuals in the vehicle has been identified as John Allen Muhammad, AKA John Allen Williams, black, male, date of birth 12/31/60. The other individual is a seventeen-year-old male, who will remain unnamed at this time because of his age."

Bouchard stepped up next. He told reporters that a search of the vehicle had yielded a Bushmaster XM-15 E2S .223-caliber rifle. The weapon had been sent to the ATF lab in Rockville for analysis. He said the ballistics tests had come back positive. "The results of forensic testing are that the weapon seized from the vehicle occupied by Muhammad has been determined to be the murder weapon in the following shootings." Then he read, one by one, the names of the eleven victims, eight of whom had died. Bouchard did not mention James Martin or James "Sonny" Buchanan by name. But he did say, "Those [murders] that are inconclusive remain linked through other evidence, and we continue to investigate them in connection with all the others. We are also continuing to investigate any other unsolved shootings that are similar in nature"—a reference to the September killings, in Maryland, at the liquor store and the pizzeria.

I returned to the microphones and said there would be a statement from the state's attorneys of Maryland and Virginia, concerning legal issues, but that, for now, we considered the two men in custody the only suspects in the shooting deaths.

County Executive Doug Duncan then came to the microphone. He said, "Tonight, people in the Washington area are breathing a collective sigh of relief." He then asked for a moment of silence to remember and honor the snipers' victims. One by one, he slowly recited the names of the dead. "James Martin. Sonny Buchanan. Premkumar Walekar . . ."

I congratulated the people who had survived the three-week ordeal. "We have not given in to the terror," I said. "Yes, we've all experienced anxiety. But in the end resiliency has won out."

I then said thank you. I needed to say thank you. There were a lot of people to thank. I said:

"We want to thank the well over one thousand dedicated local, state and federal law enforcement officers from throughout the country who worked around the clock for the last three weeks on this investigation. This joint effort is and continues to be unprecedented. The investigation continues and we still have a great deal of follow-up to do.

"Most of all, I would like to thank the public for their assistance in this case. We asked the public to remain vigilant, observant, aware, and to call us with information. As most of you know by now, it was a vigilant motorist who called 911 to report the vehicle associated with John Allen Muhammad. The local, national and even international public has been supportive of the combined law enforcement efforts and we want to say thank you.

"This has been a trying time for all concerned, including the media and law enforcement. We would be remiss not to acknowledge the cooperation of the media in conveying our messages. Even though the pressure of competition was great, there were several members of the media that held back releasing information so as not to jeopardize the investigation. Your professional ethics are to be commended.

"Lastly, I realize this has been a difficult time for everyone, especially for the victims and families of the shootings. So we will never forget. We'll never know their pain, and we only wish we could have stopped this to reduce the number of victims. Our thoughts and prayers are with you."

We were still being sort of cautious. I said something about how happy I was that this gun was off the street. Bouchard said something similar. We made several references to the weapon. We didn't talk that much about the snipers. We didn't want to say anything we couldn't prove.

Later, and then a hundred times in the weeks to come, people would ask me what it was like to finally look into the eyes of these killers. But I never looked into their eyes at all. I never even saw them. I didn't go to the detention center that night. I didn't go to Baltimore while they were being held there, and I didn't go down to Fairfax County, Virginia, where they were held later. It wasn't my job to meet them, or interrogate them, any more than it had been my job to arrest them. I had other work, elsewhere, as all the other men and women on the task force had their work to do.

At some point in the evening I finally called Sandy and told her I'd be getting away soon. I had told her in the morning to start thinking where she'd like to go for dinner. Anyplace she wanted, I said. By now, though, it was becoming obvious that our choices were going to be somewhat limited.

I told her we were about to go and do the final press conference. We had the weapon. We had the ballistics. They were almost done.

I knew she was pissed off at me. All afternoon she'd been paging me. She was using her secret code that said it was urgent. I had not been responding. So I knew she was going to be angry. I promised to be home as soon as possible.

There was one final delay. We got a phone call from the White House telling us that President Bush wanted to call and congratulate us. By this time, not many folks were around. We were about to go into another phase of the investigation, and many had gone home to get some rest. But we gathered about 150 people to listen to the phone call.

It took a while to make that happen. Leaving the building, crossing the the parking lot to the JOC, we stopped to chat, to thank people, to say hello. We were moving kind of slowly, too, feeling exhausted as the thought began to sink in that we were really done, and it was really over.

When we got to the JOC we had to wait another thirty minutes for the President to be ready to address us. The phone call came in. The President's voice came through the microphones at the podium. It was like listening to a speech on the radio. The President didn't seem to want to have a conversation. He just wanted to say congratulations.

Assistant Chief Walker said, "He makes it sound like we won the Super Bowl or something." She said it sounded like a prerecorded announcement, or like a tape they were playing for us, like the President himself wasn't really there.

I was somewhat disappointed. For three weeks we had stood up to this terrible violence in our community, right in the President's own backyard. We had handled one of the largest joint task forces in history, and run the largest single manhunt ever, and we had lost almost a dozen citizens to the snipers' bullets.

I wish the President could have rolled out to Rockville. He had a lot of federal employees working on the case, and it would have been a nice touch. But, again, the telephone call was nice, too. Maybe a little anticlimactic, but I have never been involved in any police work where the President of the United States took the time to call and say, "Good job." At the time you are living in the moment. On reflection, this was indeed a historic moment.

A lot of the task force people were going out for drinks that night. They were headed over to a place called Mrs. O'Leary's, and they invited me to come along. I told them I was going home instead. I was really looking forward to going home. I was especially looking forward to going home and knowing no one was going to call and wake me up with some more bad news. I told Captain Demme, "I get to go home and not worry tonight that someone is going to call me and say the sniper is going to strike again."

When I finally got home, it was Chinese takeout from a place in the neighborhood.

When I came through the door, the first thing I did was start apologizing. I said I was sorry for the way the thing ended. I was sorry that I couldn't have told her more, kept her more current with the way things were breaking, been more forthright with her about how it was coming to a close. I told her that even though she wasn't actively working the case along with the rest of us, I knew it was hard on her, just like it was on me, just like it was on everyone. I told her she deserved to know more than she'd been told, because of the way she'd always stuck by me in the past during the tough times.

She forgave me. We ate our Chinese takeout. It was finally over.

12. Famous, and Infamous

The weeks and months that followed the close of the sniper investigation were a remarkable roller coaster ride for me. I was hailed as a sort of hero. I was embarrassed by all the attention. I couldn't go anywhere in Montgomery County without people coming over to me—*lots* of people—and thanking me for helping to end the killing. I was invited to speak or appear or accept an award at literally dozens of events. There were church events and school events, police events and military events, events with politicians, events with entertainers and celebrities. I met Barbara Walters and was interviewed by her on national TV. I was on Ted Koppel's *Nightline*. I was treated like a celebrity.

I even had my own fan club. Some people from Australia created the "Chief Moose Fan Club" (at www.chiefmoose.com) on which they called me things like "powerful and mighty" and "eloquent and passionate." I had not ever met any of these people, and I don't know what induced them to become members of a fan club. They had T-shirts for sale, and coffee cups. It was very nice. When I found out about it, I asked the county attorney, Mike Fry, to look into it and see if we could stop them. I was afraid they might not be legitimate, and that their actions might reflect badly on the police department or the task force. He reported back that he could not stop them, but he did send them a note to post on their site saying it was not connected to the county, or to me. Anyone sending money or unhappy with the products would have to contact them—not the county. It was the beginning of a flood of fan mail, fan gifts, letters of appreciation, flower arrangements, personal cards and other gifts that began pouring into the Rockville police headquarters and district stations. At one point we had more than thirty cardboard boxes filled with letters to us—most of them, it seemed, from elementary school kids, junior high school kids, parents and teachers, or just grateful individuals who were relieved that the sniper was no longer shooting citizens in their community.

I found myself in the news even when I wasn't in the news. Even where there *wasn't* any news. It was reported that the governor had offered me a new job as the head of the Maryland State Police, and that I was considering taking the new job. I first heard about this on the radio, while I was driving somewhere, reported as fact. This was the first I knew of it. I had not been contacted by the governor. I wasn't offered any job. I wasn't even aware of the job being open. But it was reported as fact.

Somewhat later, I became a candidate for the police chief's job in Prince George's County, Maryland. This job I knew about, because I knew the outgoing police chief. We had worked together on the sniper task force. Someone had leaked my name to the media as a candidate. I had talked with the new county executive, Jack Johnson, about how important the police could be in his efforts to improve his county. That was the end of it, but suddenly I was a top contender. It was a big news story when the word got out that we had met.

The most important thing about doing my job is doing my job. I would not want my executive to start thinking I've got my eye on something else, or that I've got other things on my mind. When I'm at work, I'm all the way at work. But I can imagine how it looks from the outside. The newspapers might report that I've been asked to speak at a function at Langley Air Force Base, and that a plane is being sent from there to Andrews Air Force Base to fly me down. Now, how does that look? I can imagine my executive thinking, *No one's asking* me *to speak at Langley. No one's sending* me *any airplanes.*

You can get kind of blasé about the attention. We joke about it, my wife and I. She used to say, when I had to go out at night and do some public speaking or something, "If you don't make TV, don't bother coming home."

During the sniper siege, I had received some pretty hostile mail, and very hostile email, from people who didn't like the job I was doing. After I chewed out the media for the tarot card leak, and after I shed a tear over the shooting of thirteen-year-old Iran Brown, these messages got extremely hostile. "How did this guy get the job?" one man wrote on a Moose-related message board. "Can you imagine what the morale must be like among the people under him? Boss is a moron, and the citizens are dropping like flies." Another posting, from just after the end of the shootings, said, "Moose was in over his head. He clearly showed . . . his whole insecurity with the whole thing. The next thing I expected from him actually was the race card. He meant well but he still suffers from persecution complex . . ."

This was all new for me. I had no idea how celebrities are supposed to act, and I had no idea how a celebrity police chief was supposed to act. I just tried to be polite and answer the questions people asked me, and not let any of it go to my head. I realized that it had nothing to do with me, really. I hadn't earned it. I didn't deserve any special treatment. Or special insults. Or special psychoanalysis. Or flower arrangements.

Some of the special treatment isn't so bad. A state trooper pulled me over for speeding recently. I was in Virginia, on the freeway, and I was driving too fast. The trooper asked me for my license and registration. While

I was getting them out, he said, "Sir, I pulled you over because you were going seventy-eight miles an hour in an area where the limit is sixty-five."

Then he looked at my license. He frowned. He stared at the ground for a minute. Then he handed the license back. He said, "Chief Moose? Can I ask you to please slow it down a little from here on out?"

My wife, who describes herself as a "habitual speeder who *never* got a break," found this pretty irritating.

On the other hand, all through February of this year I was invited to go all over the place and speak on panels, in recognition of Black History Month. I was the police chief in Montgomery County for three and a half years before the sniper case. As far as I know, they had Black History Month every one of those years. And nobody was inviting me to speak on any panels then.

I try to keep that in the right perspective. I can be irritated that nobody asked me to talk about black history before. Or I can do my research, prepare my talk and show up and speak about the things that matter to me. And hope that I don't get too upset if they don't ask me to come back and speak again next year. I have to remember that for a lot of people, I might just be the flavor-of-the-month speaker.

I have always taken my job as a police officer very seriously. Maybe too seriously at times. I haven't been as good at relaxing as I could have been. I've probably brought more stress on myself than I needed to. That's just the way I've worked.

At the end of 2002, my wife and I went to Hawaii. We were gone for a little over two weeks. That's the first time in my working life that I've taken two weeks, back to back, at a time.

In Montgomery County, I'm allotted a certain number of sick days per year and a certain number of vacation days. The time accumulates. If you don't use it, the time rolls over into the next year.

The same thing was true when I was in Portland. I accumulated time for sick days I didn't use and vacation days I didn't use. Unfortunately, though, I had to resign the position in order to become chief of Montgomery County and forfeited the accumulated time. I was sorry to lose it. It took a long time to accumulate it, and I was blessed by not being sick.

In twenty-four years as a police officer in Portland, in fact, I only took one sick day. I had gone to the dentist on a Thursday afternoon, for a cleaning and a checkup. The dentist told me I had a real problem with one of my wisdom teeth. He said it had to come out, and he offered to pull it right there. I told him to go ahead.

He didn't explain too much about how this was going to make me feel. If you've had a wisdom tooth out, you know what I'm talking about. So he gave me a prescription for Percodan, and told me to take them as needed, for the pain.

I did what I was told. And I was *gone*. Obviously I couldn't go to work like that. I had to take the Friday off and spend the weekend recovering. If I'd known what it was like to have a wisdom tooth taken out, I would have scheduled the extraction for the Friday.

The point is that sometimes you wind up with something on your record that looks really good, when that wasn't part of the plan. I didn't know I was going to be a police chief. I didn't know I was going to be at the center of an international news story. I didn't know it would look good on my record that I only took one sick day in twenty-four years. I was just doing my job and collecting my pay and trying to make the most of things.

I am not sure what my legacy in Portland is. The longer you're gone from a job like that, the more they seem to miss you. I don't think there was any gaping hole in Portland society when I left. Among police chiefs, that seems to be universally true. You hear people say that the best chief is always the *last* chief—if you're the new chief. Otherwise, if you are the chief, the best chief is the *next* chief.

I was a controversial figure in Portland in some ways.

There was some animosity there when I left. I noticed that some of it flared up again during the sniper shootings. Then, when the sniper thing went well, it quieted down. Had it gone the other way, I think the animosity and criticism would have gotten louder.

Here's a funny thing, though. The police union in Portland has actually invited me to come back and speak at one of their fund-raising functions. This is amazing. This is management-versus-union stuff. Even when you *do* get along, you don't advertise it. In the time I was police chief in Portland, I went through three or four different union presidents. I had a pretty embattled relationship with all but the first one.

It's pretty shocking that they're inviting me back. They're trying to organize financial help for an officer that got injured, and that's something I can support, so of course I'll go. They'll give me an honorarium, and I will donate that to the fund. It's just a question of clearing the calendar and making sure I have the time.

It can cut both ways, though. One time, when I was a relatively new police chief in Portland, I had an accident driving to work. A bus ran a red light, and I smashed right into the side of it. Wrecked my car all up. The papers were full of it. "Bus Hits Moose" or "Moose Hits Bus," or something like that—like it was a funny story. I had to make sure that people didn't think it was my fault. But what if it had been? What if I'd been drinking? What if I'd been in the car with someone I shouldn't have been?

On the other hand, in Portland, I had the opposite experience. It was the only time ever, in my time as a police chief, that I witnessed a crime and had to become a police officer out on the street.

I was driving down the street in Portland, and I witnessed this guy actually shoot someone, or shoot at someone. I jumped out of the car and identified myself as a policeman. I think I told him to drop the weapon and put his hands up. Naturally enough he didn't. He turned and ran. So I chased him.

It was very exhilarating. It was also potentially embarrassing. You want to be a hero, and catch the bad guy, single-handedly. But you don't want to be caught in the position of not calling for help, and then having the guy get away, while you're standing there in your Sunday-go-to-meeting clothes. I was wearing a suit and tie and street shoes. I had a weapon, but I didn't have a radio on my belt. I wasn't wearing a vest. I wasn't dressed for a chase. But I took off after him anyway. And it became very clear to me, right away, that I wasn't going to catch him. He was moving *fast*. I ran after him for two or three blocks, and he was pulling away from me. I knew I wasn't going to catch him.

I ran back to my car and called for backup. I knew the neighborhood. I got the units there pretty fast. They had a K-9 unit and got the dogs out, and sure enough we found the guy hiding under a house.

It would have looked bad if he'd gotten away. If you're just Joe Patrolman, and you don't come through on something like that, it doesn't make the papers. If you're the chief, it does make the paper. Plus, to your officers, you probably end up looking like you're old, or out of touch, or have been part of the administration so long that you're not hardly a cop anymore.

I guess I was lucky. My skills were all still there. I didn't screw it up. I got the exhilaration of chasing a guy down the street with my weapon out. And then he didn't get away.

And the guy he shot didn't die, either.

During the sniper investigation, I was acutely aware of how my actions might be interpreted by people in my county and by the media. If I stopped someplace for a cup of coffee, I'd bring my police radio with me and put it on the table, and leave it *on*, so people wouldn't think I was goofing off. But I'd still get these looks like "Aren't you supposed to be *doing something*?"

So doing anything else during my private time was out of the question. Even though I wasn't needed on the case twenty-four hours a day, I wasn't going to go and catch a movie. I wasn't going to eat in a restaurant. I wasn't going to go walk around a mall. I was at work, or I was at home sleeping. That was it.

I've been a leader for a long time. This sounds like the kind of thing you say if you're running for office, but it's not bragging. As police chief in Portland, and in Montgomery County, and as a major in the Air National Guard, being a leader was a big part of my job. I have a lot of experience organizing and coordinating manpower. I've had a lot of opportunity to observe what kind of leadership is effective, and what kind isn't.

A lot of what I practice is called "situational leadership." It's something I've studied, and it's something I've taught. In practice, this is about how you stay flexible in the way you lead, the way you instruct and the way you reprimand.

A fundamental part of it is what I will allow a new police officer to do, and what kind of direction I will give him, as opposed to what direction I would give, say, an assistant chief. With an assistant chief, who's been around for a while, I just need to tell him or her what needs to be done. The assistant chief doesn't need to be told *how* it needs to be done. It would be insulting to him or her, to be told that, and it would be a waste of my time. However, I may need to tell a newer officer what to do, how to do it, when to do it and everything.

Even if a newer officer screws up, I may not want to reprimand him or her. I might need to praise the officer for the effort, or for the things that he or she did accomplish, even when the officer didn't get nearly as close as I wanted. For the same level of performance, though, I might really chew out, or even discipline, an assistant chief.

There are various things you might fire someone over. If someone is not dependable or doesn't show up or shows up unprepared, you might have to reassign him or her. If someone is withholding information or lying to his or her fellow officers or intentionally excluding other members of the team from participating in the solution of a crime, you might have to discipline that person. The challenge is to stay flexible and to judge accurately, as you go along, what response is appropriate. If you miss it enough times, it will hurt you. You will lose your ability to lead.

During the sniper case, we had a lot of leaks to the media. It was infuriating to me. It was damaging to team morale. It undermined confidence, and it could have blown up in our faces.

There were people in my department, and around the task force, who wanted me to find out where the leaks were coming from, stop them and fire the people responsible. I made a decision not to do that. I wasn't sure that I could find out who was behind it. I wasn't sure I could prove it. So I told everyone that while I was upset, while I was concerned, while I thought it was a damned shame, we were going to just move on. It didn't make sense to waste our time and resources investigating that, when we were already using all our time and resources finding out who was doing the killings.

In fact, I didn't discipline anyone, or seriously reprimand anyone, during the sniper crisis. I would have gone out of the way to avoid that. It would've been too big a distraction. It would have suggested a police force or a task force that was in trouble. And we weren't in trouble.

What I learned was that it's actually easier to lead during a time of crisis. Everyone is so focused on the job at hand that there is less time for criticism. There were so many people involved in the sniper investigation, and so many new players. There were struggles for leadership. If it had not been a time of crisis, there would have been a more serious ongoing evaluation. There would have been more complaining. More of the details would have been held up to scrutiny.

On the sniper case, though, everything was moving so fast. Details were breaking so fast. It's like there wasn't time for anyone to stop and inspect the leadership and find things to complain about—an advantage, from a leadership point of view. We didn't have time to do anything but our jobs. That made leading a little easier.

Most of the time I try to lead by example. I try to be the kind of police officer I'd like my police officers to be.

For example, I show up for work every day wearing the Kevlar body armor "vest" under my uniform. I think it's very important—not for me, so much, because the likelihood is I'm going to be behind my desk all day, but for the officers who are going to be in the field. When I was in Portland, I made the wearing of the vest mandatory. In Montgomery County, I could force the officers to wear the vest.

I would "model" it for them anyway, by wearing it myself every day. It's not that I enjoy it. I don't. It's bulky and uncomfortable, and it makes you feel hot and sweaty and itchy. But I think the officers owe it to their loved ones. It shows the people who care about them that they're doing everything possible to protect themselves.

I also try to show the officers how to do their jobs by showing them how I do *my* job. I'm real visible in the community and at the station. My door is open. I want my officers and the community at large to know I'm there, and that I'm available and accessible.

When I'm on the job, I try to show my people that I don't expect any special favors. I don't have a driver, for one thing. The chiefs before me had drivers. When the chief had someplace to be, the driver would take the wheel and the chief would . . . Well, I don't know what the chief would do. Because I don't let the driver take the wheel. If I've got someplace to go, I do the driving. That frees up the person who's supposed to be driving me to do something useful.

This backfired on me when I first got to Montgomery County. I made it known this was my policy. I drove myself everywhere. And for the first six months or so I was lost all the time. I couldn't find my way around. I was constantly running late. And I couldn't ask for help, because I'd made such a big deal about driving myself. But the tone was set: Even the chief isn't looking for a cushy deal.

I try to model the whole "free food" thing, too. I try to make sure I pay for everything I get when I'm out in the community. This can be difficult. I can't tell you how many little disagreements I've gotten into trying to pay for a coffee or a newspaper or a meal. Especially since the sniper investigation, people really want to do something nice—a free dessert, a free car wash, a free something or other.

It's nice. I appreciate it. I understand this is one way that people say thank you. But I also understand this is one way that police officers have traditionally taken advantage—by insisting, out loud or not, on getting that free meal.

I think it sets a bad example in the community. It suggests that the police officer thinks he or she is special and different and above the law. It suggests there is one set of rules for the citizens and another set of rules for the police. I don't support that.

I don't give lectures on this stuff. I don't tell the officers what to do about the free doughnut. I don't give speeches about off-duty behavior. I don't feel I have to.

Instead, I talk about values and value-based decisions. We have a poster campaign going on now. You can see these things hanging on the police station walls. They talk about "P.R.I.D.E." That stands for "pride," "respect," "integrity," "dedication" and "excellence." I encourage the officers to understand that everywhere I go, I am representing them and the rest of the department. And everywhere *they* go, they're representing *me* and the rest of the department.

All they have to do is look at a newspaper. It's always going to say, "Charles Moose, Montgomery County Police Chief," and then what I have done or what has happened to me. It's never *not* going to say what police department I work for. And because of the sniper thing, it's going to be that way for the rest of my life.

I try to get them to consider the idea that wherever they go, and whatever they do, each officer is representing all the other officers who've ever worked here, and even the officers who haven't come here yet. That's the set of pressures I feel we're under, and the set of reasons we have to do the right thing.

That's why, during the sniper investigation, I made so many comments about how hard everyone was working, how focused everyone was and how proud I was of them. I was sending a message about how optimistic I was. I said I had looked into my people's eyes, and I had seen how dedicated they were, how committed they were.

There were times when I hadn't seen any of my people in hours. I hadn't looked into anybody's eyes. And the ones I had looked into didn't look optimistic at all. But that was the example I needed to give and the message I had to send. For the people who were working really hard, it was a way of saying thank you. For the people who weren't, it was a way of saying, "This is what I expect of you."

This is why I always insisted on going down to the press conferences side by side with the men from the FBI and the Bureau of Alcohol, Tobacco and Firearms. It's one thing to say that we on the task force were working as an integrated team. I thought it would be more effective if we actually showed up as an integrated team.

I told my partners on the task force that this whole case was an opportunity for each of us to recoup some lost public relations problems we'd had in the past. The FBI was still stinging from the way it handled the Timothy McVeigh case. The ATF had taken a lot of criticism for the way it handled the Branch Davidian Waco case. And my own department was still working under a Department of Justice agreement that was the result of some charges of racial discrimination. We all had something to gain and something to lose.

That's why I was serious about this. We got into a beef with the producers of the TV news show *48 Hours*. They came and interviewed all three of us—me, Gary Bald and Mike Bouchard. That was part of our agreeing to do the interview. That was part of the deal. You want one of us, you get all three of us. But when it came time to edit their broadcast, they cut out my colleagues from the ATF and the FBI. Bald and Bouchard weren't even in there. I was the only one on the show.

I let the producers know how disappointed I was by this, and they apologized and tried to explain. Then, later, one of the shows connected to *48 Hours* came to us with another interview request. We turned them down. I said, "You were here before, and you screwed it up, and we're not giving you another chance." They were blown away. I think they thought we wanted to be interviewed. They asked us to reconsider. We didn't reconsider.

This "sending a message" thing doesn't always work. When I was new in Montgomery County, I was asked to speak at the graduation ceremonies at the police academy. I had only been chief for two or three months. I saw it as an opportunity to set a tone for these incoming officers.

I got up there onstage and made this speech. I told the graduates that they were going to be getting partners on the police force, senior partners who were going to tell them to forget all that stuff they learned at the academy. They were going to tell them to forget about ethics and all the other classroom stuff, because now they were in the real world.

I told them, "Don't do that. Don't forget what you've learned here." I wanted them to understand there was no excuse to ever compromise the ethical standards they'd been taught at the academy.

Then I hit them with my larger point. A number of officers in the department had been brought up on charges of untruthfulness—of lying on the job. To me, this is a very serious offense. In Portland, in fact, it was one of the few grounds for automatic dismissal. The rule there was "Do whatever you want, but never lie about it." You could get away with almost anything, and still keep your job, as long as you came clean to your superiors. But if you lied, you were out.

In Montgomery County, they had a list of the officers who had lied to their superiors, on the job, and were still in. I thought this was outrageous. And I said so. I referred to that list of officers and denounced them.

"They continue to carry a badge and a gun and drive about the county arresting people and going to court and testifying," I said. "So they will also tell you that you don't have to tell the truth and you can be a Montgomery County police officer. And they will have proof that that is the case."

Referring to the "code of honor" supposedly shared by police academy graduates, I said, "It's just an absolute joke and a lie because you don't have to have a code of honor in the Montgomery County Police Department. You can be untruthful and keep your job."

I told the graduating officers that I didn't want this kind of behavior on my police force. I told them I wanted officers who prided themselves on integrity and honesty. I thought I was sending a message of strength and hope, and setting a new, higher standard for the police department.

The whole thing blew up in my face. By the next morning, the media was all over me. They demanded to see this "list" of officers who had lied. The prosecuting attorney for the county demanded to see the "list." And the officers in my department were outraged: "He called us all liars!"

Not only that, but I had made another mistake. In Portland, we had an everyday uniform and a dress uniform, which included a dress coat. We never wore it, except to the most formal events—funerals and things like that. In Montgomery County, the dress coat was worn more often. Well, I didn't know that. It was a warm spring day. So I showed up at this graduation wearing my everyday uniform—which for warm weather is a short-sleeve shirt.

I was calling my officers liars and I was disrespecting the uniform.

It took months to put out the fire. My boss, the Montgomery County executive, backed me up right away. He said, "Chief Moose has told his officers he wants them to be honest and have integrity. I don't see what's wrong with that. He sends a message loud and clear that he expects the highest level of excellence of this police force."

The people in my department figured out I wasn't calling them liars.

It took longer to untangle the legal mess. For a couple of years we'd get attorneys demanding to see the "list." A defense attorney would be representing a guy for doing something bad, and he'd insist that the officer who filed the charges or made the arrest was tainted. His name was probably on the list. So the attorney would ask the judge to turn over the list, to see if the arresting officer was a liar. Sometimes the judge would agree, and the attorney would try to make a case out of that. I don't think there was ever anything in it—I know we never had a case fall apart because of this—but it added another level of complication to prosecuting criminals for a while.

It all comes down to making a little extra effort, to trying to be a little better. I make sure I send birthday cards to all the people in my department. It's a lot of people—I oversee fourteen hundred employees, so in any given month you can do the math and see it might be 100 to 150 cards to fill out. I try to say hello to everyone I meet on the street, and to give each of them a minute or two. I could just nod and move on. I try to slow down. Some of this is my wife's handiwork. She's always telling me I could be nicer. So I try to respect that, and I try to be nicer. If someone wants to stop me and talk for a minute about some problem they're having, or just wants to say thank you for the job we did on the sniper thing, I try to listen and thank them for their input. It's not my nature, I don't think, to do that. But I think it's a good idea to try.

Consider the alternative. Like it or not, I'm a public person. I get recognized everywhere I go. People are watching. People are listening. If I were acting up, I'd get busted in a minute.

Actually, my wife loves that part. She thinks it's great. Now, she says, she doesn't have to keep an eye on me. I couldn't sneak around even if I wanted to. I'm out in public a lot, and she's with me a lot. People know what my wife looks like. If I started showing up in public with some other woman, she'd have to look *exactly* like my wife or I'd be in serious trouble fast.

It all goes with the territory. There are people who feel at liberty to criticize me because I am a public figure and a public servant. I've gotten emails recently that say, "I don't know why you're writing a book, when everyone on your police department knows you can't even write a complete sentence." I've gotten more than one like that.

I react by thinking, *What did I do to deserve that?* But what can I do?

It's like with the press. I didn't complain when the *New York Times* ran a big article saying what a great job I'd done and printed it with a big picture of me smiling. I didn't call and yell at them about that. So I couldn't very well call some other paper and yell when they wrote something about me that wasn't flattering.

A lot of police chiefs live with this. Some of them seem to pay attention to it, and some don't. Most of us understand the reality—we can be fired, at any time, and we are going to be fired, sooner or later. Almost all the police chiefs get fired eventually. Something bad happens, and you were out of town. They know it's not your fault, because you were out of town. Well, that's what's your fault: What the hell were you doing out of town?

Willie Williams, when he was chief of the Los Angeles Police Department, learned a lesson in this. There was an officer-involved shooting, and he was out of town. He was in Las Vegas. He did not return to Los Angeles fast enough to please his critics. That made people start asking what kind of chief he was. It made them start asking what he was doing in Las Vegas. Turns out he was doing some high-roller gambling and taking a free room and other perks from the hotel. He wasn't doing anything against the law, or even out of the ordinary—for an ordinary citizen. But he wasn't an ordinary citizen. He was the police chief of a large and very troubled police force. It didn't wash.

The trick to successful police chief work might be knowing when to leave. I hardly ever hear about a chief who leaves when everyone still likes him. You don't hear about the ticker-tape parade down Main Street and the tearful good-byes for the outgoing chief. Maybe I could have had one of those, if I'd left Montgomery County. In about November 2002.

Too late! I missed my chance.

As for the breaks I *don't* get, or haven't gotten, I try to keep that in perspective. What I worry about most is that I'm somehow going to mess it up. The worst thing would be getting my head turned by all the attention. Or running the risk that someone would think I was being unethical by writing a book or doing speaking engagements. Or my police department becoming leaderless and falling apart because I'm too busy to pay attention to it. Or, much worse, the case against the snipers falling apart because of something I said or did.

Again, it's all a question of perspective. I was named "Person of the Week" by *Time* magazine. Well, so was Ozzy Osbourne. So how big a deal is that?

I look at a guy like Jimmy Carter, and everything he has used the platform of being the former president for. He's really used it well: speaking about peace, involving himself with Habitat for Humanity. This is the challenge for Bill Clinton, too. How will he use the platform? What will he stand for?

Not that I'm comparing myself to a President, but I ask myself that. What will I stand for? It's a good question for all of us to ask ourselves. In the end, what will we stand for?

I've spent a lot of my career trying to establish trust, as a basis for being able to do my job well. I originally decided to become a sergeant, back in Portland, because my sergeant didn't seem to listen to anything his people were telling him. So when I became a sergeant, I had this commitment to listening. I was going to earn the trust of the people under me by listening.

Then I found that one of my bosses wasn't coming to work on a regular basis. He was taking advantage of his office by not working the same hours as the people he was responsible for. So when I became a lieutenant, I had this commitment to being there when my people came in and not leaving before they left. I was going to earn their trust by showing them I was working just as hard as they were.

As a result, I think the men and woman I've commanded feel that I am in this thing right along with them, that I'm paying attention to them and that I care about them. I try to put myself in their shoes and remember what it was like, remember what the police officers need. From wearing the vest, to always wearing the uniform, to not having a driver, to not taking days off, to showing up early and staying late, I think I've demonstrated that I don't ask my officers to do anything I wouldn't do, or anything I'm not already doing.

As the years have passed, it has gotten harder. The farther you are from being a patrolman, the harder it is to remember what the patrolman's life is like. Plus, after you become chief, everyone stops talking to you. Regular officers are hesitant to tell you the truth. If you ask them how it's going, they say, "Great," every time. Everything is always okay. I find I have to stay in the conversation a little longer. I used to be able to ask how things were going and get a real report. Now, I have to ask how things are going. Then I have to ask how the family is doing. Then I have to ask how things are working out with the new radios, or the new shift configuration, or with the police officer's new house or his kid on the baseball team or his elderly parents, or whatever I can remember to ask the police officer about. Then, and only then, do I have a chance of finding out what's really going on with the people I'm supposed to be taking care of.

I make the effort. I think I've had the loyalty of the people who work for me as a result.

If there's a model for this, I think it's *The Wizard of Oz*.

This is the greatest leadership movie in the world. Think of the story. Dorothy is in trouble. She's lost in an unfamiliar and hostile world, and she has no idea how to get home. But she gets everyone she meets to do something they don't want to do, or something they don't think can be done at all. She gets them to do something that improves them as people. She gets them to help her get back to Kansas. And they all think that this is their idea.

Along the way, Dorothy and her friends vanquish evil, get the bad guy, liberate an oppressed people, expose fraud in government and become heroes.

Dorothy leads them perfectly. They all get what they want. She gets what she wants. They are all better people as a result of trying to help her. They all become leaders themselves.

I always encourage people to watch that movie and think about leadership. It's a great model for being a leader, for learning the skill of getting people to do the right thing by getting people to do what they want, when what they're doing is really what you want, and then helping them think it was their own idea the whole time.

Some things never change.

One morning, about six months after the sniper siege ended, I was working out in the little gym in the building where Sandy and I were living. We'd moved there, into an apartment building right in Chevy Chase, Maryland, around the first of the year. We were still waiting for construction to be finished on the house we were building in Gaithersburg. We had moved out of the townhouse we owned there and rented the place in Chevy Chase just temporarily. It was a two-bedroom luxury apartment, and it had its own gym.

That morning, I had just finished my workout. I was looking forward to a busy day. I'd gotten up at four-thirty and done my workout, and was finishing up at around five-thirty. I was wearing sweats and a baseball cap.

This woman came into the gym and came over to me. I guessed she was going to use the machine I had just finished using. So I came back over to wipe the machine down, just to make sure it was clean. And she looked angry, or indignant, or something. She said, "What are you doing here? Do you work here? Do you live here? Are you supposed to be using this equipment?"

I was surprised, but I said, "I'm just wiping down the machine. And no, I don't work here. And yes, I do live here. And I guess next time I'll just leave the machine dirty rather than get in your way."

I walked out. I was disgusted. All I could think was *This stuff never ends. It never ends.* I might be the chief of police. I might be a national hero. I might be "Person of the Week" in *Time* magazine. But guess what? To some people, I'm just another black man, doing something they think I have no right to do.

Does this kind of thing happen to white guys? I don't know, because I've never been a white guy. But I don't think it does. If I'm in a store, people come up to me all the time and ask me questions: Where do they keep the lightbulbs? Is there a rest room in this building? They ask me this like they know I work there—not like I'm shopping there, like them, but like I work there. I just don't think this happens all the time to white guys the way it does to me.

I was contacted by some people who thought I should find a way to tell my story, and the story of how I became the guy who led the task force that ran the largest manhunt in American law enforcement history. Those conversations led to this—the book you are reading right now.

I was also contacted by people who wanted to buy the rights to my life story, so they could make a movie about the sniper story and tell it from my own personal perspective. Those conversations have led, so far, to nothing—even though there are other sniper projects out there being made without any input from me.

The book deal and all the movie talk led to a series of terrible confrontations with some of the people in Montgomery County.

I don't know where it started, but somewhere, someone asked the question, was it ethical for a police chief, a county employee, to make a profit from work he was doing on county time? Was it right for a police chief to tell his life story, and get paid to do it, when he'd already drawn a salary for living part of that story?

A committee sat down to discuss this issue. They decided it was not ethical. They decided I would be in violation of the law if I received any money for the writing of a book or the making of a movie. They started telling reporters that I might be censured or fined or fired or even put in jail if I wrote a book about my life and got paid for it.

It would be hard for me to say how much this disturbed me. I was stunned that the people of my own county, the people whose county I had been recruited to come protect and serve, would turn against me in this way. I was shocked that anyone would call me unethical. I was particularly distressed when I saw suggestions in newspaper stories about the controversy that I was going to reveal inside secrets of the investigation that would compromise the prosecution of the sniper suspects and somehow jeopardize the legal case against them. For a person who's been in law enforcement for almost thirty years . . . it's hard to think of anything you can say that is more insulting than that. And I was real insulted.

I was also shocked that the media would take up the

story the way they did. The *Washington Post*, particularly, made a campaign of it. They wrote more than fifteen articles just on the topic of me writing this book. There was story after story about developments in my case—the committee ruled this way, the committee issued this statement and so on. In some of the stories, the *Post* admitted that they had a partial conflict of interest, because two *Washington Post* reporters had been hired to write their own book about the sniper case. The *Post* never said that these reporters had asked me to cooperate with their book and had gotten irritated when I told them I could not. The *Post* never said that some of its other employees were part of a deal to make a made-for-TV movie about the sniper story. So they never revealed all of the motives that might have been driving their animosity toward me.

I kept thinking the story would go away. I kept thinking people would understand that I would never do or say anything to jeopardize the prosecution of the suspects. I couldn't understand how anyone could misunderstand my rights and responsibilities. When I came to work in Montgomery County, I told my new employers that I was a major in the Air National Guard, and that I was sometimes asked to go and speak on panels or to special interest groups, and that I had been a college professor for a long time and hoped to find a position doing some teaching in Montgomery County, and that I needed to know I would have permission to continue doing these outside activities. I was told—in no uncertain terms, in writing, in a memo I still have—that of course I would be allowed to continue doing things like that.

How, I wondered, if those things were not ethical violations of this law preventing me from doing outside work, could my writing the book become an ethical violation of the same law? If I could teach on Monday nights, in my spare time, or be a major for one weekend a month in the National Guard, in my spare time, why in the world wouldn't I be allowed to write a book? If the average Montgomery County police officer could do side work as a security guard, or get paid to ride a motorcycle as escort for a funeral, why in the world wouldn't I be allowed to get paid to write a book?

The three-week sniper siege left a permanent mark on Montgomery County and the Washington, D.C., area. The snipers' bullets did permanent damage. They left ten people dead. They seriously wounded three others. The snipers' marksmanship shot holes in the lives of the families of these victims. Some of that damage can never be repaired. The people who died will be missed, forever, by their loved ones. Some of the people who lived through the siege will be frightened, forever, by what happened to them. The sniper shootings will be the defining moment in the childhoods of little boys and girls who had to go to school terrified that some unknown person was going to shoot them down on the playground.

The shootings left a mark on me, too. I don't know how permanent it is. I learned as much about law enforcement from the three-week crisis as I've learned in any three-year period as a police officer. If we are smart about our after-action reports, the shootings will have left behind a new template for handling certain kinds of terrorist situations.

The shootings made me famous. That's certainly not permanent, but it will have a permanent effect. No matter where I go with the rest of my life, and no matter what else I do, I will always be the police chief who led the sniper task force. Whenever my name appears in the press—whether it's because I'm picked out to head the President's Council on Law Enforcement or picked up for drunk driving—the story will identify me as the chief who led the sniper task force. My obituary, if I rate an obituary, may start by identifying me as the chief who led the sniper task force.

Right after the sniper crisis was resolved, there was a cartoon in the *Hartford Courant* newspaper, drawn by a person named Englehart. In the cartoon, I was featured as Bullwinkle, the moose from the old TV cartoon. I was wearing a uniform and a badge that said, "Chief Moose." I was holding a newspaper with the headline "Sniper Caught." And I was giving a high-five to Rocky, who had a badge on him that said, "Media."

And I'm saying to Rocky, "Good work, partner!"

I don't think the cartoonist was trying to be sarcastic. From the look of the cartoon, I imagine he was trying to show how the police and the media worked together to track down the sniper—how the media helped get the message out there about who and what we were looking for, and how the public used that to help us catch the killers.

The cartoonist probably could not have known how inaccurate this was as a picture of my feelings toward the media. I did thank them in my last press briefing by singling out the ones who helped us by giving out information when we asked them to and not giving out information when we asked them not to. But I never congratulated the media for helping us solve the case. The cartoonist probably had no way of knowing how offensive I found this drawing.

There were lots of stories that followed the capture of the killers that discussed what bumblers the task force police officers were. There were grossly inaccurate reports about how many times we had apprehended and then released the snipers, and about how many tips we had about the Chevy Caprice. According to the media, we were so fixated on the white box truck that we actually refused to consider the snipers could have been using any other vehicle.

Most of what I read was just wrong. We did not have any tips about a Caprice. We had one or two sightings that I'm aware of. And we see now, if we go back through the ledgers, that the car was stopped and checked several times. On four occasions, during the three-week siege, police officers in Montgomery County ran the car's license plates.

In each case, the police found no record that the car

was being driven illegally, was stolen or had been involved in any crime. Nor was there any indication that the people in the car had been involved in any crime. Since all of the patrol cars now have computers in them, it's easy to do, and there is a record of it. You see a car, you run the plate and see what comes up. If nothing comes up, there's nothing you can do with the car. But the press made a big thing about these snipers being talked to, time and again, and being released so they could go kill some more people.

In the case of the Washington, D.C., sighting of the burgundy Caprice, the follow-up from the District police told us this car was not related to our investigation. The car was located, it was burned out, and it did not appear to have had anything to do with the sniper killings. We stopped looking for it. And yet it has reappeared in the press as another example of the police not following through on the investigation.

The problem is this. There is a lot of desire on the part of people in this country that civil rights be obeyed. Just because a car is from another state doesn't mean you can stop it and turn it upside down. That would be against the law. It would be a violation of civil rights. And especially if the occupants of the car were two black men. Chances are the police turning their car upside down would have been white men—because there are that many more white police officers than black. How would that have looked?

It's kind of ironic that the press wants to know why we didn't find this guy and turn his car upside down. The Montgomery County Police Department, because of things that happened before I arrived as chief here, is under a decree not to violate civil rights, not to arrest or detain people based on their race. It's ludicrous that people want to come to the conclusion that we should have stopped or detained Muhammad and Malvo. Based on what? The police officers who might have had the chance to detain them all followed the Constitution. How strange!

But some of the papers decided that was bad.

I have a lot of frustration with this. It's like people think it was the Keystone Kops running the investigation. One editorial page writer even began her story by asking, "Is it just me, or does anyone else out there think Montgomery County Police Chief Charles A. Moose and his vaunted task force bungled the sniper investigation? Why are we glorifying ineptitude?"

It's almost not necessary to say that editorial appeared in the *Washington Post*.

I have to ask myself, since the snipers apparently killed people all over the place before they came to Montgomery County, how come no one else was able to catch them before they got here? How come I turn out to be an idiot, when I was on the task force that did catch them?

It was an interesting backlash to watch. First we were heroes because we caught the bad guys. We engaged the largest manhunt in history, involving a task force of unprecedented size, trying to solve a kind of crime that had never been solved before, using police techniques that had never been used before—and we were successful. We were heroes; the media sang our praises. I got an unfair amount of the praise just because I was the public face of the task force.

Then, when the story about our heroism wasn't news anymore, we stopped being heroes. Somewhere in there, we started becoming bums. We caught the bad guys, but we caught them by accident—despite ourselves, some writers said. We caught them, but we were idiots because we didn't catch them sooner. And I got an unfair amount of the blame, just because I was the public face of the task force.

None of this bothered me as much as the press coverage of my plans to write this book. Led by the *Washington Post*, the media seemed to treat the news as a serious story about serious ethical issues being raised by the book deal. Papers all over the country reported the story as a kind of "Chief Moose in Trouble" story. Some of the reporters tried to contact me. I tried to explain things to a few of them. This seemed to make matters worse. When I told one reporter, "If the Montgomery County government says I can't write a book about my life, maybe I'll have to stop working for the Montgomery County government," he wrote a story headlined, "Chief in Sniper Case Considers a Job Change."

The author of that story was the *New York Times*'s Jayson Blair. He has since had some credibility issues with his employers, who fired him for fabricating material for his stories. His story on me contained fabrications. But the *Washington Post* did a follow-up story just the same, and repeated the incorrect assumptions Blair made in his article.

What happened to the guy who solved the sniper case? It seemed like I had been that guy just a short while ago. What did I do to stop being that guy? Well, the same thing I did to *start* being that guy. Which was nothing. I didn't try to get famous. I was trying to stop the killing, by doing the job I'd been trained to do. I didn't ask to be anyone's hero. I didn't ask for any adulation. And I didn't deserve any. But I got it anyway, and then, coming down the other side, I got the insults, too.

One of the bits of fallout from the whole ethics controversy was that I started thinking, for the first time in more than a decade, whether I was going to continue being a police officer. I started thinking, *What if I lose this job? What if I stop being police chief? What if I decide not to find another job as police chief?* I started wondering what my life would be like away from law enforcement.

When I am asked whether I'd recommend a young person take a look at law enforcement as a career, I say, "Yes, absolutely." I have been extremely successful. I have had an extremely interesting time of it.

Being a police officer has given me an enormous opportunity to be of service.

I strongly support the ideas expressed by Marion

Wright Edelman, founder of the Children's Defense Fund and author of the fine book *The Measure of Our Success.*

Ms. Edelman says, in that book, "Service is the rent each individual pays for living." She defines civic duty as a debt each of us owes to our fellows. Without an awareness of that duty, without an awareness of the obligation and responsibility each of us has toward others, individuals can become isolated and disconnected. In that isolation, that disconnectedness, is where society's ills begin. In part, that's where crime begins. If you and I are not part of some connected whole, what difference does it make to me if I hurt you? Why shouldn't I take your money? What are you to me anyway?

I would argue, along with Ms. Edelman, that civic duty can turn into civic participation, and that civic participation is the very definition of civilization, and of democracy. Society evolves when all the citizens of that society are engaged in its evolution, and when all the citizens benefit from advancements. When personal responsibility becomes civic responsibility, civic pride results. From civic pride comes a healthy, lawful society.

In our society, all of that sense of responsibility seems to start from the top and work its way down. It starts with the parents and is passed to the children. It starts with the chief of police and is passed to the rank and file. It all starts with leadership.

The other thing I'm grateful to law enforcement for is the chance it has given me to be a leader.

In his book *A Higher Standard of Leadership: Lessons from the Life of Gandhi,* author Keshvavan Nair wrote that Gandhi believed the essential ingredient for leadership was courage. As a guide to successful leadership, Gandhi set forth five "commitments." In order to be a successful leader, in order to live a successful life, a leader must:

Commit to absolute values.
Commit to the journey.

Commit to training his conscience.
Commit to reducing attachments.
Commit to minimizing secrecy.

Gandhi believed in living life with a single standard for conduct—for the individual, for the citizen, for the leader—and in attempting to incorporate those five principles or "commitments" into every aspect of his life.

I think this is a wonderful set of guidelines, and I try to apply them in every job that I do in my life. I've found that applying them can make me a better husband and a better father.

I'm sure my awareness of them has made me a better leader, too.

One of the hardest decisions I ever had to make, as a police chief, was the decision to write that letter to the attorney general, over the first weekend of the sniper shootings, asking to have the crime classified as a serial crime and asking for federal help. I had no way of knowing how successful this choice was going to be. I thought it might be the wrong choice. I especially thought it might be the wrong choice for me, personally. I thought I would lose control of the case, that I would look like I was afraid of the case, that I was abrogating my responsibility as police chief, that I was attempting to pass the buck and make the case someone else's problem so that not solving it would look like someone else's fault.

I used Gandhi's five principles to make my decision. My decision turned out to be the right one.

Successful leadership requires a certain amount of imagination. My old mentor Bob Lamb used to tell a story. A teacher had instructed her third-grade students to get out a piece of paper and begin drawing whatever came into their minds. The teacher began looking over the children's papers. One child was drawing something the teacher couldn't understand. She asked the child, "What are you drawing?

"I'm drawing a picture of God," the child said.

"But you can't draw a picture of God!" the teacher said. "No one knows what God looks like."

The child continued to draw, and said, "Everyone will know what God looks like, when I'm finished."

That's the kind of imagination I'd like to continue to have, every day, as a police chief. And as a man.

We can all be social engineers. We *must* all be social engineers. We have to be angry when we see injustice done to another person, just as we are when someone commits an injustice to us. We all have that responsibility to get angry and take action.

I've decided to do that as a police officer—to ensure that there will be no injustice done where I am. We can all do that in our lives. We must all do that. We can't assume there is a Martin Luther King Jr. who's going to march, or a Jesse Jackson who's going to speak out against injustice. If you see someone committing an injustice against another person, it is your job to speak out against that.

Joe Madison, the Washington, D.C.–based civil rights activist and radio talk show host, always says the same thing when someone calls in to complain about how rough things are for black folks. He says, "Well, what are *you* doing about it? Never mind what Jesse Jackson is going to do. Never mind what Al Sharpton is going to do. What are *you* going to do?"

The other day Joe reminded me of an old story. A good man, frustrated by hard times, fell on his knees and called out to God. He said, "We got poverty! We got crime! We got hard times! When are you going to do something about that?" And God answered him, "I already did something about that. I put it in *your* hands."

It comes back, then, to personal responsibility. Civic duty and the spirit of service, which grow from personal responsibility, require that a leader reconcile his or her desire to rule with the desire to serve, that the leader focus on his or her responsibilities and not rights, and that the leader's commitment be to serving the people around him or her and not serving the leader's own selfish interests.

As Gandhi wrote, "If the single standard is the foundation of a higher standard of leadership, the spirit of service is the material with which the structure must be constructed."

I feel I have protected and served the best I possibly could have.

On the afternoon of Friday, June 13, 2003, I called the office of Doug Duncan, the Montgomery County chief executive, and asked his secretary to schedule some time for me. She said her boss wasn't available immediately. I told her I didn't want to disturb his weekend, or his Father's Day, but that it was somewhat urgent. She scheduled us for a dinner meeting on the night of Monday, June 16.

Duncan's office made the arrangements. I put on a pair of black slacks and a starched blue dress shirt and in the evening drove myself over to an Italian restaurant in Rockville, not all that far from the police department headquarters where Camp Rockville existed during the sniper siege. It was Duncan's choice, and I trusted it. Doug Duncan is the former Rockville city mayor. He was one of nine children in a family raised in Rockville. He married his childhood sweetheart and is raising five children of his own in Rockville.

Doug was already waiting for me in the restaurant when I arrived. He stood up and walked from behind his table, and gave me a warm welcome and a strong handshake. He complimented me on my new haircut— which is so close it's almost a shaved head. During the meal, he was very friendly. He was obviously pleased to see me. We had grown close during the ordeal, closer than most county execs probably get to their chief of police. The meal was a friendly one. Our waiter introduced himself, and told us he had just moved to Montgomery County, from Los Angeles, not long before the sniper siege. During the attacks, particularly after the middle school boy was shot, he considered moving back. Friends from California called him every day to ask if he and his children were safe. He felt so grateful now that he could say they were.

I didn't waste much time on cordialities. I told Duncan that I was sorry to say it, but that I was handing in my resignation. I told him I wanted my last day to be June 28, 2003. I didn't say why, but June 28, 1993, was the day I was named chief in Portland—June 28, 2003, would be ten years, to the day, that I had been a police chief. I made it clear that I had made up my mind.

Duncan told me he was disappointed and saddened by my decision. He didn't want me to leave the department. He was very pleased with how I had transformed the police during my almost four years on the job, and how I had handled the task force during the sniper attacks. He also said he understood my decision, though, and would support it. He told me again that he thought I should have been able to continue as police chief, and write my book, and even get paid to write my book, without any interference. He said he had no doubt I could have done that without endangering the integrity or prestige of my office, and without risking any dereliction of duty as police chief.

I told him I wished things could have gone differently, too. I advised him to tell the next police chief to be watchful, and to advise that person that his job would be to uphold a Constitution that would not offer him any Constitutional protection. His job would be to defend the rights of citizens who had rights that he would not necessarily have himself—like the right to unfettered free speech.

The resignation made headlines and caused the talking heads to talk again, and led the evening news when Duncan's office announced what had happened. All the headlines connected the resignation to this book. "Chief Moose Steps Down After Book Clash," said one. "Police Chief in Sniper Case Quits After Book Conflict," said another. Within days, the press decided I had done the right thing. "Sniper Investigator Free to Tell Story," one news organization wrote—before any legal ruling had said this.

This was one of the most difficult decisions I had ever made. I am not a quitter. I don't resign. I don't walk away from a fight. But the situation in Montgomery County had become untenable. I did not see how I could continue to be police chief after the questions that had been raised about my ethics and my conduct.

Duncan and I left the restaurant, parting warmly, on good terms. I called Sandy from the car. We had agreed to go out after my meeting. She was waiting in the lobby when I got home. She hopped in the car, and we drove over to a place in Chevy Chase called Clyde's. We went down to the lounge and sat at the bar. I ordered a Glenlivet, and Sandy asked for a champagne cocktail. I was a little surprised at this, but she told me, "Come on! We're celebrating!" We toasted each other. I thanked her, again, for standing by me and supporting me through one more difficult period.

In the days that followed, the press had its say. I was particularly stung by comments suggesting I was turning away from public service and choosing instead private financial gain. This was a hard thing to hear. I had, after all, spent the last twenty-eight years as a public servant. Now I was trying to write one book. I hadn't planned to leave public service, either. Montgomery County has a system that said I could not write a book, and profit from the book, and remain Chief. The committee could have granted a waiver. They decided not to. I had appealed this decision according to their rules, but the process was going to take a long time. Meanwhile, the book would be published. If I stayed it would appear to some as though I was in violation. A tough choice. But life is about choices.

It was also somewhat premature. I may not be leaving public service at all. I was contacted by search firms for two cities that were looking for new police chiefs. The search firms wanted to know whether I was interested in being a police chief again. At that point, Sandy and I did not know how to answer, and we did not know what our future held.

I wish I could see the future more clearly. I wish I knew what was coming next. When things are difficult for me, I try to remember that while this is all part of a bigger plan, I may not ever know what the bigger plan *is*. I'm the kind of guy who wants to see the whole plan, now, and then have the chance to make all the proper adjustments to the plan and sit back and watch the plan happen in a way that it doesn't have a single hitch to it. I think I drive my wife, Sandy, crazy searching for that. But that's just the way I am, and I'm not about to change now. Besides, I know that when you want to make God laugh, tell God your plan.

ACKNOWLEDGMENTS

I would like to give special thanks to the women and men of both Portland Police Bureau and Montgomery County Police Department, for their respective roles in making me the policeman I have become, and for their participation and support over the course of this project.

I am especially grateful to Agent Mike Bouchard, ATF; Agent Gary Bald, FBI; Acting Chief Bill O'Toole; Assistant Chief John King; Assistant Chief Dee Walker; and Captain Nancy Demme for the hours and days spent so intensely working for the result produced in October 2002. We got the job done!

I also would like to make a special acknowledgment to Vera Katz, Mayor, City of Portland, Oregon, my friend and former boss, for her participation and encouragement over time and during this endeavor.

Special acknowledgment to Douglas Duncan, County Executive, Montgomery County, MD, who stood beside and behind me during the entire period I served as his Police Chief; very special thanks for the important role he played during the three weeks in October and beyond.

Posthumously, to my father, David Moose, and Robert Lamb, Ph.D., a heartfelt love for the two men who so kindly molded me into the person I have become.

Posthumously, to my mother, whose life was cut short, for loving and teaching me as a young boy.

A heartfelt thank-you to Mrs. Edna Robertson, a mother to me and my community in Portland, Oregon. She has never stopped loving and supporting me and I am eternally grateful.

To my two sons, Lincoln and David, I say a sincere thank-you to each of them for their continued love and support throughout both calm and difficult times.

To my sister Dorothy, a very special thank-you for a lifetime of friendship, love and support.

A special thank-you to all others who have believed in me and reached out in love and friendship throughout those twenty-three days in October.

A special acknowledgment to those who facilitated making this project happen.

Finally, a sincere thank-you and acknowledgment to my best friend, partner and loving wife. Sandy, you are always there and I thank you.

ABOUT THE AUTHORS

Charles A. Moose was the chief of police in Montgomery County for four years. Before that, he was the police chief in Portland, Oregon, for six years. For his work on the serial sniper investigation, Charles Moose was named one of the year's ten "most fascinating people" by *20/20*.

Charles Fleming has worked as a staff reporter for *Variety* and *Newsweek*, and has been a frequent contributor to *Vanity Fair*, the *Los Angeles Times*, the *New York Times*, and other publications. He is the author of *High Concept: Don Simpson and the Hollywood Culture of Excess* and *The Ivory Coast*, and co-author of *A Goomba's Guide to Life* and *The Goomba's Book of Love*.

Charles Moose is donating a portion of the profits from *Three Weeks in October* to the Chief Moose Foundation for Justice. This foundation was created by Charles and Sandy Moose for charitable and educational purposes associated with the promotion of racial and gender equality, studying the causes and effects of poverty and injustice, aiding victims of violence, and the conduct of free speech.

If you would like more information about this foundation, please go to *www.chiefmoosefoundation.org*

TRUE CRIME AT ITS BEST

MY LIFE IN THE NYPD
by James Wagner with Patrick Picciarell
0-451-41024-6

James "Jimmy the Wags" Wagner takes readers behind the badge and into the daily drama of working New York City's toughest job in New York City's toughest precinct. It's the NYPD as no one has ever seen it before—from a street cop who walked the walk through the turbulent 1960s, the violent 1970s, and the drug-fueled 1980s. Unbelievable war stories from a man who's seen it all.

FATAL VISION
by Joe McGinniss
0-451-16566-7

The writer Joe McGinniss went to visit Dr. Jeffery MacDonald, with the intent of writing a book that would help clear his name. But after extensive interviews and painstaking research, a very different picture emerged. This is the electrifying story of a Princeton-educated Green Beret convicted of slaying his wife and children. "A haunting story told in detail." –*Newsweek*

A KILLER AMONG US:
   A True Story of a Family's Triumph over Tragedy
   by Charles Bosworth, Jr.
0-451-40854-3

Here is the incredible story of a small town crime that made national headlines, of three explosive trials, of a seething hotbed of adultery and abuse, and of a stunning verdict that ignited a legal minefield of child-custody battles and a chilling final retribution.

Available wherever books are sold or at
www.penguin.com